News Parade

News Parade

THE AMERICAN NEWSREEL AND THE WORLD AS SPECTACLE

Joseph Clark

University of Minnesota Press
Minneapolis | London

Portions of chapter 4 were previously published in *Getting the Picture: The Visual Culture of the News,* ed. Jason Hill and Vanessa R. Schwartz (London and New York: Bloomsbury Academic, 2015). Portions of chapter 5 were originally published in *Useful Cinema,* ed. Charles Acland and Haidee Wasson, 263–88; copyright 2011, Duke University Press; all rights reserved; reprinted by permission of the publisher. www.dukeupress.edu.

Published by the University of Minnesota Press
111 Third Avenue South, Suite 290
Minneapolis, MN 55401-2520
http://www.upress.umn.edu

Printed in the United States of America on acid-free paper

Library of Congress Cataloging-in-Publication Data
Names: Clark, Joseph, author.
Title: News parade : the American newsreel and the world as spectacle / Joseph Clark.
Identifiers: LCCN 2019033192 (print) | ISBN 978-1-5179-0367-1 (hc) |
ISBN 978-1-5179-0368-8 (pb)
Subjects: LCSH: Newsreels—United States—History—20th century. | Newsreels—Social aspects—United States. | Motion picture journalism—United States—History—20th century. | War—Press coverage—United States—History—20th century. | Mass media—Audiences.
Classification: LCC PN4888.M6 C57 2020 (print) | DDC 070.43—dc23
LC record available at https://lccn.loc.gov/2019033192

UMP BmB

For Andrea

Contents

Introduction "History of the Most Graphic and Thrilling Sort": The History of the Newsreel, the Newsreel as History 1

1 News Parade: The Logic of the Newsreel System 19

2 Newsreel Realism: Redefining the Real in Motion Picture News 49

3 "Heroes of the Lens": Newsreel Cameramen, the Sino–Japanese War, and Looking as Action 91

4 "Come Along. We're Going to the Trans-Lux to Hiss Roosevelt": Modernity, Virtual Travel, and the Newsreel Cinema as Public Forum 127

5 Double Vision: World War II, Racial Uplift, and Politics of Visibility in *All-American News* 167

Conclusion News Parades Gone By? 203

Acknowledgments 213

Notes 217

Index 253

INTRODUCTION

"History of the Most Graphic and Thrilling Sort"

The History of the Newsreel, the Newsreel as History

> The small boy of the future is going to have one great aid in his historical researches that men of the present day did not have. That aid will be moving pictures. He will not have to dig for all his facts through heavy and dreary volumes; he will not have to exercise his imagination in wondering what kind of man the Kaiser was; he will not have to speculate vaguely about air raids and trench warfare and the submarine. He will find reel upon reel of valuable data in moving picture form to enlighten him; he will have "canned" history of the most graphic and thrilling sort to make things easier for him.
>
> —ROBERT C. McELRAVY, *MOVING PICTURE WORLD,* 1918

> As history, as bottled samples of what is happening now, to be handed down to our great grandchildren, the newsreels are more often than not trivial, lazy, and misleading. As witnesses of great contemporary events, as impartial eyes and ears which wander over the world to record red-hot actuality, they have degenerated rather than improved with time . . . [The newsreels] have ceased to run after history or try to catch her unawares, preferring to consult the calendar and wait until, as in a St. Patrick's Day Parade, she marches past the corner with a brass band.
>
> —ROBERT LITTELL, *AMERICAN MERCURY,* 1933

When the first weekly newsreel launched in the United States in 1911, its boosters promised that it would change the way Americans saw the world. For the first time, there would be a weekly record of events that represented "indisputable evidence" of the news.[1] Not only would such a record help to inform contemporary audiences, but, as Robert McElravy argued, it would also prove a powerful educational tool for the students of the future.[2] By the time the newsreel had reached the peak of its power and popularity in the 1930s and 1940s, critics had already become skeptical of this early optimism. Writers like Robert Littell charged that, in an attempt to entertain rather than inform or simply out of laziness, the newsreel had forsaken its responsibilities to its viewers—current and future.[3] One hundred years later, McElravy's vision is finally becoming reality . . . sort of. Newsreel archives that for decades were closed to the public are gradually making their way onto the internet. British Pathé recently uploaded 80,000 hours worth to YouTube, hundreds of *Universal Newsreel* stories held at the National Archives are now available in the public domain through Archive.org, and archivists at institutions like the Moving Image Research Collections (MIRC) at the University of South Carolina and the UCLA Film and Television Archive are working to digitize their massive collections of newsreel material. These archives include footage of everything from graphic warfare and terrible natural disasters to fashion shows, horse races, and countless parades. The availability of these newsreel archives represents a potential boon to students, teachers, researchers, and documentary filmmakers, but this "canned history" is neither the grand collection of enlightening and valuable data that McElravy envisioned in 1918 nor the trivial and misleading sampling of the past over which Littell despaired. Or rather, it is both and neither. It is a rich but uneven collection of sounds and images that poses as many questions as it provides answers about the past. Most of us encounter the newsreel only as footage in documentary films and television programs or as the occasional historical curiosity on social media. These fragments do little on their own to illuminate the past, in part because contemporary audiences lack the context to understand them beyond the binary possibilities posed by McElravy and Littell. The newsreel has gone largely unexamined by film historians and those interested more broadly in the politics and culture of the United States in the 1930s and 1940s. A sustained analysis of the history of the newsreel industry, its images, and its audience reveals a media system that had a profound effect on American culture. In particular, the newsreel transformed the very notions of reality, representation, and their relation to one another that lay at the heart of both McElravy's and Littell's observations about the newsreel's historical potential. In doing so, the newsreel did indeed change the way Americans saw the world, though perhaps not in the way its original supporters had imagined.

The newsreel shaped as much as it documented the twentieth century. In order to better understand the newsreel images now found in the archive, we must understand the newsreel itself, the context in which it was made, and the key role it played in transforming American culture. This is what this book explores. It asks: What was the newsreel? What did it represent to those who made and watched it? How did the newsreel alter the relationship Americans had with one another as well as their increasingly mediated world? And what were the social and political stakes of this change for Americans and others?

This book combines an examination of the newsreel's methods of production, distribution, and reception with an analysis of the form's representational strategies in order to understand the newsreel's place in the history of twentieth-century American culture and film history. The newsreel was more than a genre or an industry; it was a total system. Looking at this interconnected system using the film industry's own metaphor of the "news parade" reveals how the newsreel's specialized modes of production and address shaped and reflected its content. The logic of the news parade posited world events as a passing pageant and the newsreel audience as a privileged spectator. The serialized and segmented format of these films, combined with the power of the medium to make the news visible to its audience, offered the newsreel's publics a new way to view the world. By emphasizing the mediated watching of reality—and by framing that reality as a kind of parade—the newsreel privileged spectatorship over other forms of knowledge. For the first time, the commodified experience of watching the news became as important as the news itself. In doing so, the newsreel helped redefine the public through spectatorship and the public sphere as a site of identity formation and participation mediated by the screen. In a world now completely suffused with images and screens, the consequences of this shift continue to impact our notions of reality and the public sphere today.

Writing the Newsreel into Twentieth-Century Media History

Pathé introduced the first weekly newsreel in the United States in 1911 after successfully launching similar reels in France and Great Britain.

Actualities—short nonfiction films documenting events, people, or places—had been an important part of early motion picture programs since the introduction of film in the 1890s, but Pathé's was the first attempt to make a regular serial including a variety of news items. Many imitators would follow. Newsreels quickly became an important and near ubiquitous part of the American moviegoing experience. These seven- to ten-minute reels typically contained between six and a dozen individual stories on topics ranging from the pomp and ceremony of royal weddings, to the devastation of natural disasters, to a fashion show in Paris, to the latest horse race at Belmont Park. Indeed, one of the principle characteristics of the newsreel was its variety. Shown alongside cartoons and other short subjects before the feature presentation at most cinemas, newsreels had something for everybody. In the silent era, this diverse format was relatively inexpensive to produce and, in the years before World War I, independent newsreels—both national and regional—abounded. Many of the smaller reels were short lived however, and, by the mid-1920s, an estimated 85 to 90 percent of the 18,000 cinemas in the United States exhibited one of six widely available national weekly newsreels.[4] Increasingly, exhibitors came to see the newsreel as a necessary part of the motion picture program and sought out brands that their audience would come to recognize and respect.

A series of factors in the late 1920s and early 1930s transformed the newsreel industry and further entrenched its place in American culture. Major news events like the historic transatlantic flight of Charles Lindbergh proved to be huge box office draws, establishing the newsreel's relevancy in moments of collective crisis and celebration. The consolidation of the movie industry made it difficult for independent newsreel companies to compete with those affiliated with the major studios, further reducing the number of newsreel producers. Finally, the introduction of sound in 1927 made the newsreel a multisensory experience that promised even greater access to the news. The introduction of sound also made possible the voiceover commentary that quickly became a crucial element of the newsreel's mode of address. Although the sound newsreel retained much of the variety that had characterized its silent offerings, its stories were now grouped into newspaper-style departments with announcers linking the stories together and directing the audience's gaze.

Despite the introduction of sound, the newsreel's visuality remained paramount in the 1930s and 1940s. The newsreel premised its appeal on allowing audiences to see for themselves the events of the day and equated its realism with this mediated vision. By exploiting the tension between its ability to capture filmic evidence of the news and the ability to display that evidence to its audience, the newsreel emphasized the power and privileges of looking. In this context, spectatorship was not framed as passive. Instead, the newsreel offered its audience a mobile and active form of looking. As engaged newsreel audience members, Americans were invited to inspect the onscreen evidence and judge the images for themselves. This spirit spilled over into the theater itself where newsreel audiences frequently vocalized their approval and displeasure at the people and events on screen. Through its mediated vision, the newsreel offered audiences a way to participate in the media events of the day and an opportunity to enter into a new public sphere.

Despite its proliferation and importance to prewar popular culture, the newsreel remains largely overlooked by film historians. The 2018 collection *Rediscovering U.S. Newsfilm: Cinema, Television, and the Archive* (Cooper et al.) represents a long overdue movement to consider the place of the news in film history, but no monographs have been published on American newsreels as a film form since Raymond Fielding's 1972 industrial history, *The American Newsreel, 1911–1967*.[5] Most recent work on the broader film culture of the 1930s and 1940s in the United States either ignores the newsreel altogether or addresses it only briefly.[6] These omissions are unfortunate, as virtually every member of the moviegoing public watched the newsreel as part of the film program at their local cinema during this period. This project begins to address this lamentable gap in recent film scholarship.

Although little work has been done on the newsreel itself, there is a growing literature on the history of movie culture in the United States outside of feature film and Hollywood productions. Scholars have begun to examine scientific, educational, and industrial films, as well as amateur filmmaking, in order to better understand how film culture has operated beyond Hollywood's feature productions.[7] As these authors have begun to look at film in these new contexts, they find motion pictures were used as far more than entertainment and escape. Although the mainstream newsreel was produced largely within the studio system, its ephemeral nature and its unique format make the newsreel part of the diverse film culture that existed alongside the classical studio film. The histories of these neglected film genres and forms don't just provide a fuller picture of the diversity of film culture, they offer insightful perspectives on how film functions as a medium of representation and as a tool for education.

Documentary studies has raised many questions about film's representational authority and its relationship to the real. Since the publication of Bill Nichols's 1991 book, *Representing Reality: Issues and Concepts in Documentary,* and Michael Renov's important collection, *Theorizing Documentary,* there has been a renewed interest in the theory and history of the documentary film.[8] This work builds on classic documentary theory while incorporating new insights from other areas of film theory.[9] Much of the work in this area has been directed toward theorizing the documentary's distinction from fiction film, as well understanding its different subgenres—or what Nichols calls the documentary modes of representation. In particular, many of the authors in this field have attempted to think through the documentary's claim to represent reality given their skepticism of film's transparency and the well-understood ideological functions of realism.[10] Although there is a good deal of diversity of opinion within this literature, several authors have turned to theories of the spectator in order to solve the dilemma. Nichols and others, such as Jane Gaines and Brian Winston, have argued—albeit to different ends—that documentary's claim on the real rests not in its ability to represent the world as it is (i.e., transparently) but in the spectator's ability to recognize the world represented as their own. If the reception of documentary images rests on the audience's experience and understanding of reality, then any change to that understanding becomes particularly relevant to discussions of documentary film. This book examines just such a change—one brought on by the newsreel's unique claim on the real.

Scholars who study the history and nature of television have raised similar questions with respect to the status of reality on screen and the relationship between spectacle and news. As with documentary studies, scholars interested in television have devoted considerable attention to the question of the medium's ability to represent reality—in particular, writers like Jane Feuer have focused on television's rhetoric of "liveness" as key to constructing the medium's authority and authenticity.[11] Although the technologies of the newsreel did not allow for news to be seen live per se, Feuer's focus on the ideology of liveness rather than its technological basis allows us to link the newsreel's claims to immediacy, authenticity, and timeliness to these same impulses in television news. Along with the notion of liveness, a number of television scholars have also focused on television's role in what has come to be called the "media event." According to Daniel Dayan and Elihu Katz, the media event transforms viewers "from casual, tired, consumer-oriented pleasure seekers . . . into expectant witnesses of a historic moment."[12] Years before the advent of television, the newsreel offered its audience similar access to the media event through spectatorship. Moreover, as we can see from the commentary of both Robert McElravy and Robert Littell, the newsreel, like television after it, had the potential to transform the mundane into the historic and, in turn, fundamentally alter its audience's relationship to history and memory.

The Newsreel and the Mediation of the Public Sphere

The newsreel's emphasis on relations of looking had profound ramifications for the public sphere in the United States in the 1930s and beyond. The newsreel's expansion and influence came at precisely the moment when Americans were wrestling with the status of the public sphere and the role of the media in the democratic process. As intellectual heavyweights like John Dewey and Walter Lippmann debated the potential and desirability of popular participation and the role of the media in instructing or educating the public to this end, the newsreel intervened in a way not anticipated by either of their positions.[13] Rather than providing a means to educate the masses or generate consensus on questions of public policy, the newsreel refashioned the public sphere and the nature of civic participation in the United States. By emphasizing relations of looking, the newsreel created a new mediated public sphere—one where participation rested not on information and knowledge but on what I will call collective spectatorship.[14] Focusing on the nature of this shared experience and how it helped to shape ideas of American collective identity in the 1930s and beyond poses broader questions relating to the role of the mass media in democracy.

The newsreel's rise to prominence in the 1920s coincided with one of the key debates in American social and political theory. In the aftermath of World War I, John Dewey and Walter Lippmann sought to understand how democratic institutions could function in modern, technologically advanced nations and what role the public ought to play in those institutions. In his 1922 book *Public Opinion,* Lippmann argued that modern societies like the United States had become too complex for the citizens to "acquire a competent opinion about all public affairs" and that instead experts ought to guide the public.[15] Dewey acknowledged the problem Lippmann described but called for a different solution. In *The Public and Its Problems,* he argued that it was the role of the press to supply the public with the information necessary to participate fully in the democratic life of the nation.[16] The experience of the world war had convinced Lippmann that such participatory democracy was no longer workable in complex industrialized societies. He suggested that the press should be a tool for technocratic elites to shape public opinion in what he called the "manufacture of consent" rather than as means of public education.[17] Edward Bernays took Lippmann's arguments in favor of elite opinion leaders to their logical conclusion in his advocacy for the art of public relations. In *Propaganda,* Bernays argued that the "manipulation of the news and the inflation of personality" were simply the means by which "ideas were brought to the consciousness of the masses."[18] While he acknowledged that these instruments might be misused, he asserted that they were nevertheless necessary for the competition of ideas and the organization of public opinion. Although these debates about the nature of public opinion made no mention of the newsreel, they centered on the role of the press in democratic societies. Should the media educate or persuade? As we shall see, the newsreel was routinely criticized for failing to be sufficiently edifying, and, despite the cooperation of Hollywood studios with the United States Office of War Information during World War II, for most of its history the newsreel was not engaged in what most would define as propaganda. The newsreel certainly did influence public opinion, but the impacts of the newsreel system were more fundamental. While Dewey, Lippmann, and Bernays focused on the content of the news media and its ability to shape the public's mind, radical changes to the mass media meant that the nature of the public sphere itself was undergoing a profound transformation.

In the 1920s and 1930s, the development of new technologies was changing the news media. Along with the newsreel, the advent of radio altered the way that Americans consumed information and related to one another. Both radio and the newsreel mediated the experience of reality for their audiences. In doing so, these new media provided audiences with not only new or different information but also new ways of experiencing the world and one another.

For the first time, radio broadcasting brought the news—along with sports, music, entertainment, and advertising—directly into the homes of millions of Americans.[19] As Susan Douglas points out, in doing so, radio created new audiences and new connections between listeners. Whether they were listening to momentous news or simply listening to the Yankees beating the Cubs in the World Series, the shared listenership fostered a new sense of American identity. "Millions were engaged, simultaneously, in the same cognitive and emotional work: to create a mental representation of a history-making occurrence. Certainly it was this common activity, as well as living through the same times, that created a sense of national culture."[20] In addition to bringing Americans together, radio also represented a challenge to the traditional boundaries between public and private spheres. By bringing the world into American homes, Jason Loviglio argues it helped to "produce a new kind of social space—the intimate public—in which the terms 'public' and 'private' came to represent a complex web of social performances perpetually in play rather than distinct and immutable categories."[21] What Loviglio calls the "intimate public" was the contested terrain on which the new sense of American identity described by Douglas would be negotiated.

The changes brought on by radio were profound and in many ways paralleled those of the newsreel, but the newsreel's visuality set it apart. Like radio, the newsreel fostered a new sense of national identity and shared experience, but while the radio brought the world into American homes in an unprecedented way, the newsreel changed the way Americans saw the world beyond their homes by redefining the news in visual terms. Where radio's challenge to old notions of the public happened in the "intimate" space of the home, the newsreel's challenge occurred in the theater. In this shared space, collective spectatorship took on new power, and the experience of watching the news came to be more important than its content. Even as radio troubled the traditional boundaries between public and private spheres, the newsreel's visuality transformed the public sphere itself and the public's relationship to it.

Scholars of the public sphere since Jürgen Habermas have regarded the mass media with varying degrees of suspicion.[22] Habermas, like others in the Frankfurt School, saw the mass media as part of a culture industry fundamentally beholden to the ideological interests of capital and the state. As such, the mass media represented a profound threat to the independence and rational discourse he associated with the bourgeois public sphere of the nineteenth century. Such a view both underestimates the powerful discursive constraints present in those bourgeois publics and overestimates the culture industry's power to determine its own public. In his book *Publics and Counterpublics,* Michael Warner productively complicates the idea of the public sphere by redefining it as a "multicontextual space of circulation, organized not by a place or institution but by a circulation of discourse."[23] By shifting attention from the institutions to the space of circulation, Warner opens up room for contestation and negotiation within the public sphere without simply discounting the ideological power of institutions. In the 1930s, the newsreel represented as much a symptom as a cause of a newly emergent public sphere premised on the circulation of images.

The newsreel addressed a new public defined by its shared relationship to the screen and the images on it. While Habermas and others might have regarded this new public sphere as entirely determined by the hegemonic power of the culture industry, a careful study of the newsreel yields a more nuanced picture. As Michael Warner reminds us, "publics exist only by virtue of their imagining."[24] As we shall see, the new mediated public sphere that emerged in the United States in the 1930s was imagined as much by its spectators as by the newsreel itself. The newsreel did not simply indoctrinate the masses, it posed a new relationship between the masses and the world on screen and invited its viewers to engage with that world. The public sphere was not determined by the images themselves (or the industry that produced them) but by the circulation of images between the screen and the audience. It was in this new space that American publics and counterpublics began to imagine and debate their relationship to the state, the world, and one another.

This transformation of the public sphere into a mediated space of shared spectatorship continues to have profound repercussions on American society today. Media scholars often attribute the so-called postmodern media environment to the relatively recent developments of television, satellite, and internet technologies.[25] Renewed attention to the newsreel demonstrates that many of the changes that led to the current media landscape were anticipated decades before the advent of television. Moreover, although technological developments were central to the newsreel's rise, it was the cultural shifts that accompanied the news film that fundamentally changed Americans' relationship to reality and the public sphere. In particular, the visual representation of the news, and its display in the arena of commodified leisure that is the movie theater, transformed reality into a series of consumable images. By making the mediated viewing experience a kind of commodified reality, newsreels anticipated what the French theorist Guy Debord called the society of the spectacle. Debord argued that in a spectacular society, the line between reality and representation blurs to the point where one becomes indistinguishable from the other, and "everything that was directly lived has moved away into a representation."[26] In such a world, images mediate all social relations. By no means did the newsreel complete the shift that Debord identified and critiqued, but its focus on the power of looking and on mediated vision as a way to experience and participate in the public sphere can certainly be seen as making a spectacular society possible. In the newsreel, American audiences encountered the world as a collection of moving images on the screen. Increasingly, the public's relationship to that world, and to one another as spectators, was mediated by the screen.

In her article "Early Cinema, Late Cinema: Permutations of the Public Sphere," Miriam Hansen asks, what is the point "of thinking about cinema in terms of the public?"[27] Hansen argues that doing so allows us to analyze reception "in terms of multiple and conflicting identities and constituencies" and that it might even "function as a matrix for challenging social positions of identity and otherness, as a catalyst for new forms of community and solidarity."[28] As we shall see in chapter 5, the critical reception of *All-American News* and the debates it provoked within its African American counterpublic reveal exactly the kinds of overlapping identities and challenges Hansen had in mind, but the vocal audiences described in chapter 4 show that the studio newsreel was also a venue for conflicting constituencies to generate and contest "new forms of community." Hansen suggests that the advent of classical Hollywood cinema displaced the vital public dimensions of film's early years—the boisterous crowds of the nickelodeon era were replaced by respectable silence in the picture palace, and the "social audience" became an increasingly "private consumer."[29] The evidence of the newsreel and its publics counter such a narrative of decline. Newsreel spectatorship was quintessentially public. For those fully engaged by the news parade's mode of collective spectatorship, as well as those relegated to its margins, the newsreel represented a contested public sphere where American identity and democracy were asserted and debated.

Although contestation and disruption within the newsreel theater reflect the vitality of the mediated public sphere in the pre–World War II era, the public dimensions of the newsreel were not limited to such vocal resistance or to the physical space of reception. As Julian Hanich argues, when an audience comes together to watch film, it is a kind of joint action, and "even quiet attentive viewing implies a type of collective experience."[30] This was certainly true for the newsreel; its mode of address and appeal to realism invited audiences to participate in an active process of looking and to see themselves as part of a shared experience. But the newsreel prompts us to think further about the nature of collective spectatorship. Both Hansen and Hanich consider the public and collective nature of reception only within the confines of the space of the cinema. As this book shows, the newsreel hailed its spectator as part of a collective—one that went beyond the audience in the theater itself. Indeed, the public nature of the news parade implicitly bound the real audience in the cinema to the crowd on screen, as well as an imagined audience of viewers throughout the nation. To watch the newsreel was to participate in an imagined community of spectators where American identity became increasingly linked to the privilege and power to look.

This book's examination of the public nature of the newsreel draws attention to how the news parade functioned as a site of contestation and negotiation, but it also acknowledges that the newsreel's collective spectatorship took place in the venues and on the terms provided by capitalist consumer culture. As Michael Warner neatly states, "publics do not exist apart from the discourse that addresses them."[31] Indeed, the newsreel's unique mode of address was inextricably linked to the system's modes of production and distribution. By recognizing the power of the newsreel's parade mode to shape if not fully define the conditions of reception, "the concept of the public forestalls the idealization of consumption that has become habitual in some quarter of cultural studies."[32] Instead, thinking of the newsreel in terms of its publics and its role in the public sphere allows us to avoid such idealization and account for collective spectatorship and reception at the same time, the text and its context at the same time, cultural power and resistance at the same time. Each of the following chapters aims to do just this while addressing how the industry and culture of moving picture news changed the relationship between Americans, current events, and the public sphere, as well as the consequences of these changes.

Chapter 1 examines how the newsreel system—its content, form, and industrial organization—changed the way Americans consumed the news. The newsreel, more than other film genres and areas of the motion picture business, demands to be studied as an interconnected system—where representation is examined alongside production, distribution, and exhibition. Although each of the five chapters addresses the relationship between these various aspects in some way, chapter 1 explicitly details the connection between the newsreel's mode of production and its logic of representation. Using Charles Lindbergh's transatlantic flight as an illustrative example, this chapter details the changes to the newsreel industry at the end of the 1920s and the beginning of the 1930s. Not only did this singular news event effectively launch the sound newsreel, it proved that news film could be a major box office draw. This chapter details the studio newsreel's unique system of production, distribution, and exhibition that developed after 1927 and how these elements worked together to force out the remaining independent competition. It also describes the mode of address that emerged as a result. Exploiting the tension between the presence of its spectacular onscreen display and the absence of the event of which it provided evidence, the newsreel brought its audience closer than ever to the news while paradoxically maintaining it at a safe distance. I use the newsreel industry's own metaphor of the "news parade" to demonstrate how its audience members were invited to watch the world but also to indulge in the visibility of that world and their own status as spectators. The news parade did not simply offer the audience an opportunity to look and be part of the crowd; it also represented a new relationship between the crowd and the reality on screen.

Chapter 2 examines the newsreel's mode of representation more closely to demonstrate how the tension between display and evidence discussed in chapter 1 produced the newsreel's unique realism. By moving from a discussion of the newsreel system as whole to a more focused analysis of individual newsreel stories, this chapter shows how mediated vision and a populist notion of participation in the media event helped form the basis of the newsreel's reality effect. Two case studies help illustrate these ideas. Both the coverage of the U.S. Presidential Inauguration of 1933 and the Lindbergh kidnapping show how the newsreel applied its unique logic of representation to engage audiences with current events in a way that fundamentally redefined reality in an increasingly mediated world. The newsreel's parade mode facilitated a new kind of realism in three ways. First, the newsreel system fostered media events where the shared viewing of the news was part of the story itself. Second, the newsreel made the world visible in an unprecedented way and, in doing so, privileged the experience of watching the news over other kinds of knowledge. Finally, by privileging this experience, the newsreel invited viewers to judge the events on screen for themselves. By allowing the audience to see and hear the news, the newsreel offered a new kind of realism—one where the real was neither a transparent fact nor an authentic truth but was instead a mediated experience.

Chapter 3 takes up the newsreel's emphasis on looking explored in both chapters 1 and 2 by examining the figure of the newsreel cameraman. In the 1930s, the newsreelman and the tales of his heroic exploits became a key way for studios to promote their newsreels and their sensational scoops. Emerging as both a model of masculinity and a symbol of the imperial gaze in the 1930s, the cameraman represented the newsreel's commitment to go out into the world and "capture the news," bring it back to the United States, and allow audience members to see for themselves. This chapter examines the figure of the cameraman in the newsreels made of the Sino–Japanese war—in particular the bombing and invasion of Shanghai and Nanking in the summer and fall of 1937—as well as a series of fictional representations of the cameraman in Asia that were made in the war's aftermath. Embodied in the newsreel cameraman, looking did not signify passive observation but rather a modern, active, and powerful means to explore the world. This chapter argues that the cameraman played a double role, both as a heroic adventurer-explorer braving the dangerous war-torn locales of the Far East but also as a representative of America and the West in Asia. At a time when American public opinion opposed intervention in the Sino–Japanese conflict, the figure of the heroic cameraman addressed potential anxieties over the United States' policy of neutrality. Drawing on discourses of masculinity and orientalism, newsreel photographers could show on-the-ground images of the war while holding it at a safe distance for their viewers in the United States. In doing so, the newsreel cameramen mediated the relationship between West and East as well as the distance between film audience and film object. The play of distance embodied in these mediations—as well as the deployment of racial and gender categories—is key to understanding the newsreel's power to bind local audiences to the reality of the media event. The newsreel cameraman acted as the agent of the spectator's gaze, at once testifying to the authenticity of the image, authorizing a masculine and imperial form of vision, and reinscribing the power of looking on screen.

Chapter 4 takes up the audience for the newsreel to show how the exhibition context itself furthered the notions of mobility and activity through spectatorship. Using the architecture and history of specially designed newsreel theaters, this chapter shows how companies like the Trans-Lux Corporation and the Newsreel Theatre chain presented the newsreel as part of a modern culture of speed—in both transportation and communication. This chapter also shows how newsreel audience members took up the role of active viewers and transformed the theater into a kind of "public forum of the screen." This chapter examines the conditions of newsreel reception from three different but related perspectives. First, an institutional history of the Trans-Lux Corporation shows how it marketed its theaters as the ultimate in modern moviegoing. The rise of the company, its technological innovations, and its forays into the moving picture industry helped transform newsreel spectatorship into an experience that spoke of modernity and luxury in the machine age. Next, a broader analysis of cinemas from across the country examines the newsreel theater as a physical space and considers how this structured the viewing experience. Building on the newsreel's associations with modernity, architects and designers interpreted the newsreel theater as part of a new global information environment, playing up the role of the camera in bringing the world closer than ever before to American audiences. At the same time, these men helped transform the newsreel experience into one of virtual travel and the theater itself into a kind of vehicle for reaching to distant and exotic places. Finally, an analysis of the lively newsreel audience shows that the newsreel theater was a public place where the news was not simply seen but also commented on and interacted with. In these vibrant spaces, audiences reworked the newsreel's associations with modernity and mobility and used them to inform their experience of the newsreel theater as public and plural. In a world that technology and the mass media had made at once closer and further away, the newsreel cinema became a place to engage with both the reality on screen and those sharing the space of the theater itself.

Departing from the rest of the book's focus on the studio newsreel, chapter 5 takes up *All-American News,* an independent news film series made to cater to African American audiences in the late 1930s and 1940s. This chapter shows the consequences of the mainstream newsreel's emphasis on visuality and looking for a community that was marginalized on screen and in the theater. The privileges of looking that formed such a key part of the studio newsreel were not available in the same way to African Americans as they were to white Americans. Chapter 5 shows how *All-American News* responded to the limits placed on its audience by embracing a politics of visibility linked to the traditions of racial uplift and to the specific context of the Double Victory campaign during World War II. The newsreel's emphasis on visuality and the experience of watching the news made onscreen recognition important. Reality was increasingly defined in terms of mediated looking and the newsreel's invitation to examine the visual evidence. In this context, the *All-American News* offered African Americans the opportunity to be represented—both in the sense of being depicted but also in the sense of having a delegate to speak for their concerns. In the racial politics of the 1940s, this dual representational power of the newsreel seemed to present a potent weapon in the battle for the uplift of the race. Indeed, many saw the visual power of the newsreel as a crucial tool in achieving recognition and respect—by displaying evidence of black accomplishment but also by educating African American audiences. By looking at how *All-American News* deployed its unique pedagogical address and the rhetoric of uplift in the context of wartime race relations and a Jim Crow motion picture industry, this chapter shows how the newsreel contested racial inequality while accommodating segregation. Images of achievement implicitly refuted racist portrayals of African Americans on film and encouraged its audience members to advance the race through their own talents and diligence. Nevertheless, *All-American News* largely ignored the issue of racism itself, and critics and audiences began to question a politics of visibility that put the onus for change on the newsreel's black viewers rather than white America. Between *All-American News* and its audience, we can see a critical counterpublic emerge—a counterpublic that recognized the deeply unequal possibilities to engage in the privileges of collective spectatorship offered in the news parade.

To conclude the book, I return to the questions raised by the epigraphs at the beginning of this introduction in order to examine the legacy and relevancy of the newsreel as history. The newsreel's emphasis on visuality and looking reshaped the public sphere in the United States in ways that are still being felt today. And while newsreel images may not provide the kind of "canned history" that Robert C. McElravy predicted, they do offer insight into how the power and privileges of looking revealed, and continue to reveal, gaps and fissures in America's mediated public sphere. My conclusion looks forward from the era of this study to see how the history of the newsreel can help us to understand our mediated public sphere today. Notions of the real and the nature of the public sphere are once again undergoing a profound shift. Social media like Twitter, Facebook, and Instagram now allow for unprecedented interaction with news events and among news consumers while the proliferation of news sources, the rise of hyperpartisan media, and so-called fake news cast doubt on the reliability of all information—including visual evidence. As we grapple with these changes today, the newsreel offers an instructive historical model of how media technology and culture can fundamentally alter our relationship with the world and how these changes are felt differently by different communities.

This book shows that the power of media to change the way people see reality cannot be understood narrowly in purely technological terms. Instead, media must be understood as both symptoms of and catalysts for broader cultural, social, and political shifts. In the newsreel, notions of the real were tied not so much to the images on screen but the audience's experience watching them in the theater. As such, the newsreel shifted the onus of the real from relations of representation to relations of looking. By drawing attention to this shift, this study demonstrates that realism and reality itself are historically contingent rather than universal categories and that they must be understood in context. Only by examining the film text in the full context of its circulation is it possible to understand the newsreel and its role in shaping the public sphere of the 1930s and 1940s. Whether one regards the newsreel archive naively like McElravy or cynically like Littell, one must acknowledge that it was never in the text alone that the newsreel made its meaning. The newsreel's power—its appeal to realism and collective identity and as a venue for political participation and resistance—lay in the circulation of these images and the collective spectatorship they engendered. As Michael Warner states, "a public is understood to be an ongoing space of encounter for discourse. No texts themselves create publics, but the concatenation of texts through time."[33] This book traces the concatenation of newsreel images through time—examining the newsreel's modes of production, distribution, and exhibition to determine how the newsreel system (i.e., the news parade) served as a site for the creation as well as the contestation of new publics and counterpublics. As scholars of new media recognize the need for increased attention to circulation in thinking about the power and effect of platforms like Facebook and Reddit,[34] the news parade demonstrates the power of decentering the text in the study of media histories as well. By seeing the newsreel archive in its broader context, this book goes beyond the film record to examine the transformation of America's mediated public sphere. In doing so, it shows the extent to which the news parade transformed the way Americans saw themselves and the world.

CHAPTER 1

News Parade

The Logic of the Newsreel System

> For posterity, the newsreel has President McKinley, leaving office after his first term; Czar Nicholas reviewing his troops in 1914 . . . Taft making his inaugural address in a snowstorm; Teddy Roosevelt hunting in Africa . . . soldiers of all nations going to fight in the World War . . . The Wright brothers at Kittyhawk; Byrd flying over both poles; Lindbergh in Paris; Hauptmann on the witness stand; Dillinger on a slab; Jack Johnson, Jim Jeffries, Tilden, Dempsey, Nurmi, Hitler, Mussolini, Stalin, and countless other figures of earth, and the earth on which they trod—the earth of floods, fires, panics, earthquakes, volcanoes, tidal waves, tornadoes, and parades, parades, parades.
>
> —THOMAS SUGRUE, *SCRIBNER'S MAGAZINE*, 1937

On June 13, 1927, New York City's Canyon of Heroes was host to the largest ticker tape parade since the end of the Great War. Millions of people thronged the streets of Manhattan to celebrate Charles Lindbergh's historic transatlantic flight. These crowds were photographed by dozens of newsreel cameras placed along the parade route, and moving pictures of Lindbergh sitting in an open-top car, passing through a storm of ticker tape on New York's Fifth Avenue remain iconic images of the United States at the height of its confidence in the 1920s. The Lindbergh parade was a celebration of American achievement, but it was also a watershed moment for the American newsreel. Lindbergh's triumph presented newsreel producers with an ideal opportunity to demonstrate the power and reach of their news organizations. Moreover, the dramatic contrast between the singularity of Lindbergh's individual achievement and the sheer mass of his innumerable well-wishers made for a vivid symbol of the United States' emergent celebrity culture as well as the motion picture industry's key role in fostering it. Images of this parade through the streets of New York epitomized a new way of looking at the world. The ticker tape parade, with its celebrity, spectacle, and fascinated crowds, was the ultimate newsreel event. The parade, however, was more than that. It was also a fitting metaphor for the newsreel system itself. It is important to analyze the newsreel as a complete and interconnected system because, more than other film forms, its specialized modes of production, distribution, and address shaped and reflected the newsreel's content. The newsreel system combined to produce a logic of representation that mirrored the ticker tape parade by inviting audiences to watch the world as a passing pageant. Tracing the origins and development of this logic and the unique place of the newsreel in the history of American media is key to understanding the role the news parade played in changing the way Americans viewed the world, their relationship to it, and to one another.

Charles Lindbergh: "The Greatest Newsreel Subject of the Age"

The story of Lindbergh's flight and the hero's welcome he received upon returning to the United States ushered in a "golden age" for newsreels. Since their introduction in 1911, regularly released news films had become a fixture of the silent motion picture program. American audiences expected these ten-minute shorts before the feature presentation or between the "A" and the "B" movies. Patrons and exhibitors largely took these collections of political speeches, natural disasters, sporting events, and novelties for granted, seeing them as a necessary part of the program but rarely as a box office attraction in and of themselves.[1] The Lindbergh story changed that. For the first time since the Great War, American movie audiences sought out the best coverage of the news, and the newsreel drove the box office.[2] This spike in interest in the newsreel was partly a result of the enormous public attention given to Lindbergh's flight. Newspapers, magazines, and radio stations all devoted significant column inches or airtime to the celebrated pilot, but the Lindbergh story was especially compelling to newsreel producers. It combined familiar elements of several popular newsreel subjects with the added appeal of its historical importance. Moreover, the story offered studios a chance to demonstrate the power of their distribution systems and, for at least one of them, the opportunity to show off their new sound technology. The wide appeal of the Lindbergh films proved to exhibitors that newsreels could be a draw and to producers that they could be profitable.

No news story captured the imagination of the American public like Lindbergh's flight.[3] When news reached New York on May 21 that the young pilot had landed safely in Paris, municipal steam whistles, fire truck sirens, and ship horns blared while Broadway took on a jubilant atmosphere not seen since the Armistice. But the celebrations of May 21 paled in comparison with those of June 13, when Lindbergh arrived back in New York City. After receiving commendations from President Coolidge in Washington, D.C., a day earlier, Lindbergh flew himself to Mitchell Field, Long Island, where an amphibian plane took him to Pier A in lower Manhattan. From there, Lindbergh was driven first to City Hall and then up Fifth Avenue. At each stop along the way, Lindbergh was met by hordes of media and enthusiastic crowds. Some 3.5 million people lined the streets of the city to welcome "Lindy" home. Several New York–area radio stations presented live coverage of his arrival, placing reporters at various points along the parade route. The local newspapers provided blanket coverage: including photographs, the *New York Times* devoted fifteen pages to Lindy's Day while the *New York American, New York Herald-Tribune,* and *New York World* set aside ten, nine, and eight pages respectively, and the tabloid *Mirror* allocated over twenty-three of its forty pages to the festivities in honor of the young pilot.[4] Likewise, the newsreel devoted a huge proportion of its resources to the story. *Pathé News* alone reported shooting 7,430,000 feet of film of Lindbergh's comings and goings—easily giving him the record as the most photographed person in motion pictures.[5]

For the newsreel, this enormous excitement represented an extraordinary opportunity. Even apart from the public interest, the Lindbergh homecoming was tailor-made for the newsreel. In his history of the American newsreel, Raymond Fielding states that newsreel subjects all fell into one of the following types: "catastrophe, international celebrities, pageantry and ceremony, sports, political and military events, technology, and spectacle and novelty."[6] Lindbergh's transatlantic flight could fit in virtually all of these categories. The Orteig Prize, which was to be awarded to the first team successfully to complete the nonstop flight between New York City and Paris, made for a sporting event with both political and military relevance. While Lindbergh himself made the journey with little incident, previous attempts to cross the ocean by plane had ended in catastrophe. Two of René Fonck's crewmembers died when his plane crashed on takeoff while he attempted the crossing in September 1926, and, just weeks before Lindbergh succeeded, Frenchman Charles Nungesser went missing over the Atlantic. Lindbergh's unique achievement was both human and technological. Finally, the pageantry and ceremony that greeted him in France and the United States was spectacular. For the newsreel, this was a compelling story with striking visual interest. Moreover, unlike risky war pictures, natural disasters, or political speeches, the Lindbergh achievement offered a history-making event that was relatively safe and predictable. News crews knew well ahead of time where and when Lindbergh would make his takeoff and landing, and the ceremonies that followed were well-planned events for which the press could prepare. At a time when newsreel cameras were still relatively large and cumbersome, such lead time was extremely valuable. It's little wonder, then, that the *Motion Picture News* described Lindbergh's achievement as "not only the greatest news story of the age but the greatest newsreel subject," adding that it had "given a prominence to the news film such as not even the World War lent it."[7] Indeed, the interest in the Lindbergh story made the newsreel more relevant than ever before, and the industry was poised to make the most of the opportunity.

Studios poured huge resources into recording and distributing scenes of Lindbergh's triumph. In addition to offering the perfect newsreel subject, the story represented a chance for news film services to demonstrate the potential of their medium. In all, the newsreels produced four "specials" on the aviator—covering his takeoff from Roosevelt field, his landing in Paris, and his arrivals in Washington and New York. The *Moving Picture World* reported that the industry set new records for speed in getting the story of Lindbergh's takeoff to the screen. It praised the *International Newsreel* in particular for "showing pictures of the hop-off, which occurred on Friday morning, on Broadway Friday afternoon, at 9:15 p.m. in Chicago, and in Los Angeles theatres Saturday evening."[8] Americans had to wait over a week for scenes of Lindbergh's reception in Paris, as the ocean liner *Majestic* carried the negatives for each of the news services from France. This time it was *Pathé* that scored the scoop. Having received detailed descriptions of the scenes shot in Paris, editors in New York planned the continuity and wrote the titles in advance so that all that remained was to identify the scenes and insert them between the titles. According to the *Motion Picture News,* a cutter, sent to intercept *Majestic* on its way to New York, meant that *Pathé*'s footage reached Broadway before the liner had even docked.[9]

These efforts were nothing compared to the resources devoted to filming and distributing scenes of Lindbergh's return to the United States. *Variety* estimated that together the newsreel companies spent $75,000 to turn out film of Lindbergh's reception in Washington—not including their regular expenses of salaries, film, and laboratory costs: "One firm spent $9,000 for aeroplane delivery, another donated $4,000 in air mail stamps to distribute the stuff, and International broke a record in getting a special train between Washington and New York in three hours and seven minutes over the Pennsylvania."[10] The train had three cars: a complete lab for developing the negatives and creating positive prints, a projection car where the footage was cut, and an editing room where titles were written and added. By the time the train arrived in New York City, six prints were ready to be delivered by car to Manhattan theaters where the film was seen less than four hours after the event.[11] On the day of Lindbergh's arrival in New York, the news services again raced to beat each other to the screen. Each company had a dozen or more cameras in position throughout New York to capture all the views of that day. According to the *New York Times,* "one company alone had twenty-five cameramen covering places of vantage and employed a dozen airplanes to transport the films to [various distribution hubs across the country]."[12] Again newsreel companies broke records for speed. Representatives of *Pathé* told the *Times* that "by the time Lindbergh arrived at Pier A, films recording his arrival at Mitchell field were being distributed and that they were exhibited before the aviator was through receiving the city's welcome,"[13] or about two hours later. Truman Talley, Director-in-Chief of *Fox News,* called the effort and resources spent on producing and distributing the Lindbergh story "the greatest display of newsreel energy and enterprise in the history of the industry" and suggested that it proved the tremendous strides taken in the production of news film in the United States.[14] The news companies had done their best to assert their relevance and succeeded in generating greater interest from exhibitors and audiences in the years that followed. Lindbergh's transatlantic flight marked the beginning of a new era of prominence for the newsreel.

The Lindbergh story was especially important to *Fox News,* as it used the event to promote its new sound technology. Although the company had debuted its *Movietone* newsreel several weeks earlier with scenes of cadets marching at West Point, Lindbergh's takeoff from Roosevelt Field on May 20, 1927, marked the first time the talking newsreel was used to cover a story of wide public interest.[15] The film itself was visually unremarkable. The stationary camera showed Lindbergh's aircraft as it taxied into position on the runway but lost sight of the plane as it gathered speed. Interestingly, it was only the cheers of the assembled crowd that attested to the successful takeoff.[16] Nevertheless, the film was well received.[17] Playing at Broadway's Roxy Theatre just hours after news of Lindbergh's safe arrival in Paris, the *New York Times* called the film "impressive" and reported that, "more than 6,000 persons arose and cheered, drowning out the noise of the recording machine."[18] Likewise, audiences enthusiastically received sound film of Lindbergh's reception in Washington, D.C., and President Coolidge's commendation. Reviewers for both the *Times* and *Variety* commented on the shared enthusiasm between the onscreen crowd and the theater's audience. Mordaunt Hall wrote that the applause at the Roxy Theatre preceded those on screen by a mere fraction of a second, proving "that both crowds were of one mind."[19] Truman Talley's assertion that the "'talking newsreel' gained tremendous impetus" from the Lindbergh story proved correct, as over the next few years each of Fox's competitors introduced sound to their news offerings.

The American moviegoing public enthusiastically embraced Lindbergh, and it was this reception that was the true measure of his impact on the newsreel. After reading reports and seeing news films of Lindbergh's tour of the capitals of Europe, many were eager to greet the returning hero. Millions of people turned out to see Lindbergh parade up the streets of New York—and in the movie theater. According to *Variety,* "the news stuff on Lindbergh drew business. It started around dinner time Saturday and reached its peak after the Fifth Avenue parade when everyone seemingly flocked to a deserted Broadway to jam practically every grind house on the main alley."[20] Lindbergh was in demand. The newsreel companies received letters and telegrams from all over the country requesting more Lindbergh footage as soon as possible.[21] Exhibitors told the *Motion Picture News* that "they had made more money on the newsreels of Lindbergh's arrival in Europe than on any feature within their recollection."[22] At the Roxy, where *Fox Movietone*'s sound coverage had an exclusive engagement, *Variety* attributed a nearly 20 percent jump in grosses to the drawing power of the talking newsreel of Lindbergh. The Lindbergh story proved to producers and exhibitors that the newsreel could be profitable and that it could be more than just a necessary part of the motion picture program; it could be a box office draw.

The success of the Lindbergh films, combined with the new power of the sound newsreel, ushered in a period of growth and consolidation for the newsreel industry. The films documenting Lindbergh's achievement were the most dramatic demonstration to date of the system's potential to capture and represent the world to an enthusiastic audience. However, these films—especially those of the New York parade—demonstrated more than just the newsreel's popular appeal and its financial viability. The image of the ticker tape parade—with its pageantry, cheering crowds, and celebrity idols—exemplified the logic with which the newsreel imagined the world. In framing the news as a kind of passing spectacle, the newsreel presented audiences with a particular version of reality: a series of sensational images that studios continuously selected, edited, narrated, produced, distributed, and sold. Before further analyzing the logic behind this representation, it is necessary to understand first how the medium "worked"—both as an industry and in terms of its mode of address.

Newsreel as Industry: The Newsreel's Modes of Production and Distribution

In the late 1920s, the newsreel industry underwent a series of changes that entrenched the major Hollywood studios as the sole newsreel services in the United States. The early years of the American newsreel had been characterized by a dizzying array of independent players, new alliances, and short-lived ventures. By the mid-1920s, the industry had stabilized around a few recognized producers. Key changes in 1927 made sure that independent newsreel companies could never again compete with their well-funded rivals. The introduction of sound made newsreel production more expensive, and the growing power of the studio system made it increasingly difficult for independent producers to find exhibitors to show their films. The vertical integration of the major motion picture companies and their extensive networks of production and distribution further centralized the newsreel industry in the United States. Such centralization was key to producing the standardized newsreel of the 1930s.

As Douglas Gomery and others have documented, the motion picture industry was highly integrated by the end of the 1920s.[23] Heading into the 1930s, the so-called "Big Five"—Paramount, Loew's (parent company to the production company Metro-Goldwyn-Mayer), Warner Bros., Fox, and Radio-Keith-Orpheum (RKO)—dominated the movie business. Each of these companies "owned substantial production facilities in Southern California, a worldwide distribution network and a sizable theater chain."[24] This vertical integration made these companies formidable. Although together the Big Five only owned about 16 percent of the nation's first-run theaters, according to Gomery these accounted for three quarters of the revenue from motion picture exhibition.[25] Studio-owned theaters tended to be the largest cinemas in the best locations in the biggest markets. Affiliation with the major studios ensured these movie houses first-run rights to the most popular studio films and, often, exclusive runs in many cities and neighborhoods. These efficiencies gave the big studios a distinct advantage over independent exhibitors and producers as well as smaller studios like Universal, Columbia, and United Artists, which had production and distribution units but not their own theater chains.

The vertical integration of the studio system had a profound effect on the newsreel industry in the United States. The ability to provide their own theaters as well as unaffiliated cinemas with a "complete line" of films, including features, comedy shorts, and newsreels, was key to the Big Five's success.[26] It was the need to provide this complete line that prompted the reorganization of the newsreel. Fox had been producing its own newsreel, *Fox News,* since 1919 and had made it an important part of its brand image for several years. The introduction of its sound reel,

Fox Movietone News, in 1927 gave it a further advantage in the market. In order to compete, other studios established their own newsreel divisions. Paramount introduced its *Paramount News* in 1927 as a silent reel but soon added sound. That same year, Loew's forged an agreement with William Randolph Hearst's successful *International Newsreel* operation to release the silent *MGM International Newsreel* and later the talking newsreel, *Hearst Metrotone News* (the name was changed to *MGM's News of the Day* in 1936). With this increased competition from the major studios, independently produced newsreels such as *Pathé News* and *Kinograms* found it increasingly difficult to turn a profit. One estimate suggested that "in 1925 when only four newsreels were being made, the cost of producing all four was about $75,000 per week and the total income about $115,000 per week, while in 1928, when six newsreels were being made, the cost of production was $125,000 per week and the total income about $110,000 per week."[27] With the added costs of recording sound as well as pictures, independent producers were left with few options. In 1931, RKO merged with Pathé and became the fourth major studio to offer newsreels along with the rest of its films. Hit hard by the new competition and the introduction of sound, Educational Pictures attempted to continue *Kinograms* as a silent reel. But as more and more theaters converted to sound, the company was forced to discontinue the newsreel after an ill-fated attempt to keep it afloat as an advertiser-sponsored short subject. By 1931, the newsreel industry in the United States had been completely absorbed into the studio system. Warner Bros. was the only major studio that did not have its own news service, while Fox, MGM, Paramount, and RKO could offer a complete line to their exhibitors, as could Universal Pictures, whose *Universal Newsreel* was the only national newsreel not distributed by one of the Big Five.

Although the consolidation of the motion picture industry brought the newsreels under the major studio umbrella, their production remained largely separate. Headed by separate management, each of the companies maintained their main newsreel offices in New York rather than Southern California. Organized along the lines of a daily newspaper, an editor-in-chief headed up the newsreel divisions and oversaw an operation whose success hinged on a steady flow of news pictures.

The key to maintaining the flow of newsreel images was securing quality footage. Each of the newsreel companies maintained a regular staff of about one hundred cameramen stationed throughout the world.[28] These workers were paid between fifty and two hundred dollars per week. The cameramen received some instructions from an assignment editor in New York, but it was often up to them to locate newsworthy, unusual, or simply visually interesting subjects. In addition to these staff cameramen, the newsreels regularly bought footage from freelancers who were paid by the foot for film used—these rates could be anywhere between fifty cents and one hundred dollars per foot, depending on the subject and how the material was used.[29] Cameramen had to be extremely technically skilled. While editors looked for compelling stories, the clarity and timeliness of the film shot were of primary importance. A form letter sent from Universal's offices in 1933 listed twenty-seven possible reasons footage might be rejected. While some of these referred to the subject being of insufficient "news interest" or "too tame," most referred to the technical quality of the film submitted—editors might reject footage for being incomplete, fogged, scratched, overexposed, underexposed, out of focus, shaky, having too many panoramas or their being too fast, having too few scenes or their being too short, or, of course, for the film being received "too late."[30] Newsreel cameramen were expected to produce footage to much the same standard as cinematographers working on any other Hollywood film but without the luxuries of a studio set or multiple takes. Given these technical requirements, it is little wonder that the newsreels and their cameramen preferred subjects that were scheduled and that could be shot under more controlled conditions. As one commentator dryly observed, "of all the things which a newsreel editor hates, war is first. It is expensive, it is dangerous for the cameramen, and it seldom if ever produces pictures worth looking at."[31] This attitude helps explain why the newsreel gave so much of its attention to sporting events and "human interest" stories—one study of the five major newsreels in 1935 determined that these subjects accounted for almost 50 percent of their content.[32] Indeed, the Lindbergh parade was so appealing to newsreel editors because it was not only newsworthy and historic but also on schedule and easily shot by their large stationary cameras. For newsreel editors, quality newsreel images were not simply those of the greatest news value but also those that met their high technical standards.

Cameramen forwarded their raw negatives, along with "dope sheets" that detailed the shots taken and any other relevant information (names of individuals, locations, final scores, etc.), to the newsreel offices in New York.[33] Here the editorial staff examined the footage and cut down the many thousands of feet of film received each week to a reel of less than one thousand feet. A highly specialized division of labor was involved in this process as film needed to be developed and edited. After an editorial team had chosen the stories for release, audio technicians mixed music with natural sound and studio sound effects, while writers scripted the titles and commentary. Following a few rehearsals, the story was projected in studio, and, to get the timing just right, the commentator added the voiceover to the audio mix in a single take. Finally, the print shop added titles along with dissolves, wipes, and any other visual effects. All of this was done in a single day twice a week—on Mondays and Wednesdays—in order to reach theaters in time for them to change their programs.[34] Once completed, the prints of each issue were sent out by plane or train to theaters all over the country.

Distribution for the newsreel was handled through the studios' regular system of exchanges, and it was here that they reaped the financial benefits of vertical integration. Agents in thirty-two major cities in the United States negotiated licenses with exhibitors and delivered films to the theaters. By distributing their newsreels, features, and shorts through the same offices, studios kept their per unit costs low while capitalizing on the advantage of the "complete line" of products.[35] Some larger theaters subscribed to several services and combined the best stories from each to create their own reels—in 1928, for example, the Strand Theater in New York combined footage from *Kinograms, Fox News,* and the *MGM International Newsreel* to screen its own *Strand Newsreel.* In the mid-1930s, several specialized newsreel theaters opened in major American cities. These theaters offered the best of the week's newsreels, showing the most compelling stories from all the major news services.[36] However, most exhibitors bought only one company's newsreel, usually purchasing a year's worth or 104 issues at once. This tended to favor the major studio newsreels, as it meant that overall reputation, consistency, and price outweighed individual scoops or exclusive pictures. Moreover, the savings and convenience of ordering the "complete line" from a single exchange meant that independent exhibitors usually showed the newsreel from the studio with which they already had a contract, and studio-affiliated theaters simply showed their own company's reel. Depending on the size and market, theaters paid anywhere from $1.50 per week to $300 per week for newsreel service.[37] Large, first-run theaters paid more for their news service but in return received the news as soon as it was released, including special delivery of "extra" specials. Smaller theaters in rural locales paid less, but they received the newsreel days or weeks after it was released. It was up to sales agents working out of the local exchanges to negotiate these contracts. The total life span of an issue was up to four weeks, as a single print could be passed down from a first-run house in New York all the way to a small town theater before the film stock itself was sold for scrap.[38] Once again, this arrangement favored the Big Five studios as their theaters were larger and tended to be concentrated in major metropolitan areas. Thus, they could sell their reels at a premium to these cinemas and then offer discounts to those further down the line. With comparable production costs but no theater chain of its own, *Universal Newsreel* was left to compete with the big studios for the less lucrative contracts from unaffiliated cinemas.

Although the newsreel industry was highly centralized in New York, most reels attempted to appeal to local markets by offering some special regional coverage. In one issue of *Hearst Metrotone News,* for example, Boston exchanges received coverage of the Boston Red Sox playing the Braves, while the rest of the country was treated to an "aerial sight-seeing trip above the famous landmarks in beautiful Washington, [D.C.]."[39] But even these regional stories needed to be edited and voiced in New York. This led to some circuitous paths for news footage. For example, a story about the University of Toronto gymnastics team, shot by the Associated Screen News in that same city, was requested by the Canadian Universal Film exchange. In a memo to the New York offices of the *Universal Newsreel,* they requested the story be edited to seventy-five feet for inclusion in the next week's issue.[40] In order for this to happen, the negatives needed to be shipped to New York, where they were developed, edited, and merged with the voiceover, and then sent to Montreal—along with the rest of the issue—where distribution prints were struck for release in the Canadian market.[41] While cumbersome, this centralization ensured a consistent tone and a standard level of quality for each newsreel.

The newsreel's modes of production and distribution might well be compared to Fordist models of continuous flow manufacture, where standardization, automation, and the division of labor created the efficiencies of the assembly line. Some critics have likened the entire Hollywood studio system of the 1930s to such a model of mass production: films churned out mechanically by a system that had little regard for creativity or art. The motion picture industry of the 1930s did rely heavily on Taylorist management techniques and the specialized division of labor. Nevertheless, such an analogy oversimplifies. David Bordwell, Janet Staiger, and others have argued that the studio system is more accurately described as a kind of serial manufacture—where "skilled specialists collaborate to create a unique product while still adhering to a blueprint prepared by management."[42] In such a system there was still room for individual creativity and innovation. But while these qualifications were true of Hollywood feature film production, the newsreel of this same period adhered more closely to the assembly-line analogy. Production units were not created and disbanded, there were no highly paid stars, no elaborate sets, no pretense of art, and, given the fast pace of twice-weekly production, very little space for innovation. The newsreel was, by and large, a standardized product that secured and improved its brand image by maintaining a certain level of quality and predictability (of scheduling as well as of content). To be sure, individual cameramen might occasionally go to great lengths to capture unique and spectacular footage, and the newsreel companies did release special "extra" editions when news events demanded, but, in the end, scoops and exclusive pictures were just a way of enticing new audiences to watch the regular newsreel. Ten minutes of film twice a week guaranteed that much news film was neither sensational nor particularly newsworthy. Instead, editors opted for prescheduled and predictable happenings, such as sporting events, beauty pageants, and parades, to fill out most reels. The consolidation of the film industry in the late 1920s further entrenched this factory production model, as newsreel divisions were increasingly integrated into the studio structure of production, distribution, and exhibition. Thus organized, the newsreel industry was, in many ways, the epitome of continuous flow production. Like any mass-produced commodity, the newsreel capitalized on the economies of scale offered by integrated production and well-coordinated distribution networks to offer customers a steady supply of a standardized product. Centralization, along with the specialized division of labor, was crucial to maintaining these standards. As we shall see, when combined with the newsreel's mode of address, the assembly-line mode of production and distribution was also key to the system's logic of representation.

Voiceover Commentary and the Talking Newsreel's Direct Address

The same forces that brought about the standardization of production and distribution—the rise of the Big Five and the introduction of sound—also affected the onscreen organization and representational strategies of the newsreel itself. The centralized nature of the news film business favored consistency over innovation, the streamlining of production methods encouraged segmentation and the predictable ordering of news stories, and the advent of sound allowed the various companies to distinguish their reels using the voices and personalities of their commentators. In the 1930s, the silent newsreel—a more or less loosely arranged collection of actualities—gave way to the talking newsreel and its familiar casts of personalities and regular features. These changes had profound effects on the way the newsreel addressed its audience. Although some critics complained that the new emphasis on commentary and sound effects distracted from the visual power of the newsreel, voiceovers often highlighted the presence of the image in front of the audience. By addressing the viewer directly, commentary created a sense of immediacy that became key to the newsreel's reality effect. Indeed, it was the sound newsreel's direct address, along with its factory-style model of production and the key elements of display and evidence, that produced the newsreel's parade-like logic.

With the steady flow of footage arriving on a daily basis from cameramen across the country and around the world, the major newsreels had an abundance of material with which to fill their biweekly issues. To organize this material and to take advantage of the predictability and popularity of certain kinds of footage, the newsreels began to create more or less regular sections. By the mid-1930s, most of the newsreels had introduced sports and other departments, often separated by a standard title screen and narrated by a different commentator. *Fox Movietone* was the most rigidly divided of the major reels. Lowell Thomas was the main commentator, Louise Vance voiced ladies fashion features, Ed Thorgersen covered sports, and Lew Lehr described novelty stories.[43] Each of these commentators was introduced within the reel itself, and Lehr even had his own title sequence, featuring him in costume offering such bon mots as "cheerio—let's have a go at it" and "23 skidoo."[44] In many ways this growing compartmentalization was modeled on the various sections of the daily newspaper. By 1938, *MGM's News of the Day* made this reference explicit, naming its main news section "The Front Page," narrated by John B. Kennedy, and featuring the commentary of Adelaide Hawley for the "Woman's Page" and Bill Stern on the "Sporting Page."[45] By dividing their content in this way, newsreels efficiently created biweekly editions that capitalized on the abundance of easily shot lifestyle, novelty, and sports stories. And if the creation of regular departments meant less time for "hard news," the adoption of newspaper formats gave such moves an added aura of legitimacy.

As these examples of compartmentalization illustrate, the division of content into sections was also an opportunity for the competing news services to introduce new voices to their reels and set themselves apart from the competition. Universal, with smaller production budgets and far less sound equipment in the field than the other newsreels, highlighted their commentator, Graham McNamee, in many of their publicity materials. A popular radio announcer for the National Broadcasting Company (NBC), Universal named McNamee the "talking reporter." Appearing "by special arrangement" with NBC, Universal boasted that McNamee added, "that human touch that gives life and fire to the events as they flash on the screen."[46] Similarly, in 1934, *Hearst Metrotone News* suggested exhibitors could use the acquisition of commentator and journalist Edwin C. Hill as a means to excite interest from local newspapers and thus secure additional publicity.[47] By adding popular radio personalities and respected journalists to their reels, the news services sought to borrow celebrity and authority from other media—even as they featured more sports and lifestyle coverage.[48]

Although the newsreels argued that entertaining and creative personalities added "life and fire" to their pictures, some critics suggested the additions of music, sound effects, and overeager commentary detracted from what had always been the newsreel's primary virtue: its realism. In 1931, one critic observed that while the introduction of synchronized sound had initially served to heighten the credibility of the newsreel, the addition of pun-riddled voiceovers and studio sound effects had made it "forced and unnatural," adding that "the newsreel continues to be pictorially accurate, but the tone becomes entirely false."[49] Similarly, in a 1935 article titled "Newsreels Should Be Seen and Not Heard," John Erskine lamented the effect of studio sound on the news film:

> The introduction of artificial elements has cheated me of what I came for—the opportunity of seeing exactly what happened. The pleasure should be primarily for the eye. But the firm voice pursues me, distracts my eye, and wrecks my pleasure.[50]

Written several years after the introduction of the talking newsreel, Erskine's criticism captures a crucial question for the study of the newsreel's mode of address in the sound era. Erskine may have been distracted by the constant commentary and felt it an "artificial" addition to the purity of the silent news film, but retrospectively we must recognize it as an enduring and integral aspect of the newsreel system from the 1930s on. Indeed, although the visual power of the newsreel remained primary in the sound era, its voiceover, and the direct address to the audience in particular, was, in fact, key to producing the newsreel's unique mode of address.

The newsreel had always offered to show its audience the world as it "really was." Despite examples of early newsreels "faking" their shots, the industry had built its reputation on the basis of the purity of the cinematic record.[51] At first, the addition of sound only enhanced this quality. In its first years, *Fox Movietone* simply added synchronized sound to its news pictures to offer audiences the novelty of a multisensory document. *Variety,* in its review of the *Movietone*'s debut, suggested that the reel would be a program standout and marveled at the mere fact that audiences were "listening and looking at something that [had] actually happened."[52] Before the introduction of music and voiceover commentary, sound was ostensibly a way of more fully capturing the world as it was. But, as the novelty of sync sound wore off, the newsreels added audio elements to their subjects as a way of heightening interest. Commentators could provide background information, the identities of persons on screen, and litanies of statistics. They could also alert viewers to the most spectacular moments, while music could add considerable dramatic tension. Moreover, adding sound effects and an amusing commentary to a novelty subject was one way of trying to keep it fresh—after all, one baby fashion show looked very much like the next.

Whether it was adding humor to a novelty or tension to the story of a natural disaster, the newsreel voiceover of the 1930s always directly addressed its audience. Film scholar Mary Ann Doane has pointed out that, "as a form of direct address [the voiceover commentary of documentary film] speaks without mediation to the audience, bypassing the 'characters' and establishing a complicity between itself and the spectator."[53] As Doane and others suggest, this complicity, along with the disembodiment of the voiceover, helps to produce the commentary as unquestionable truth.[54] Unlike the image of a politician giving a speech for the camera, the voiceover avoids questions like, "Who is speaking? And for whom?" Such elisions in the newsreel were critical and have rightly been linked to its hegemonic function and potential for propaganda.[55] But while it is important to acknowledge the power inherent in the newsreel voiceover, we should not simply see this power in the commentary's ability to distort the truth or represent opinion as fact. Indeed, to focus solely on its distortions begs the question as to how the newsreel, and its use of voiceover commentary in particular, worked to produce a reality effect in the first place.

I would suggest that the newsreel's voiceover facilitated another kind of complicity between commentator and spectator. By speaking directly to the viewers, it performed a critical spatial and temporal shift—from the past of the events represented on the screen to the present of the audience. All film images are, by the nature of the apparatus, representations of the past. The objects, people, and events shown on screen are, by definition, absent. The newsreel did not deny this absence. In fact, companies often trumpeted the lengths to which their cameramen went to capture spectacular footage and frequently boasted of the historical value of their pictures. Nevertheless, once inside the theater, the newsreel invited its spectator to revel in the presence of the images. Rather than casting the events of the screen as past, the voiceover typically spoke in the present tense. By essentially narrating events as they happened on the screen, the commentary created a sense of immediacy for the audience, echoing the experience of a radio broadcast of a live sporting event.[56] A striking example of this "play-by-play" was the *Universal Newsreel*'s coverage of the 1934 assassination of King Alexander of Yugoslavia and the French Foreign Minister, Louis Barthou. Commentator Graham McNamee offered the following account:

> You are about to see the most amazing pictures ever made, the assassination of King Alexander of Jugoslavia . . . It's gala day in Marseilles. Literally hundreds of thousands are jammed along the main street—the Cannebière—to see this greatest show—royalty on parade. Republican France enthusiastically greets the visiting monarch. Vive Alexandre! Vive le roi! [sound of gun shots] Oh! They've been shot! The king is dying and Barthou's fatally wounded.[57]

Accompanied by graphic images of a dying king and the melee that ensued following his murder at the hands of a "Croatian conspirator," this voiceover demonstrated the extent to which newsreel commentary brought the re-presentation of the past into the present. Given the fact that these events took place several days before reaching the screen, audiences would likely have been aware of Alexander's death, and, if not, the preceding title screen, "Alexander Murdered," left little doubt. Yet, despite the audiences' prior knowledge of events, McNamee's commentary invited them to experience the news as if it were happening right before their eyes. The use of the present tense voiceover suggests that the sound newsreel of the 1930s offered more than a simple record of the past. It offered the immediacy of reality itself.

There is an apparent contradiction between the presence of the moving image and the absence of the profilmic event (i.e., the events unfolding in front of the camera). But rather than easing this tension, the direct address of the voiceover commentary heightened the play between past and present, absence and presence. Indeed, the voiceover itself brought a new layer to this tension, as it was added after the news had happened and before it was seen by an audience. This spatial and temporal play heightened the visual pleasure evoked by the newsreel, which was in turn derived largely from another tension: that between the twin aspects of display and evidence.

Display and Evidence: Tension in the Newsreel's Mode of Address

Since its introduction in the silent era, the newsreel capitalized on film's indexical power to display reality, making its visuality central to its appeal. News services regularly advertised their images as both "spectacular" and "real" as a means to entice exhibitors and audiences. Even after the advent of sound, the newsreel remained primarily concerned with the visual and, indeed, with its own visuality. *Hearst Metrotone News,* for example, described its year-end review of 1935 as "an exceptionally spectacular panorama." Amongst others, this reel included "vivid scenes of storms in Florida . . . graphic views of the mid-West's great dust storms, [and] spectacular scenes from Britain's Royal Jubilee."[58] Although the issue also featured stories apparently chosen for their newsworthiness and general interest, the promotional emphasis placed on the visual nature of these stories is telling. As we have seen, the visual quality of news footage was a key consideration to editors. Given this, it is hardly surprising that the year-end review was not just an opportunity to look back on the important events of the year but a chance to redisplay the most visually engaging footage as well. This emphasis on visuality points to an important and productive tension at work in the newsreel's mode of address. The newsreel's appeal relied on both its ability to capture evidence of the news on film and its ability to display that reality as a spectacle for its audience.

The newsreel was by no means the first medium to exploit the pleasures of spectacle and display. Media and art historians have pointed out that the spectacular display of reality began well before the advent of the cinematic apparatus. In *Spectacular Realities,* Vanessa Schwartz traces this history in Paris through the popularity of the sensationalist press, the emergence of wax museums, the panorama craze of the 1880s, and ultimately the arrival of early cinema at the end of the century. Schwartz argues that "the visual representation of reality as spectacle in late nineteenth-century Paris created a common culture and a sense of shared experiences" that were crucial to the foundation of "mass society."[59] In many ways, it is possible to see the newsreel as an extension of these spectacular realities. Indeed, Schwartz describes the filmed actualities of early cinema as "not merely a naïve and technologically unsophisticated early film genre, but rather [as] part of a late-nineteenth-century trope in which real life was packaged, labeled as 'current events,' and . . . incessantly represented."[60] With its highly developed system for the production, distribution, and exhibition of reality as visual spectacle, the newsreel continued and developed this trope in the twentieth-century United States.

The newsreel of the 1930s also shared key aspects of its mode of address with early cinema. As Noël Burch and Tom Gunning have pointed out, the theoretical models of film spectatorship, aesthetics, and editing based on traditional narrative films do not seem to apply to early film. According to Gunning, early films held a different appeal than those that would come later—one focused on spectacle rather than narrative. He calls this the "cinema of attractions."[61] He writes, "the 'attractions' fundamental hold on spectators depends on arousing and satisfying visual curiosity through a direct and acknowledged act of display, rather than following narrative enigma within a diegetic site into which the spectator peers invisibly."[62] The newsreel elicited a similar visual curiosity through its voiceover urging viewers to watch, and it directly acknowledged its audience by addressing them in the second person (e.g., "You are about to see . . ."). Gunning further argues that without the lure of narrative, "attractions have one basic temporality, that of the alternation of presence/absence which is embodied in the act of display. In this intense form of present tense the attraction is displayed with the immediacy of a 'Here it is! Look at it.'"[63] As we have seen, the newsreel's present tense commentary literally gave voice to these statements. So, while writers such as Gunning and Noël Burch have looked to these examples of early cinema as radically different from later film styles, the rupture they identify fails to take the newsreel into account. Early film's modes of temporality and display persisted, not only, as Gunning notes, as "underground" components in certain narrative film genres and the avant-garde but as a part of the mainstream moviegoing experience in the United States throughout the 1930s and 1940s. The newsreel, with its insistence on displaying the real, was a direct descendent of the cinema of attractions.

Although the newsreel retained important aspects of the cinema of attractions, its spectacular mode of address went beyond early film's reliance on novelty to attract its audience. Part of the appeal of the early films Gunning discusses was a fascination with film's technological means of representation as well as the fairground tradition of the curiosity.[64] By the 1930s, however, audiences were more familiar with motion picture technology; camera tricks and exotic scenes were no longer new. To some extent, the need for novelty could be generated by news events themselves, but given the readiness with which news information was available from other sources and the lack of newsworthy content in many reels, this alone cannot explain the enduring appeal of the act of newsreel display. In his analysis of spectacle in Leni Riefenstahl's infamous Nazi propaganda film, *Triumph of the Will,* Steve Neale suggests an alternate view. He argues that the appeal of spectacle is not about making the world visible but rather about displaying the visibility of the world. In so doing, spectacle offers its audience more than the object of the gaze; it offers them the privilege and power to look. Neale defines spectacle as "a signifying system . . . whose basis lies in a specific form of the evocation and satiation of the scopic drive, a system which is especially concerned . . . to stress, to *display,* the visibility of the visible."[65] Looked at in this way, newsreel spectacle can be seen as having been about more than the visual—it too was about its own visuality.

The newsreel invited its audiences to revel in the visibility of the world, the power of the film medium to re-present it, and their own privilege to look. Even the newsreel's use of voiceover commentary emphasized this visuality. The present-tense narration implored the viewer to look and, in doing so, stressed the moment of display, not the historical moment on screen. Through the act of displaying spectacular realities, newsreels continually enacted a play between the presence of the spectacular image on screen and the absence of the world of which it was a record. As Neale points out, the spectacle privileges the processes of display and looking over the object or events on screen:

> Spectacle is content neither with simply rendering visible the observable nor with inscribing the spectating subject simply in position as observer. It is much more concerned with the processes of rendering visible and of looking themselves. What counts in spectacle is not the visible as guarantee of *veracity* (of truth, of reality), but rather the visible as mask, as lure. What counts is not the instance of looking as *observation,* but rather as fascinated gaze.[66]

This perspective draws attention to a key pleasure to be found in the newsreel; namely the pleasure of looking itself. To reinforce its fascination with visibility, *Triumph of Will* inscribes the activity of looking directly into the diegesis itself. Repeated shots of Germans peering into the distance mark the centrality of looking as well as the importance of the object of their fascinated gaze: Hitler himself. The newsreel also frequently represented the activity of looking by showing sports fans, parade goers, and other crowds watching excitedly. As Lindbergh was driven down the Canyon of Heroes in New York City, the cheering crowds lining the streets and peering from skyscraper windows embodied this fascinated gaze. By representing the gaze on screen, the newsreel fetishized a steady stream of celebrities, politicians, and sportsmen, but, more importantly, it reveled in the visibility of reality itself. Through the newsreel, the spectator in the cinema could identify with the mass of onlookers and share in the pleasure of looking.

Despite the importance of spectacle in the newsreel, the moment of display provided only one part of its visual appeal. Equally important was the fact that the spectacular realities it displayed were just that: realities. Unlike other popular spectacles, film—like photography—is an indexical medium. Roland Barthes, in his work *Camera Lucida,* argues that this quality distinguishes photography as a privileged field of representation. The photographic index says above all that *"the thing has been there."* Barthes states that the indexical nature of the medium "possesses an evidentiary force and that its testimony bears not on the object but on time. From a phenomenological viewpoint, in the photograph, the power of authentication exceeds the power of representation."[67] This is to say that no matter what a photograph is of, it always points to a *past* reality. In other words, the photograph is evidence of a past that is no more. John Ellis extends Barthes's argument from photography to cinema. He points out that "the cinema image is marked by a particular half-magic feat in that it makes present something that is absent . . . This is the irreducible separation that cinema maintains (and attempts to abolish), the fact that the objects and people are conjured up yet known not to be present. Cinema is present absence: it says, 'This is was.'"[68] Despite the spectacle in the moment of display, the indexicality of film insists on its status as evidence of past events.

Nowhere is this peculiarly contradictory aspect of film's address more apparent than in the news film. Indeed, the present absence Ellis identifies as a component of all film took on added significance in the newsreel because its evidentiary power pointed to the real world rather than a fictional one arranged for the camera. News services frequently extolled the medium's evidentiary power, often highlighting the technology of film itself. For example, early in the sound era, *Hearst Metrotone News* featured footage of an assassination attempt on Crown Prince Humbert, the heir to the Italian throne. Just before the film reached its climactic moment, a title screen instructed audiences to "listen for the shot." And indeed, seconds later, the newsreel featured the distinct sound of a single gunshot followed by the roar of the panicking crowd.[69] By drawing attention to this piece of evidence, *Hearst* announced the footage as a re-presentation of reality, alerting audiences to its pastness even as it made the event present on the screen. Unlike fiction film, which Ellis suggests attempts to abolish the irreducible separation between the presence of the image and the absence of the profilmic, the newsreel used its direct address to highlight this gap.

When the novelty of the technology waned, news services could always rely on the cameraman to testify to the evidentiary power of the newsreel. Implicitly and often explicitly, news services described the actions taken by their cameramen to capture the past as it happened. In promotional materials, newsreels often highlighted the exploits of their cameramen. *Universal Newsreel*, for example, trumpeted the "courage and daring" of its cameraman, Mervyn Freeman, who apparently lashed himself to the periscope of a naval submarine to capture the ship's diving maneuvers.[70] War offered a special opportunity to praise the courage of news cameramen. In the voiceover for a *News of the Day* story on the Sino–Japanese War, for example, the commentator announced, "These sensational pictures, made by cameramen 75 yards away, show the building swept by machine gun fire at the height of the assault . . . filmed for the first time is this unusual scene of modern war . . . note the bullets striking."[71] This commentary is particularly interesting because the voiceover slips between the past tense—when describing the efforts of the cameraman to capture the image—and the present tense—when describing the images themselves. In doing so, the commentator invited the audience to enjoy the visibility of the image ("note the bullets striking") even while highlighting the absence of the events on screen. Implicit in the present absence of the image was the past presence of the camera in the field of current events—in this case just seventy-five yards away from the action.[72] Whether under a hail of bullets or lashed to a submarine, the past presence of the cameraman testified to the authenticity of the images on screen and to their "evidentiary force." Ultimately, however, the appeal of the news film lay in neither this evidentiary power nor the moment of spectacular display. Instead, it lay in the tension between the two—it was the presence of absent, distant, and historic events on the screen, as well as their visibility, that made the newsreel powerful.

News Parade: The Newsreel's Logic of Representation

The direct address voiceover, the play of present absence, and the tension between display and evidence were key to the newsreel's mode of address, but they alone did not distinguish it from other nonfiction film genres. After all, we can see similar elements at work in actuality, ethnography, and propaganda films like Riefenstahl's, each of which employ one or more aspect of the newsreel mode, even if they don't seek to exploit the tensions between them in the same way. Ultimately, then, what sets the newsreel apart from these other nonfiction genres is what I shall call its processional mode—or the news parade. The news parade, however, was not simply a component of the newsreel's mode of address. Rather, the analogy of the parade offers a way of synthesizing an analysis of the newsreel's mode of address with an understanding of its modes of production and distribution. Together, these modes reflected and produced the underlying logic of the newsreel system as a whole.

The newsreel system's modes of production, distribution, and address mediated representations of current events in a unique and unprecedented way. The introduction of sound and the factory model of mass production, with its continuous flow of footage and integrated distribution networks, helped shape a mode of address that relied on the tension between display and evidence for its authority and power. But another key aspect of the newsreel, both of its address and its production, was the regularity of its appearance. Unlike other film genres—even film serials—the newsreel had a steady and predictable release schedule.

Twice a week, every week, the newsreel offered audiences a ten-minute compilation of news, sports, and novelty footage. As we have already seen, to meet this demanding schedule, the newsreel relied on events that could be easily shot and planned for well in advance. Sporting events and beauty contests worked well in this regard, but the quintessential newsreel subject was the parade. One contemporary critic estimated that "a good third of any newsreel consist[ed] of processions, parades, and ceremonies of various kinds which required of the newsreel staff nothing more resourceful than a reading of the calendar."[73] Yet the parade was not simply a convenient newsreel subject; it was also a fitting metaphor for how the newsreel represented the world. The newsreel, like the parade, offered spectators a passing pageant. As images passed across the screen—both within each issue and twice weekly, 104 times a year—the spectator was treated to a vision of the world as a continuous procession. Taken up by the industry itself, the parade was a way of ordering otherwise unrelated events. As we shall see, it made sense of the world and positioned the newsreel spectator in a particular relationship with the reality on screen. While the processional mode was a product of the newsreel's methods of production and distribution, the parade also served as the logic that underlay the entire newsreel system.

The motion picture industry took up the metaphor of the parade as a way to describe the newsreel as early as 1928. In that year, Fox Films released the romantic comedy *The News Parade* starring Sally Phillips and Nick Stuart. The studio billed the film as a "heroic tale of newsreel romance and adventure," but, featuring actual newsreel cameramen and plenty of their most sensational footage, it was also designed as a promotional vehicle for Fox's *Movietone News.* As the press sheet headline "Thrills Pass in Review Through 'The News Parade'"[74] indicated, the parade was a useful conceit for including some of these spectacular scenes. By the 1930s, others in the newsreel industry had begun using the parade as one of their principle motifs. In 1937, the *Motion Picture Daily* began grouping its coverage of the newsreel industry in a section called "The Newsreel Parade."[75] Several years earlier, *Hearst Metrotone News* took up the metaphor by calling its year-end review "The News Parade of. . . ." In 1934, this special edition of *Hearst Metrotone News* was promoted as "a spectacular panorama of the history-making events, outstanding thrills and highlights of the year!"[76] Once again, the news parade was a useful way of grouping together the unrelated events of the past twelve months. It allowed segments on "Europe's Tragic Year" to be followed by "History-Making Flights," "Outstanding Disasters," "The War on Crime," and "A Year of Speed and Thrills." This year-end parade allowed the newsreel and its audience to indulge, once again, in the visibility and re-presentability of the world while exploring the tension between display ("spectacular panorama") and evidence ("history-making events"). Moreover, in employing the metaphor of the parade, *Hearst Metrotone News* stressed the continuous flow of information—stories followed one another without any necessary connection. Although the year-end special was commemorative in tone, its parade format simply reflected the processional mode that was a feature of every newsreel issue.

While the news parade was a device for connecting otherwise unrelated stories, it was also a key way in which the newsreel made sense of world events. If nothing else, it put them in sequence. In his work on the cinema and historicity, Philip Rosen identifies sequenciation as key to the coherence of history and documentary film. Echoing the notion of history put forward by Hayden White, he argues that it is through sequence—and narrative in particular—that historians synthesize historical documents and create meaning.[77] According to Rosen, "while the documentary tradition is not locked into highly conventionalized narrative forms, it does share a commitment to the centralization of meaning through internal sequenciation."[78] By aligning the documentary with modern notions of historicity, Rosen distinguishes between the indexicality of the document and the synthetic process of making meaning. He writes:

> If shots as indexical traces of past reality may be treated as documents in the broad sense, documentary can be treated as a conversion from document. This conversion involves a synthesizing knowledge claim, by virtue of a sequence that sublates an undoubtable referential field of pastness into meaning.[79]

In other words, like the historian who must tell a story about the past using primary documents, documentarians create meaningful accounts of the past by making a narrative sequence out of raw footage (indexical traces). But narrative was highly attenuated in the newsreel—there were almost never narrative connections between newsreel items, while, as discussed above, the individual items themselves presented the news in the manner of the cinema of attractions. The procession of events presented in the news parade was often barely more than a collection of "indexical traces." The organization of these events into the newsreel's regular departments, their placement within the reel, and even the addition of titles provided a kind of sequence. Although this basic sequenciation did not necessarily create a "synthesizing knowledge claim" with regards to the newsreel's content, it nevertheless structured the recent past as a procession of images.

By ordering the news as a passing pageant, the newsreel shifted the way its viewers encountered the world. As we have seen, much of the newsreel's appeal rested on the repetitive display of absent presence. This tension between display and evidence was not primarily interested in knowledge but rather in the pleasures of looking. The processional mode served to further highlight these pleasures. It eschewed narrative per se but made sense of the world as a series of more or less unrelated events, as a parade, and as a set of looking relations. While this ordering of events did not provide the synthetic function Rosen sees as key to documentary, structuring events as a parade did make newsreel images meaningful. As we shall see in the next chapter, the newsreel's focus on looking and spectacle frustrated critics on all sides of the Lippmann–Dewey debate—it provided neither the context nor the information necessary to educate the masses as Dewey desired; nor did it offer the persuasive synthesis Lippmann thought necessary to properly shape public opinion.[80] But if the content of the newsreel failed to represent the complexity of modern society to the public, its parade mode embodied this modernity by reflecting and helping to shape an entirely new relationship between the public and the news.

Parades have long been seen as an important way in which societies and cultures represent themselves. Writing about the nineteenth-century American tradition of the citizens' parade, Mary Ryan suggests that "filing neatly by in a parade, the parade participants presented a compact documentation of how 'society takes cognizance of itself, its major classifications and categories.'" Although the ticker tape parades of the twentieth century differed markedly from the participatory parades of the nineteenth, it is possible that these too revealed, "in a particularly powerful, publicly sanctioned way, how contemporaries construed, displayed, and saw the urban social order."[81] While these nineteenth-century parades represented the ethnic and class divisions of that era, the ticker tape parades of the 1920s and 1930s embodied the new social order of a consumer culture fostered, in part, by the motion picture industry. Instead of a society divided by ethnicity or class, the ticker tape parade exemplified a mass society—one in which individuals were joined in their roles as consumers and spectators. Of course, such a vision of American society elided all kinds of differences—as we shall see in later chapters, the privileges of newsreel spectatorship were implicitly white and male—but it did represent the aspirational vision of the nation shared by advertising and the mass media.[82] Unlike the participatory parades of the nineteenth century, the ticker tape parade turned citizens into spectators.

Seen in this way, the parade honoring Charles Lindbergh and his historic flight in 1927 exemplified an emerging social order and a set of looking relations that were both reflected in and reinforced by the newsreel's logic of representation. News film of Lindbergh's car making its way slowly down New York's Fifth Avenue showed the aviator as the privileged object of the gaze. Significantly, the footage also captured an adoring crowd lining the streets, peering out of windows, and even running to keep up with the motorcade.[83] Thus, this iconic footage displayed not just the world as image but also the crowd as spectator. As Walter Benjamin pointed out in "The Work of Art in the Age of Mechanical Reproduction," "in big parades and monster rallies, in sports events, and in war, all of which nowadays are captured by camera and sound, the masses are brought face to face with themselves."[84] Indeed, the newsreel's relentless portrayal of parades, ceremonies, and sporting events constantly represented the image of the crowd—crucially, a crowd that looks. Joined in spectatorship with the masses on screen, newsreel audience members were invited to watch the world but also to indulge in the visibility of that world and their own status as spectators. The news parade did not simply offer the audience an opportunity to look and to be part of the crowd; it also represented a new relationship between the crowd and the reality on screen. The close-up and multiple camera angles of the newsreel allowed audiences to get closer and to see more of the world than ever before while still holding it at a safe distance. Benjamin argues that the reproducibility of images in the first half of the twentieth century fostered the desire to bring the object "closer . . . by way of its likeness, its reproduction."[85] But while the newsreel seemed at first to satisfy this desire, as we have seen, its visual appeal was predicated on the tension between the closeness (presence) of the world as spectacle and the distance (absence) of the profilmic. In the play of this apparent contradiction, the newsreel offered to close the gap between spectators and the world while simultaneously presenting spectators with images of exotic locales and larger-than-life celebrities. The image of Lindbergh being watched by millions of New Yorkers captured the newsreel's ability to represent the world as well as the logic by which it ordered those representations. By encouraging audiences to identify with the onscreen crowd, the newsreel offered them a vantage point from which to watch the world and, as we'll see in the next chapter, engage with it.

The processional logic of the newsreel, the continuous flow of images presented as a non-narrative sequence, combined with its looking relations and implied social order make the news parade the perfect metaphor for the newsreel system. For historians, the news parade is a way to think about the newsreel's modes of production, distribution, and address as intertwined while it helps explain how the newsreel changed the way Americans viewed the world and their relation to it. The processional mode of the news parade addressed its spectator as part of a virtual crowd watching as the world passed by on the screen. Moreover, the newsreel's frequent portrayal of real crowds attending parades, rallies, and sporting events linked the spectator in the theater to the masses represented in the films. By encouraging audiences to identify with these onscreen crowds, the newsreel offered them a sense of shared identity as well as a privileged vantage point from which to watch the world. The crowd, once identified with the visual spectacles of the street, now became a global and technologically enhanced spectator position mediated through the screen.[86] This collective spectatorship defined not only the audience members' relationship with the newsreel but their relationships with one another as well. As we'll see in the next two chapters, the privileges of looking were tied to participatory citizenship as well as gendered and racially defined notions of American identity. Those invited to join in the news parade entered into a new mediated public sphere where the real could be experienced in the theater and looking was an active process.

CHAPTER 2

Newsreel Realism

Redefining the Real in Motion Picture News

The consolidation of the newsreel industry, its vertical integration, and the introduction of sound changed the way critics regarded the newsreel. Most notably, in the 1930s some began to question the newsreel's ability and willingness to represent reality. What critics once had seen as a transparent representation of the real world, they now frequently described as phony, superficial, or biased, often dismissing the newsreel as propaganda. Even as the newsreel became a near ubiquitous part of motion picture programs in the United States, reaching an audience of as many as eighty million Americans each week, critics became increasingly skeptical.[1] How can we reconcile the increased prominence of motion picture news with criticism of its realism? The newsreel's mode of address combined with its mode of production to create the representational logic of the parade. The news parade segmented and regimented the news and, by engaging its audience in the alternating presence and absence of events, made the world into a mediated spectacle. In order for this spectacle to be effective as "news," however, the newsreel needed to engage its audience with the screen image as reality. As we saw in chapter one, this was achieved, in part, by exploiting the tension between display and evidence. This chapter will explore aspects of this tension further in an effort to understand better how the newsreel created a reality effect in spite of the criticism it received. The newsreel's parade mode facilitated a new kind of realism in three ways. First, the newsreel system fostered media events where the shared viewing of the news was part of the story itself. Second, the newsreel made the world visible in an unprecedented way and, in doing so, privileged the experience of watching the news over other kinds of information. Finally, by privileging this experience, the newsreel invited viewers to judge the events on screen for themselves. By allowing audiences to see and hear the news for themselves, the newsreel put claim to a new kind of realism—one where the real was neither a transparent fact nor an authentic truth but was instead a mediated experience.

In order to examine the newsreel's realism more closely, it is necessary to shift focus from the newsreel system as a whole to how that system represented individual news events. Two case studies illustrate how the newsreel worked to create its reality effect. The coverage of the U.S. presidential inauguration of 1933 and the Lindbergh kidnapping illustrate how the newsreel applied its unique logic of representation to engage audiences with current events in a way that fundamentally redefined reality in an increasingly mediated world. Although these were exceptional news events that garnered special attention from the newsreel, they also provide important insights into how newsreel realism worked in its everyday offerings. Because of their high profile, these events put newsreels in competition with their rivals—both within the motion picture news business and in other media—requiring them to focus explicitly on their distinctive ability to represent the real. Indeed, major news events such as these were important opportunities for newsreels to establish their claims to realism and legitimate their regular coverage. Examining the newsreels' coverage of these events and how they promoted this coverage reveals the notions of the real at work throughout the newsreel system of the 1930s.

Above all, the newsreel premised its realism on its unique system of production. The extensive network of cameramen allowed the newsreel to claim to bring the audience closer than ever to the events of the world. In coverage of the 1933 inauguration of President Franklin Delano Roosevelt, the newsreel constantly invoked the power of its system, either directly—through references to the means of newsreel production itself—or indirectly—through the deployment of specific camera techniques designed to give the audience visual mastery over the world on screen. These invocations shifted the locus of the real away from the news event itself and onto the newsreel representation of that event. The coverage of the kidnapping of Charles Lindbergh's young son and the subsequent trial of Bruno Hauptmann for the boy's murder shows how notions of display and evidence worked together to draw audiences into the visual nature of the newsreel's reality. The coverage of this case gave newsreel companies an opportunity to re-inscribe the supposed evidentiary power of film onto the newsreel and to bind that power to the demands of the American justice system. The Lindbergh case also demonstrates how the newsreel invited audiences to engage with the world on screen. By examining how the newsreel emphasized the power of its own mode of production as well as the tension between display and evidence, this chapter will show how motion picture news developed its own unique brand of realism—one that privileged the experience of watching the news over the news itself. Newsreel audiences were invited to see, hear, and examine the world through the screen. The newsreel was more than a simple record of what happened; it was a way for audiences to participate in the events of the day through the act of looking.

The Course of Realism

Beginning with its introduction in the United States in 1911, the newsreel filled its promotional material with claims of vivid realism. Ads for newsreels in the trade press referred to recording "things as they are," the "actual drama of life," and "real battle pictures."[2] This language aimed to convince audiences of the authenticity and power of the newsreels' images. Early observers endorsed and even echoed such language, but while newsreel companies continued to use realism as a way to promote their films in the 1930s, critics grew increasingly wary of such pronouncements. Exploring these contemporaneous debates about filmic realism and the newsreel in the 1930s helps explain the production of newsreel reality. Criticism of the newsreel came from both the popular press and early film theorists. Reflecting a commonsense view of realism, popular critics focused on the degree to which the newsreel provided (or failed to provide) a faithful representation of the important events of the world. Others, including filmmakers and early theorists of the documentary, focused instead on the newsreel's lack of creative penetration and synthesis. These different critiques reflected differing views of realism itself. Should the newsreel aim to provide a simple and faithful copy of the world, or should it compile actuality into a more synthetic and potentially more authentic truth? These debates shaped the critical reception of the news film in the 1930s even though the newsreel's own realism did not conform comfortably to either view of the real.

Many early observers described the introduction and growth of the newsreel with admiration and an apparently genuine belief in the news film's ability to realize the most utopian promise of motion pictures.[3] Stephen Bush, writing in the *Motion Picture World,* for example, called newsreel images of the First World War "real, incorruptible, [and] utterly without bias."[4] Emanuel Cohen expressed even more confidence in the power of the newsreel to represent reality in an article for a special issue of the *Annals of the American Academy of Political and Social Science* in 1926. He wrote that "the deadly accuracy and the vivid realism of the newsfilm has brought it to the heights of purpose and utility which it now occupies. It has reeled its way into the confidence of millions of persons."[5] Such faith in the power of the newsreel to represent reality is remarkable, but typical, of early observers of motion picture news, swayed in large part by the apparent indexical power of film.

By the 1930s, much of this goodwill was gone. The introduction of sound was greeted with skepticism by some critics who saw it as a threat to the purity of the film image. In addition, a number of notorious (though sometimes apocryphal) stories emerged in the 1920s and 1930s of newsreel footage that had been faked in one way or another.[6] These developments called into question the newsreel's objectivity, and, by the mid-1930s, there was a growing cynicism with respect to the newsreel's realism in general. Articles in the popular and trade press complained that newsreels were either vehicles for propaganda, superficial fluff, or both.[7] In a 1935 article titled, "Are the Newsreels News?," *The Nation* questioned the impartiality of the United States' newsreel services. Pointing the finger at *Hearst Metrotone News* in particular, the magazine accused studios of red-baiting and right-wing bias, as well as promoting militarism. The article lamented that the newsreels "won their popularity largely because they seemed such a random sampling of the mad world. One felt that one was getting a more direct contact with simple actuality than one could achieve in any other way."[8] The anonymous editorial suggested that newsreel producers, and Hearst in particular, were forsaking this tradition in favor of their personal ideologies and predicted that unless the newsreels acted to eliminate editorializing, the public would soon discover that "though photographs can't lie, liars certainly can photograph."[9] Criticisms of the newsreel's superficiality were equally vehement. Critics complained that the newsreel had given up on "real" news in favor of inconsequential pap. Indeed, newsreel companies were loath to cover anything controversial and, for example, regularly ignored the economic and social hardships brought on by the Depression in favor of lighter fare.[10] In a particularly scathing feature for the *American Mercury,* Robert Littell called the newsreel "trivial, lazy, and misleading"[11] and concluded that:

> While history is digging twenty-four hours a day in her garden and hope and worms and the future squirm together in the upturned sod, the newsreel camera continues placidly, lazily to feed us on a diet that is mostly marbles champions, prepared statements, parades, puns, and young men who can play piano with mittens on their hands.[12]

Littell had a point. Indeed, as we saw in chapter one, the consolidation of the newsreel and its factory mode of production meant that its biggest bias was toward the predictable. Although criticism based on the newsreel's triviality took up slightly different perceived problems than those based on its biases, both critiques shared a common concern for the "real," and both invoked "realism" as the proper goal and standard by which the newsreel ought to be judged. For *The Nation* and others who criticized the newsreel industry for its lack of objectivity, the newsreel was in danger of losing the one thing that had made it unique—its capacity to represent the world directly, without editorial comment. Those who felt the newsreel had become superficial worried that it had given up on representing the real altogether in favor of amusements and novelties. Both of these concerns reflected the idea that the newsreel could and should depict the important news of the world in a more or less transparent way.

In addition to the skepticism of popular and trade presses, newsreels were also subject to criticism from a group of filmmakers and theorists who had begun to think more seriously about documentary film. In the 1930s, writers on the documentary, like John Grierson and Paul Rotha, were defining a genre against other forms of film expression. In this context, the newsreel was often criticized or dismissed outright.[13] Rotha, in his 1937 book *Documentary Film,* rejected the newsreel as having "little in common with the characteristics of the documentary except that they both go to actuality for their raw material," and he argued that the newsreel allowed for neither the time, selectivity, nor creativity necessary to produce documentary film.[14] John Grierson elaborated a similar critique in his 1937 essay, "The Course of Realism." In this essay, Grierson called for cinema to revitalize itself with a return to the real. Lamenting the rise of melodrama and artifice in popular motion pictures, Grierson urged filmmakers in Britain and the United States to believe in cinema's "separate and original destiny" by taking up the realist tradition.[15] Praising filmmakers like Robert Flaherty, Alberto Calvalcanti, and Sergei Eisenstein, he extolled the virtues of documentary and fiction films that depicted real life and tackled contemporary issues. Significantly, in making his argument, Grierson dismissed the one film genre that had consistently claimed to bring reality to movie screens in the United States and beyond: the newsreel. He wrote:

> Looking down the history of the actuality films, of what has seemed on the surface most natural and most real, there was, until the late thirties, a lack of fibre. From the beginning we have had newsreels, but dim records they seem now of only the evanescent and the essentially unreal, reflecting hardly anything worth preserving of the times they recorded . . . Among the foundation stones, the pompous parades, the politicians on pavements, and even among the smoking ruins of mine disasters and the broken backs of troubled ships, it is difficult to think that any real picture of our troubled day has been recorded. The newsreel has gone dithering on, mistaking the phenomenon for the thing in itself, and ignoring everything that gave it the trouble of conscience and penetration and thought.[16]

Grierson regarded the newsreel's attention to the purely visual spectacle as a distraction from the kind of realism he hoped to see on film. For Grierson, realism was neither a profusion of detail nor a mere parade of people and events. He categorically rejected the model of the newsreel that *The Nation* described affectionately as a "random sampling of the mad world." He famously defined documentary as the "creative treatment of actuality," and it was creativity and treatment that Grierson viewed as crucially missing from the newsreel.[17] Because the newsreel was characterized by the non-narrative sequence of the parade, and given its modes of production and address, it aimed at re-presenting the world for the viewing pleasure of its audience with a minimum of context and emplotment. This non-narrative structure all but eliminated the kind of "creative treatment" Grierson demanded of the documentary film. In Grierson's terms, it was pure "actuality," and, as such, the newsreel neither aimed for nor achieved the penetration he saw as necessary "to [get] behind the news, [observe] the factors of influence, and [give] a perspective to events."[18] For Grierson, documentary and cinematic realism in general required a kind of synthesis that could educate the viewer by revealing the truth that lay beyond the surface phenomena of the visual. The newsreel made no attempt to illuminate this reality.

Grierson's critique of the newsreel's realism was both philosophical and politically pragmatic. He put a great deal of faith in the power of the mass media—and documentary film in particular—to educate the masses. Citing Walter Lippmann's concerns over the difficulty in maintaining democracy in a modern society where citizens could not be expected to "know everything about everything all the time," Grierson argued that documentary film could perform a crucial social function in "both the practice of government and the enjoyment of citizenship."[19] Because film had the potential to reach across socioeconomic and other divisions, it had an important role to play in shaping the public mind. This social function could not be achieved by simply recording the events of the world. Instead, films should skillfully craft their realism so as to enlighten the audience. This task could not be left to just anyone. As Philip Rosen has argued, Grierson believed that documentary's "overriding social and civic virtue [could] be grasped and manifested by an educated, liberal elite seeking the social good."[20] Only such a group of dedicated filmmakers could fulfill film's social and educational potential. Because the newsreel industry was dominated by the financial interests of the Hollywood studios, and because newsreels made no apparent attempt to edify the audience, newsreels failed to meet Grierson's standard of realism.

Grierson's notion of realism was grounded in his philosophical education at Glasgow University prior to 1924. As Ian Aitken has argued in his work on Grierson and cinematic realism, Grierson was heavily influenced by the idealist philosophies of F. H. Bradley, A. D. Lindsey, and the Kantian and Hegelian traditions upon which they drew.[21] Unlike other critics who have seen Grierson's philosophy as primarily Hegelian, Aitken makes the case that Grierson combined Kantian and Hegelian ideas in his epistemology and his aesthetics.[22] In terms of his ideas about realism, the key elements of this synthesis were Grierson's Kantian suspicion of the purely phenomenal world along with his adoption of the Hegelian view of reality as an "organic totality," comprehension of which required an intuitive or aesthetic experience rather than simple observation. By highlighting his Kantian anti-empiricism, Aitken further illustrates the importance Grierson placed on the synthetic potential of "creative treatment" over a more conventional faith in simple "actuality." According to Aitken:

> This implied that, in order to be effective, art and education should use generalized and symbolic, rather than overtly didactic or pedagogic, modes of expression. This also applied to the documentary film which, according to Grierson, should not convey didactic factual information, but should use dramatic and symbolic material which: "strikes out the more useful patterns of modern citizenship . . . and conveys patterns of appreciation, civic faith and civic duty."[23]

Aitken shows how Grierson used this kind of symbolic expression to demonstrate the interconnection of social practices in his film *Drifters* as well as others from the documentary film movement, of which Grierson was the leading force. Aitken's analysis of Grierson's philosophical idealism helps contextualize Grierson's critique of the newsreel. For Grierson, realist film needed both to reveal and comprehend underlying reality. In his "Course of Realism" essay, he invokes the Kantian notion of the "thing in itself" to describe this concept of the real and contrasts it with the surface phenomena presented in the newsreel. Inasmuch as the newsreel did concern itself primarily with the visual and the factual, Grierson's critique was accurate—the newsreel could never achieve the kind of penetrating realism he demanded and, as such, never fulfill the social and political potential of documentary film.

Grierson was not alone in his suspicion of purely surface representation. The relationship between realism—be it literary, cinematic, or documentary—and the superficial has long been a subject for critical debate. Marxist critics, in particular, had questioned the value of purely empirical realism and its ability to represent the world truthfully. Much of this writing drew from Marx's notion of the commodity form and its ability to mask the social relations of production.[24] According to this view, the physical properties of commodities obscure the social reality that produces them, but because of the fetishism of the commodity form, these objects are experienced as real. In the 1930s, Georg Lukács developed the classical Marxist suspicion of visuality and surface into a complete aesthetics. In his essay on "Realism in the Balance," Lukács rejected the formal experimentation of the expressionists and pushed for an art that reflected the objective truth of social relations. For Lukács, like Grierson, objective truth was not a simple matter of reflecting the world as it appeared. He argued that, for Marxists, form and surface were simply not sufficient subjects for art. "If literature is a particular form by means of which objective reality is reflected, then it becomes of crucial importance for it to grasp that reality as it truly is, and not merely to confine itself to reproducing whatever manifests itself immediately and on the surface."[25] For Lukács, the surface of reality was inevitably false—like Marx's commodity form, it masked the true social relations that lay beneath. As with Grierson, Hegel's notion of the objective totality informed Lukács's position. In his essay "Narrate or Describe?," Lukács opposed epic literature to new forms of naturalism that had eschewed narrative in favor of meticulous description. This latter literary form, represented by Emile Zola, failed to distinguish the objective significance of certain social phenomena, failed to relate the particular to general, and in turn fell prey to the perils of what Lukács called subjectivism. Lukács argued that realist literature, which he associated with Balzac, Scott, and Tolstoy, made these necessary connections and, in doing so, captured something of the totality that lay at the heart of the real. Lukács wrote: "The decisive ideological weakness of the writers of the descriptive method is in their passive capitulation to [the surface] phenomena of fully-developed capitalism and in their seeing the result but not the struggles of the opposing forces."[26] Thus, for Lukács, the job of the artist was to look beyond the surface—to mediate reality—and reveal the objective truth of social relations and the class struggle.[27]

Although one should be careful not to conflate the two, the similarity of Grierson's and Lukács's language is remarkable. While Lukács and Grierson differed on the nature of the totality they believed was at the heart of the real, both regarded realism as a means to reveal a truth that lay beyond the immediate phenomena; and both regarded the surface—of detail and phenomena—with suspicion with respect to its ability to reveal that underlying totality. This shared suspicion of the superficial and desire for synthesis in literary and filmic realism reflected a growing intellectual movement in the United States and elsewhere. In his book, *The Real Thing: Imitation and Authenticity in American Culture, 1880–1940,* Miles Orvell describes this shift as a movement away from an interest in the "faithful reproduction" in favor of the "authentic." According to Orvell:

> The nineteenth-century culture of imitation was fascinated by reproductions of all sorts—replicas of furniture, architecture, art works, replicas of the real thing in any shape or form imaginable. It was a culture inspired by faith in the power of the machine to manufacture a credible simulacrum . . . The culture of authenticity that developed at the end of the century and that gradually established the aesthetic vocabulary that we have called "modernist" was a reaction against the earlier aesthetic, an effort to get beyond mere imitation, beyond the manufacturing of illusions, to the creation of more "authentic" works that were themselves real things.[28]

Grierson's critique of the newsreel and Lukács's critique of literary naturalism can be seen as part of this modernist position and part of the emergent "culture of authenticity" Orvell describes. For Grierson, it simply was not enough for the newsreel to record events and re-present them to audiences; it needed to go beyond the surface to reveal an authentic reality.

Newsreels were, however, more than mere faithful copies of the world in the nineteenth-century tradition Orvell describes. Although in its early years newsreel producers had promoted their product on this fairly limited basis, by the 1930s they presented a somewhat more nuanced notion of the real. As we shall see, the newsreel's unique brand of realism neither simply showed the world "as it really was" in the way that popular critics might have hoped nor revealed the authentic truth behind the surface in a way that might have corresponded to the modernist realism of Grierson or Lukács. The power of the newsreel lay not in its ability to represent reality but rather in its ability to allow audiences to experience the real on screen. The newsreel system achieved its realism in three ways: by stressing the power and scope of its modes of production and distribution, by exploiting the tension between display and evidence to emphasize the visual nature of the news, and by investing the shared experience of watching the news with its own sense of importance. Newsreels offered audience members more than the chance to discover what had happened in the world; they offered the opportunity to see for themselves and gain access, albeit mediated access, to current events. By engaging in the collective spectatorship of the news parade, newsreel audiences participated in a public sphere mediated by the screen.

Newsreel realism offered its audience a real world made up of images—one that viewers could engage with through the screen. In doing so, the newsreel participated in the creation of what Guy Debord would later call the society of the spectacle—where the line between the real and its image became increasingly blurred.[29] What Grierson regarded as a terrible mistake might then be understood as part of a process of change in the representation of reality. In other words, the newsreel's realism reflected a shift in the notion of the real itself—not toward one more or less interested in what Grierson called the "thing-in-itself" nor one more or less concerned with imitation or the faithful copy. Instead, the experience of watching the news itself was defined as real, and the newsreel's ability to make the world visible is what gave it power. The newsreel's realism, then, lay not in the image, but in the watching.

Producing Realism: The Inauguration of Roosevelt

Although theoretical debates about cinematic realism have tended to focus either on the ontology of the filmic apparatus or the aesthetic choices made by directors, it is important to recognize that, in the case of the newsreel, realism was an effect of the entire system of production and distribution, as well as representation.[30] As a number of scholars have shown, paying close attention to the institutional basis for specific modes of realism reminds us that notions of the real are historically contingent.[31] Realism is produced by a complex interaction between economic systems, media institutions, technologies of representation, and textual strategies. Given the newsreel's highly integrated mode of production, the newsreel system itself became a crucial means of producing and buttressing realism in motion picture news. Newsreel editors worked hard to remind their audiences of the power and efficiency of the newsreel system in an effort to close the gap between the profilmic news event and the experience of watching the image on screen. The inauguration of Franklin Delano Roosevelt on Saturday, March 4, 1933, provides an excellent example of such an effort. Although it was by no means a typical newsreel story, media events like the inauguration served to demonstrate the power of the newsreel system and thus legitimate the realism of its regular offerings. Given the nature of presidential inaugurations, their highly choreographed ceremony and detailed planning, newsreel companies were able to put considerable efforts toward ensuring the event was captured on film and that the footage was distributed and screened as quickly as possible. An examination of how this was done, as well as how this process was represented—explicitly and implicitly—in the newsreel's coverage of the inauguration, will help illuminate how the newsreel system itself produced its reality effect.

Given the public interest in the inauguration, studios mobilized the full power of their news organizations to secure footage and get it to the screen as quickly as possible. The day before the event, the *Motion Picture Daily* reported that companies were "guarding their strategy like generals in opposing armies."[32] *Fox Movietone News, Hearst Metrotone,* and *Pathé News* each refused to divulge their plans, but, according to the report, Paramount had seven sound units, four silent cameras arrayed around Washington, and a fleet of chartered planes ready to fly their negatives from the capital to New York. Universal, meanwhile, assigned twelve men to cover the event and made extensive plans to coordinate their coverage. A memo from *Universal Newsreel* editor, Charles E. Ford, dated February 24, 1933, detailed their preparations.[33] The strategy called for five camera teams to be deployed throughout the capital and included a hand-drawn map of Washington, D.C., with camera placements marked. The first camera was designated to cover the White House and secure close-ups of Roosevelt and Hoover leaving the building together in their open car. Following the ceremony, this same crew was to get shots of the president and first lady arriving back at the White House and close-ups of the family watching the inaugural parade from the reviewing stand. Camera number two was assigned to the U.S. Treasury Building where it could follow the president on his way to and from the inaugural ceremony. According to Ford, this was "a choice position for parade shots coming up Penn[sylvania] Ave with [the] Capitol in [the] background." The third camera was Universal's only sound unit assigned to the event, and it was to set up on the photo stand facing the Capitol building where the unit could record the oath of office and Roosevelt's inaugural address. Camera four was to pick up additional shots of the inaugural stand and the parade, while camera five was assigned to take high shots from the Library of Congress and the House Office Building where Ford suggested they could get good views showing the Capitol with the crowds. In addition to camera locations, Ford suggested camera lenses for some of the units—noting, for example, that the distance from camera three's location to the ceremony stand was 138 feet and would therefore require a seventeen-inch lens for close-ups. He also included suggestions for specific shots as well as the estimated length of Roosevelt's speech and of the whole ceremony. The high degree of planning contained in Ford's memo is hardly surprising given the nature of the event, but it does reveal the extent to which the newsreel organized itself in advance of the news. Given the system's preference for pre-scheduled events, this detailed preparation suggests that any discussion of newsreel realism must begin with the decisions made before the cameras started rolling.

Of course, the extensive planning and the deployment of multiple cameras meant that the newsreel companies could provide coverage of the inauguration from many angles. For example, in their special release coverage of the event, *Universal Newsreel* included everything from an aerial view of the crowd at the Capitol building to close-ups of the new president.[34] By cutting between these different perspectives, the newsreel offered audiences a privileged view of the event. Aerial shots and high-angle footage taken from rooftops gave newsreel audiences an omniscient overview of the inauguration (Figure 1). Panning shots taken from

Figure 1. The inaugural parade moves down Pennsylvania Avenue. Still from "Extra Special: Roosevelt Inaugurated," *Universal Newsreel,* March 4, 1934.

the parade route mimicked the experience of watching the inauguration from the crowd. Close-ups of Roosevelt, Hoover, and others provided viewers with unprecedented access to the personalities and events of the day (Figure 2). The power of such multiperspectival coverage was twofold. On the one hand, it created the effect of a comprehensive record that placed the audience in the privileged position of seeing the entire event. The newsreel viewer saw more of the inauguration than any of the thousands of Americans who were in Washington that day. In this sense, at least, the newsreel could claim to be "better than being there." Moreover, by moving from one perspective to another, the newsreel made the world visible in an unprecedented way, transporting its audience throughout the capital and creating a sense of omnipresence that interpellated the spectator in a position of control and power. On the other hand, by cutting from an aerial shot of the Capitol building to a medium close-up of the new president taking the oath of office, Universal also demonstrated the power of the newsreel system itself. Each cut pointed to the elaborate

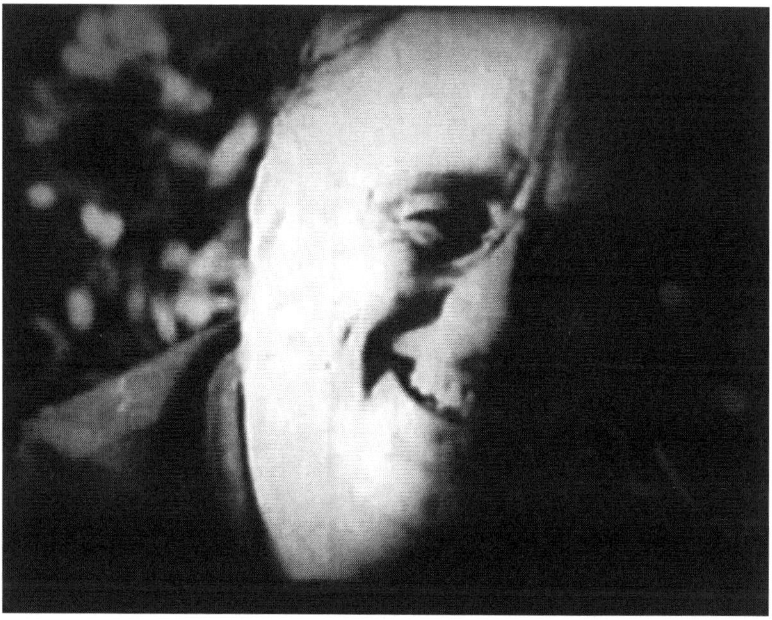

Figure 2. "More power to you, President Roosevelt. The entire country's behind you, filled with hope and patriotism." Still from "Extra Special: Roosevelt Inaugurated," *Universal Newsreel,* March 4, 1934.

planning and significant resources required to bring the inauguration to the screen. In the end, it was the power of the newsreel system itself that created a viewing experience that was arguably more real than any "simple record" of events. The newsreel system offered audiences a privileged view of the inauguration unavailable to those present and brought the inauguration to the local theater.

Universal's advance planning for its inauguration coverage did not stop at the deployment of its cameras. Getting the footage to movie screens as quickly as possible took just as much organization. Ford's memo also detailed these preparations. A chartered plane was to wait at Washington, D.C.'s Hoover Field and fly to New York's Floyd Bennett Airport. Ford calculated that at a speed of 230 miles per hour, the "approximate" flight time would be fifty-three minutes. From the Bennett airport, a waiting police escort would rush the negatives to Universal's laboratory where six special rush prints were to be made for New York–area theaters. These plans were apparently successful. Universal reported that it was the first newsreel company to show pictures of Roosevelt's swearing-in ceremony. Its films were screened at the Strand Theatre on Broadway at 6:50 p.m., just hours after the new president had finished his speech.[35]

For newsreels, speed was a crucial element of their realism. Although ostensibly the goal was to get the news first, in practice scooping their competitors by a few minutes or even hours achieved little. After all, as the *Motion Picture Daily* reported following the inauguration, "each reel claimed a scoop of some kind."[36] While Universal said it was the first to show pictures of the actual swearing-in, Paramount claimed it had preliminary shots of inaugural activities on screen at the Paramount Theatre in New York City as early as three o'clock. Pathé claimed its reels were the first to reach the screen in Los Angeles. With scoops and beats of events like the inauguration canceling one another out, the practical rewards of rushing news to the screen were minimal, but the ideological power of speed was significant. As Jane Feuer points out in her work on live television, concepts such as "liveness" are as much ideological as they are ontological properties of media. So, according to Feuer, "as television becomes less and less a 'live' medium in the sense of an equivalence between time of event and time of transmission, the medium in its own practices seems to insist more and more upon an ideology of the live, the immediate, the direct, the spontaneous, the real."[37] While, in the 1920s and '30s, radio offered the simultaneous broadcast of news and sporting events to its listeners, newsreels did not and could not claim to provide the same kind of live coverage. Nevertheless, their rhetoric of speed and efficiency worked to achieve a similar ideological effect. By reaching the audience faster than their newsreel competitors, studios implied that their coverage was more direct, more immediate, and more real.

Universal made the connection explicit in its self-referential coverage of the inauguration. The first three minutes of their eight-minute special release covering the event detailed the company's own efforts to bring the news to theaters in New York before their competitors. Beginning with a shot of footage being loaded onto a waiting airplane, narrator Graham McNamee announced that while viewers may not have been able to attend the inauguration, the newsreel would provide the next best thing:

> Two hundred and fifty thousand people are in Washington for the inauguration, but for those unable to get there, the *Universal Newspaper Newsreel* is rushing pictures of the epic by the fastest Air Express plane in the country. The speedy plane takes off and soars over the National Capital even while President Roosevelt is still on the inaugural stand. At 230 miles an hour, the record-breaking Air Express whisks its historic freight to the screen, arriving at New York while newspaper wires are still hot with the story of the great event and while the radio still roars with acclamations for the new president.[38]

By comparing the newsreel to radio and newswires, Universal implicitly acknowledged that its film coverage was not live. However, by offering the audience footage as fast as it could be turned around, McNamee invoked an immediacy that was key to the newsreel's reality effect. The speed of the newsreel's distribution did not provide a more accurate or more insightful account of events; instead, it, ostensibly at least, provided a more direct and immediate one. This rhetorical emphasis on speed and immediacy hints at the new way in which the newsreel deployed the real.

Universal's discussion of speed, its emphasis on its own processes of production and distribution, and its deployment of multiple camera angles to provide audiences with a more complete visual experience of the inauguration point to a realism different from those articulated by the newsreel's critics. All of these devices did not make the newsreel's coverage more accurate or true. Instead, the newsreel's rhetoric about itself emphasized the virtues of its own system for making the world available to the viewing audience in a more immediate and direct way than ever before. Indeed, Universal's coverage of Roosevelt's inauguration shows the degree to which the newsreel's realism relied on creating and maintaining a mediated link between the news event and the theatrical audience. This link made watching the event part of the news itself, fostering an early form of what scholars have identified in the television age as the media event.[39] In these moments of collective viewing, the audience shares in the news event through the experience of watching it on screen, often, in turn, making this communal spectatorship part of the news story. By highlighting this shared experience through the use of camera shots and editing, as well as emphasizing the newsreel's own means of production and distribution, Universal reflected a notion of the real that was based on more than film's ability to record the world. Instead, its realism was based on the newsreel's power to allow audiences to participate in the media event itself. As we'll see, by emphasizing this mediated connection between the audience and the events on screen, the newsreel privileged the act of looking over other forms of knowledge.

Displaying the Evidence: Making Absence Visible

There was no shortage of spectacular and historic events in the decade before the outbreak of the Second World War for the newsreel to demonstrate its realism, but no single news story received as much sustained coverage over a prolonged period of time as the kidnapping of Charles Augustus Lindbergh Junior. In 1927, Charles Lindbergh became the quintessential newsreel celebrity after his transatlantic flight. He remained in the public eye over the next few years with a series of goodwill tours of the United States, Asia, and Latin America, as well as his well-publicized marriage to Anne Spencer Morrow. The kidnapping of his nineteen-month-old son in 1932 instantly transformed this larger-than-life hero into a tragic figure, and Lindbergh's private grief became a national obsession. Many observers described the abduction of Charles Lindbergh Jr. as a moment of lost innocence for the United States. At a time when the country was mired in the worst of the Depression and the public was questioning an economic system that had apparently failed, the Lindbergh case raised the specter of organized crime and posed difficult questions about the consequences of the United States' emergent celebrity culture. Had Lindbergh's fame made him a target? Was the media somehow complicit in the crime, or did it at least hamper the investigation and recovery efforts?[40] But if some saw celebrity culture and the culture of looking personified by the newsreel as part of the problem at the heart of the Lindbergh story, the newsreel presented itself and its emphasis on the visual as part of the solution. By displaying the evidence of the crime on screen and making the search for the kidnappers visible to audiences, the newsreel bound its viewers to the story in ways that newspaper and radio coverage could not. The unique visual power of the newsreel allied its audience with law enforcement efforts to recover the child and solve the crime while simultaneously breaking down the traditional boundary between Lindbergh's public persona and his private life. In doing so, the newsreel made its viewers more than just witnesses to the Lindbergh kidnapping; it made them a part of the story.

Charles Augustus Lindbergh Jr. was kidnapped on the evening of March 1, 1932, from the family's estate near Hopewell, New Jersey. The baby's nurse, Betty Gow, discovered the child missing when she went to check on him in his room. She found the nursery empty and spotted muddy footprints from the child's crib leading to a nearby window. She immediately alerted the Lindberghs, who, after checking the house for the child and discovering a ransom note demanding $50,000, called the police. What followed was one of the largest police operations in history as the local police, New Jersey State Police, and the Federal Bureau of Investigation all joined the search for the kidnappers. Besides the ransom note, few clues were available. In the woods nearby, searchers found a makeshift ladder, which was apparently used to access the open window to the child's bedroom, along with some footprints in the muddy ground. The paucity of evidence in the case added to the mystery, and as the law enforcement investigation began, so did media speculation. The obsession with which the press had covered Lindbergh's triumphant flight and subsequent exploits was now directed toward speculating about suspects, motives, and possible underworld connections.[41]

Almost as soon as the police were called out, so was the press. In his memoir, *Newsreel Man,* Charles Peden—a cameraman and sound engineer for *Hearst Metrotone News*—recalled being awoken by his assignment editor in the middle of the night. Despite doubting the legitimacy of the story, Peden hurried to Hearst's Manhattan office where he read the 11:03 p.m. wire from the Associated Press: "LINDBERGH KIDNAPPED. DETAILS FOLLOW."[42] Peden and a camera crew sped to Hopewell, where they rushed to put together footage for a special release. Of course, the newsreel was not alone in its fascination with the Lindbergh story. Along with the newsreel crews, newspaper and radio reporters descended on Hopewell in unprecedented numbers. News of the abduction dominated the front pages of the nation's newspapers for weeks, with several giving over entire front sections to news of the kidnapping. For the first time, radio broadcasters replaced regularly scheduled programming with extended coverage and, in the push to break news first, networks interrupted popular broadcasts with frequent but sometimes erroneous updates.[43] The intense press interest in the case, combined with a relative lack of reliable information, fostered a great deal of speculation and uncertainty. Amid this charged atmosphere, the newsreel was able to emphasize its visuality to reassure audiences while still engaging their fascination with the kidnapping.

Commentators and historians have criticized the press frenzy as overwrought and ultimately detrimental to the course of justice in the Lindbergh case. Historian Kenneth Davis called the press "a force inimical alike to the apprehension of the criminals and the safe return of the child."[44] He argued that, by ratcheting up the atmosphere of hysteria, the press made it more difficult for the police to operate and forced them into mistakes; it also made it more difficult for Lindbergh to communicate with the kidnappers. Some observers at the time were already suspicious of the influence the press was having on the case. Walter Lippmann suggested the Lindbergh's relationship with the press prevented him from devoting his complete strength and attention to the search for his son.[45] Silas Bent, a commentator writing in *Outlook* magazine, went further:

> Charles S. Lindbergh has suffered more, probably, than any other citizen at the hands of the newspapermen. They capitalized for revenue only a stunt flight to France. They built up around his personality a myth which he has never been quite free to dissipate. They outrageously invaded the privacy of his honeymoon and his marriage and now they have made more difficult if not impossible the return by the kidnappers of his son to Mrs. Lindbergh's arms. Colonel Lindbergh has an ugly score against the daily press.[46]

Indeed, the press—the newsreel included—did exploit the Lindbergh myth of heroic achievement followed by tragedy and loss for melodramatic effect. In her book, *Kidnapped, Child Abduction in America,* Paula Fass discusses the press coverage of the Lindbergh case at length. She argues that the national press told a story "about the ravishment of the home and the vulnerability of even the most famous and beloved."[47] "In the Lindbergh case," she continues, "the rabid commercialization of grief, which was attached to an already insatiable curiosity about the famous, turned horror into another kind of sensation—a kind of salacious pity."[48]

While the newsreel certainly indulged in the "commercialization of grief" along with other members of the media, its focus was less on pity than on justice. The Lindberghs would not appear for the cameras in the days following the kidnapping, so, in part by necessity, the newsreel's coverage emphasized the police efforts.[49] Thus, instead of aligning itself with the grieving parents of the child, Universal and the other major newsreels used their cameras to ally audiences with law enforcement as they aimed to solve the case. The newsreel used its unique mode of representation to display the evidence in the case and to engage its viewers in the search for the missing boy.

By the time of the Lindbergh kidnapping, the American public was already being encouraged to identify with the work of the police. In her book, *Calling All Cars: Radio Dragnets and the Technology of Policing,* Kathleen Battles details how radio crime dramas of the 1930s helped to shift citizen attitudes toward the police. While popular culture of the early twentieth century often depicted police officers as corrupt or ridiculous, radio drama framed them as respectable. What Battles calls the "intimate authority" of radio allowed programs to "address listeners both as members of a larger community and as private individuals," and the police were depicted as "'public' servants entrusted with the responsibility of protecting 'private' persons and property."[50] Since the Lindbergh kidnapping represented a breach of the private realm, the notion of the police ensuring or restoring the sanctity of the Lindbergh home was a powerful one. By aligning itself with the police, the newsreel implicitly suggested that its looking too could safeguard rather than threaten the private sphere.

Universal Newsreel provides a good case study of how the major studios covered the Lindbergh kidnapping and the subsequent search for the child.[51] Universal produced a special reel on the Lindbergh kidnapping for early release to the East Coast on the evening of March 2, 1932. This story was subsequently included in Universal's scheduled release on March 3 and followed by regular updates over the next several weeks.[52] In its coverage of the kidnapping, Universal focused on the evidence in the case, but it also replayed home movie footage of the child and repeated images of the police and others participating in the search. In doing so, and by linking its own networks of production and distribution to the machinery of justice, Universal placed itself and its audience at the heart of the law enforcement effort to locate the missing boy. Even in this case of disappearance, the newsreel made the processes of looking—for its audience and for police—central to the story.

Universal's first story on the Lindbergh kidnapping framed the newsreel's coverage of the crime in terms of technologies of communication and looking. The item opened with shots of news of the kidnapping being sent over police wires—a police operator was shown receiving the teletype message and relaying it to police units, while the voiceover stressed the sense of urgency.

> The message that shocked the world comes in on the police teletype—a message that stunned the imagination—that made every parent shudder—and that brings into instant action the entire facilities of the nation's law-enforcing agencies. Out over the wires! And immediately there begins the greatest man-hunt in the history of modern crime.[53]

This focus on the speed of police communication recalls the frequent references in the newsreel to its own technologies of production and distribution. Thus, while ostensibly detailing police speed, this framing device indirectly underlined the newsreel's own immediacy. During coverage of Roosevelt's inauguration, for example, Universal's emphasis on its speed stressed the power of the newsreel to bring audiences closer to the event. In the Lindbergh case, references to police communication and speed served to link the newsreel and its audience to the police efforts to find the Lindbergh baby. The newsreel system went into "instant action" along with the "nation's law-enforcing agencies." Subsequent reports detailed these efforts. In its second story on the search for the missing boy, Universal opened with shots of the press frantically communicating the details of the story, echoing the footage of police communication shown in the previous report: "Reporters, cameramen, radio-announcers, typewriters, the telegraph, everybody working at top pressure—a mad house—so that the latest news can be flashed to the four corners of the earth."[54] As with other self-referential scenes, these shots stressed the news as media event, making the coverage of the kidnapping part of the story itself and placing the media in general, and the newsreel in particular, at the heart of the unfolding drama. But, by linking the technologies of media communication to those of the police, Universal went further. It aligned the police operation to find the missing child with its own efforts to report the story.

The alignment of the newsreel with law enforcement was not limited to the pairing of their communication networks. It can also be seen in the newsreel's display of the evidence in the case, in its detailing of the police efforts to locate the Lindbergh baby, and in Universal's efforts to enlist the public in that search. In each of these ways, the newsreel camera's gaze was clearly yoked to the activities of police looking.

Universal's first report on the kidnapping included a detailed account of the evidence discovered so far, along with the police's initial theory of the crime. Despite the limited number of clues available, the newsreel presented this evidence to its audience like the facts in a detective story:

> [The baby was] stolen in the dead of night from his crib on the second floor of the home in the Sourland Hills. The crime was committed by means of a ladder placed against the house. The baby stolen, dressed in his little sleeping suit, by two men and a woman, we believe. The kidnapper wore heavy woolen socks to disguise his footprints, but the search goes on just the same . . . looking for the writer of this message.[55]

Universal accompanied this list with footage of the evidence in question: a shot of the second-floor window and the makeshift ladder leaned up against the house demonstrating how the kidnappers entered the Lindbergh home; a close-up shot of the indistinct footprint found in the mud nearby the home, indicating stockinged feet; and an enlargement of a handwritten note addressed to Chas. Linberg [*sic*], reading: "BABY SAFE. INSTRUCTIONS LATER. ACT ACCORDINGLY." Although this litany of clues ostensibly presented the facts in the case, the display of evidence was not simply about providing the audience with new information. After all, by the evening of March 2, newspapers across the country had already published details of the evidence discovered by police.[56] Instead, this display confirmed for its audience the information they had read about in the paper or heard about on the radio and, perhaps more importantly, made that evidence visible. By showing the evidence to the audience, the newsreel worked to engage its viewers in the act of looking. In this case, looking was aligned with the police search for clues and more specifically the detective's investigative gaze.

In an essay on Walter Benjamin's *Arcades Project* and the figure of the detective, Tom Gunning has pointed out that the detective story of the late nineteenth and early twentieth centuries had a lot in common with film and other spectacles. "Like the visual attractions of popular culture," he writes, "the detective story activate[d] the complex dialectical optics of modernity, an optics based not only on the visual mastery of surveillance but also on the uncanny experience of transformed vision, glimpsing a presence where it is not, a space where it does not belong, and triggering a frisson of possible recognition."[57] As Gunning explains, the detective must search the exterior traces of the crime in hopes of uncovering the truth that they conceal. The newsreel's display of the evidence in the Lindbergh case invited its audience to participate in a similar kind of transformed vision: to search the clues on screen for their hidden meaning. The crudeness of the kidnapper's ladder, the indistinct nature of the footprint, and the odd handwriting in the ransom note all seemed to demand special scrutiny. By making the evidence visible, the newsreel engaged its audience in the experience of police looking in a way other media simply could not. In doing so, it drew its audience into the police search for the answer to the mystery of the child's disappearance.

If the display of evidence first invited audiences to engage in the investigative gaze of the detective, then the newsreel's coverage of the search for the missing child further married the newsreel to the machinery of police looking and urged its viewers to join the effort. The police search was featured prominently in Universal's initial coverage of the kidnapping: "Through every inch of the adjacent woods, trappers and State Troopers beat their way, seeking clues, while every law enforcement agency of three surrounding states presses with redoubled energy, the search for the missing infant."[58] The newsreel included nighttime footage of state troopers "going through the neighborhood with a fine-toothed comb" and shots of police searching cars on the New Jersey side of the Holland Tunnel and the entrance to the George Washington Bridge "in the search for the most famous baby in the world."[59] These images of police scanning the woods with their flashlights and opening car trunks framed the search for the missing boy in visual terms. Finding the child and solving the crime was a matter of uncovering clues and making the hidden visible. By framing the story in this way, the newsreel implicitly aligned itself with the police's efforts to locate the child. Moreover, given its ability to make the world visible, the newsreel was uniquely positioned to allow its audience to participate in the search through the act of looking itself.

With few clues in the kidnapping, the search for the missing boy continued to be the focus of Universal's subsequent reports. The newsreel reported that "the whole machinery of the law [was] in operation," but despite that, in desperation, the Lindberghs had turned to underworld figures Salvy Spitale and Irving Bitz, "hoping that gangland [could] succeed where the law [had] failed."[60] But it wasn't just the police and gangsters who were shown helping in the effort to locate Lindbergh's son. One Universal update detailed the efforts of police to recruit ordinary civilians to the search:

> The first circulars reach the East and are handed out by Police Chief Walter of Trenton, with instructions to plaster the whole community. This means that the United States Department of Justice has entered the picture by distributing these circulars to more than 1400 different cities. Millions of people will see the appeal and there's a chance that somebody might notice one of the posters, who'd recognize little Charles Lindbergh and so furnish a valuable clue.[61]

In these scenes, the newsreel showed a concerned crowd of citizens thronging the posters of the Lindbergh boy as they were distributed by police officers and stuck to streetlights. As with images of crowds at events like Roosevelt's inauguration, these crowds could act as proxies for the newsreel audience itself. Looking was once again part of the news story, and the audience was implicitly asked to join police and the crowds on screen in this act of collective viewing.

While the newsreel's display of evidence and its detailing of the search efforts implicitly recruited its audience to the task of finding the missing baby by linking the newsreel's gaze to police and civilian looking, its use of home movie footage of Lindbergh's son explicitly asked its audience to participate in the search through the medium of film itself. This homemade footage became a crucial element of the newsreel's coverage of the kidnapping. From the moment camera crews arrived on scene in

Hopewell, they wanted shots of Charles and Anne Lindbergh, presumably consumed by grief and worry. Unfortunately for them, the Lindberghs declined to appear on camera.[62] In a note to his editors, Universal's cameraman Roy Edwards expressed his frustration at his inability to secure images of the grieving parents. He wrote, "Lindbergh was never outside the house but once and his wife not at all. I was on the lookout all the time to get Lindy or wife at a door or window but they never appeared."[63] In the end, Universal used file footage of the Lindberghs in its report. Without new pictures of the parents, the home movies of Lindbergh's son took on added importance for the newsreel. They provided evidence of the child's appearance and an unusually intimate glimpse of Lindbergh's family life. Universal showed the images in its first release following the kidnapping, calling them "enlargements of small films photographed by Col. Lindbergh himself, [showing] the youngster in the last pictures ever taken of him."[64] In fact, the motion pictures had not been filmed by Lindbergh himself but by his brother-in-law Dwight Morrow Jr. at the Morrows' nearby estate. The footage showed the baby playing in his crib and crawling around on the grass. The Morrows turned over the pictures to *Pathé News* on March 2. The company enlarged the images and, after showing the footage on Broadway in New York and ensuring their scoop, made copies available to the other newsreel companies and to the press. As the *New York Times* reported, "the pictures were clear and informative as to the appearance of the child," and they "were distributed from coast to coast in the hope that by some chance a person seeing them might be of help in discovering the whereabouts of the kidnapped baby."[65] Indeed, Universal showed the footage again in its next issue, explicitly asking its audience to look at the pictures in order that they might "memorize his pretty face and report any news of him at once."[66] Calling on its audience to inspect the images to help the police, the newsreel placed itself and its audience at the heart of the unfolding story.

By framing newsreel spectatorship as part of the search for the missing child, the newsreel used the amateur footage as an opportunity to align its own systems of looking with both the justice system and the family. As Paula Fass points out, the kidnapping came to represent not just a loss of innocence for the United States but, because the kidnapper had literally broken into the Lindbergh home, also a tragic "violation of domesticity."[67] Critics like Walter Lippmann and Silas Bent suggested that the media, and its obsession with Lindbergh and his family, was somehow complicit in this violation. As an editorial published in the *New York Times* remarked, the Lindbergh home was built as a refuge from the publicity and media attention that had been the result of Lindbergh's fame:

> [It represented] the beauty and the sanctity of romance and youth. Somehow it seemed unspoiled and untouched by the mundane evil and ugliness, and remained apart as a sort of common ideal. The ravishment of that home by crime becomes a challenge, a personal affront to every decent man and woman, and a disgrace to the nation in which such a thing could occur.[68]

By representing the kidnapping as a violation of the domestic retreat that Lindbergh had been forced to build to avoid the "ugliness" of his own celebrity, the *Times* suggested that the press posed a threat to this domesticity, but the kidnapping had completely destroyed it. While such statements clearly implicated the newsreel along with the rest of the media, Universal's use of the home movie footage was a way for it to counter such discourses, to present itself as a defender of the domestic ideal, and to align itself and its audience with the Lindbergh family. Calling the child "well worthy of the love of *any* parents," Universal concluded its first report on the kidnapping by showing images of the baby again, along with an editorial plea for the restoration of the Lindbergh home and the domesticity it represented:

> The whole world wishes that the Lindbergh home'll soon see its baby safe in his crib, the very same crib they took him from. I'd sure like to have that kidnapper alone for just about 4 minutes. Come back soon, Little Lindy, our hearts are with you.[69]

By using the metonym of the home to refer to the Lindbergh family, Universal articulated the rupture of domesticity in spatial rather than visual terms, implicitly drawing a sharp distinction between the physical violation of the abduction and the camera's gaze. The use of the home movie footage framed film itself as a domestic medium. Far from posing a threat to the privacy of the family, these films, distributed via the newsreel, offered the possibility of its restoration. Ignoring its own cameraman's efforts to capture an illicit picture of Charles or Anne Lindbergh at the window of their home, Universal used the home movie footage as a means to offer its audience intimate access to Lindbergh's private life while paradoxically presenting itself as the defender of the sanctity of the home. Thus, while the critiques leveled by Bent, Lippmann, and others suggested that the celebrity culture of looking, of which the newsreel was an important part, was somehow complicit in the kidnapping of the Lindbergh baby, the newsreel's use of the home movie footage and its marshalling of its viewers to participate in the police search positioned its cameras and the looking of its audience as part of the effort to preserve and restore the family in the face of external threats.

Framing the newsreel gaze as part of the effort to find the missing baby and symbolically restore the sanctity of the American family was crucial for Universal because the newsreel's realism and authority rested, in part, on its ability to make the world visible and the invitation to its audience to look. The newsreel could not tolerate any implication that this looking was illicit or unwelcome. Universal's use of the home movie footage, its displaying of the evidence in the case, and its focus on the police search allowed—even obliged—its audience to participate in the news through the act of looking. In other words, the newsreel rested its realism not on its power to represent the real transparently but on its ability to engage the audience with the real through its own systems of looking. By allying these systems to the police's own technologies of communication, the newsreel ostensibly offered its audience an opportunity to engage in the Lindbergh case in a way other media could not.

Despite the efforts of law enforcement, the newsreel, and the public, and despite Lindbergh's payment of a $50,000 ransom after receiving his son's sleeping suit from persons claiming to be the kidnappers, the search for the missing baby failed to bring him home alive. On May 12, 1932, the child's body was found just a few miles from the Lindberghs' home. While revisiting its own themes of mediated communication and the massive search efforts, Universal's coverage of the grisly discovery once again presented the story as a media event:

> Once more a shocking message is sent out over the wires—once more a grim story is flashed to a horrified world—by telephone—and radio—and telegraph—and the great newspaper presses grind out a tale too horrible for belief—the final solution of a hideous crime—ending one of the greatest man-hunts in the history of

> criminology—a search that occupied thousands of men and crept into every corner of the globe—a search that carried with it the prayers and hopes of all decent men and women that the Lindbergh home would soon ring again with the laughter of a child. But it was not to be. Four miles from Hopewell, they found him—the pitiful little form unrecognizable except for its clothes—73 days after he disappeared, stolen from his distinguished parents by the vilest creatures that walk—found by four laborers on this very spot. The cradle's empty now—the nursery hears no more the happy crooning of an innocent baby. The world bows its head in sorrow. Sleep well, little Lindy.[70]

Accompanying this overwrought elegy were aerial images of the Lindbergh estate, the search efforts of police, and the spot where the child's body was ultimately discovered. These images underscored the enormity of the search and the difficulty of finding the now "unrecognizable" body of the child. Just as importantly, however, Universal's coverage provided its audience with a venue for the nation's shared grief, however much it had been commercialized by the media coverage. Unlike the individual experience of reading the newspaper or the intimacy of hearing the news on the radio at home, the newsreel made movie theaters into a public space for audiences to share their sorrow. By ending its story with a virtual moment of silence, Universal once again framed newsreel spectatorship as a way to participate in the media event.[71]

The Lindbergh kidnapping story did not end with the discovery of the child's body; it simply moved into a new phase. As events unfolded and the case went to trial, the newsreel's ability to make the world visible and to display evidence would once again be key. In the case of the kidnapping, Universal and its competitors displayed the evidence available to engage its audience in the search for the Lindbergh baby. In the trial of the alleged kidnapper, Bruno Hauptmann, the newsreel once again asked its audience to examine the evidence. This time, the evidence was displayed to establish the guilt or innocence of the accused.

"What Do You Think? Is That Man Guilty?"

After the discovery of the Lindbergh baby's body, it was over two years before there was a break in the case. That changed on September 18,

1934, when Bruno Richard Hauptmann was arrested after passing a ten-dollar gold certificate bearing a serial number from the ransom money that Lindbergh had paid in 1932. Once again, the Lindbergh case was front-page news and the lead story in the nation's newsreels. Under the headline "Lindbergh Kidnapping Sensation," *Hearst Metrotone News* announced that the "abduction which shocked world [was] near solution after two years with arrest in New York and recovery of $13,750 paid as ransom money."[72] Of course, Hauptmann's arrest was hardly the resolution of the case—instead it was the beginning of a series of legal proceedings that lasted over a year before culminating in Hauptmann's execution in April 1936. After being extradited to New Jersey on a murder charge, Hauptmann's trial began in Flemington on January 2, 1935. Dubbed the "trial of the century" by many observers, the proceedings garnered unprecedented radio, print, and motion picture news coverage. The newsreel's coverage, however, offered something different from that in the print media and on the radio. By capitalizing on its ability to make the trial, the evidence, and its personalities visible, the newsreel once again invited its audience to engage in the proceedings through the act of looking.

As it had during the investigation, the newsreel displayed the evidence of the case for its viewers and invited them to inspect it, offering up the ladder and the ransom notes for examination. But it was Hauptmann himself that represented the most decisive evidence: did he look guilty? Unlike during the investigation, the evidence was not presented as clues to a detective mystery but rather as a means by which the audience might decide whether or not Hauptmann was the kidnapper. Yet, although the newsreel could claim to provide its audience with visual evidence, it did not claim to provide proof. Unlike the prosecutors who argued their evidence was proof of guilt, the newsreel deliberately left this question open. Indeed, as we shall see, the display of evidence in the newsreel was done in part to allow for audience members to examine this evidence and come to their own conclusions. Once again, the newsreel aligned itself and its audience with the American justice system, but instead of allying itself with the state and its case, the newsreel put its audience in the position of the jury. This invitation to look at the evidence, not its ability to display the truth, was the key to the newsreel's realism.

The trial, like the investigation before it, was a massive media event. The small town of Flemington, New Jersey, where the trial was conducted, saw an influx of approximately one thousand journalists, growing its population by 30 percent. In order to accommodate the output of these reporters, Western Union and others installed telegraph facilities equivalent to those needed by a city of one million people. The courthouse itself was transformed into the nerve center of this newly installed network, with teletype machines, telephone booths, and typewriters filling every available space. The Associated Press alone dedicated three of its teletype wires to sending out a complete transcript of the trial every day. Several newspapers, including the *New York Times,* published these transcripts in full throughout the five-week trial.[73] Radio also offered unprecedented coverage of the trial. Although broadcasters were not permitted to air the actual proceedings, the Press Radio Bureau issued regular bulletins that were carried on several stations across the country. Others, including WABC and WOR offered listeners daily eyewitness accounts from their own radio commentators who were attending the trial. For legal perspectives, WHN featured nightly analysis by attorney Samuel Leibowitz, and WINS turned to Alexander H. Kaminsky, Assistant District Attorney for New York County.[74]

The scale of this media attention led some to question whether or not Hauptmann could get a fair trial. In an editorial titled, "Trial by Newspapers," The *White Plains Daily Reporter* called the media coverage "hysterical," accusing the press of "trying Hauptmann more completely, and perhaps more convincingly, than will be done during the trial" and turning "the trial into a modern Circus Maximus with the victims Hauptmann, and Colonel and Mrs. Lindbergh."[75] Respected journalist William Allen White lamented the sensationalism of trial, while prominent Americans, like Eleanor Roosevelt and Clarence Darrow, wondered if the media frenzy even made a fair trial possible. White argued that "the disgrace and scandal of movietone trials like the Hauptmann case reflect[ed] upon American intelligence and undoubtedly lower[ed] the tone of American justice."[76] As White's reference to "movietone trials" suggests, he and others saw the newsreel coverage of the trial as particularly emblematic of the media's sensationalism. Indeed, newsreels offered their audiences unprecedented access to the courtroom and certainly contributed to the trial's circus-like atmosphere. Universal reported on the "scramble for seats" at the beginning of the trial, showing a huge crush of people attempting to enter the Flemington courthouse—some even climbing into the building through an open window.[77] *Hearst Metrotone News* peppered its coverage with superlatives and adjectives, describing the "enthralling court drama" as "surpassing in its compelling, fascinating, heart-stirring intensity any make-believe drama of stage or motion picture."[78] Despite their sensationalism, newsreels like *Universal Newsreel* and even the florid *Hearst Metrotone News* worked hard to present their reports as impartial. The newsreel companies ostensibly left the task of judging Hauptmann's guilt to their audience. By putting the evidence and the personalities in the case on display, newsreels offered their viewers the opportunity to decide for themselves whether or not Bruno Hauptmann was guilty.

Much of the state's case against Hauptmann—and the newsreel coverage of the trial—focused on the physical evidence: the ransom money discovered in Hauptmann's garage, the makeshift ladder, and the handwritten note that Universal had featured in its original coverage of the kidnapping became crucial evidence against the accused. As the state rolled out this evidence, so did the newsreel. In a story detailing the initial grand jury testimony against Hauptmann, Universal detailed the "strong chain of circumstantial evidence . . . being forged by police to bind Bruno Richard Hauptmann to the Lindbergh kidnapping." What followed were shots making this evidence visible to the audience: the nearly $14,000 in marked bills were shown off for the camera as police officers silently placed them inside and then removed them from the can in which they were found in Hauptmann's garage; a close-up of two pieces of wood—one from the makeshift ladder used to access the Lindberghs' upstairs window, the other from Hauptmann's garage—showing similar grain and handwritten numbers on both; and finally, shots of the ransom note and a sample of Hauptmann's handwriting. The commentator informed the audience that the "man who wrote the two messages is said by experts to have been the same man."[79] The newsreel revisited much of this physical evidence during the trial proper, sometimes pairing it with the testimony of the state's expert witnesses. In one issue, a witness for the prosecution was shown pointing at the wood taken from the ladder and the garage while testifying that the two were made using the same carpenter's plane.[80] In another, the camera scanned a poster made by the prosecution comparing the idiosyncratic penmanship and spelling mistakes in the ransom notes to samples of Hauptmann's own. The state's handwriting expert, Albert S. Osborn, testified, "Hauptmann must have written the kidnap notes," but the newsreel followed this with footage of defense attorney, Edward J. Reilly, stating emphatically that "Bruno Richard Hauptmann did not write those notes."[81] By pairing shots of the evidence with expert testimony and defense rebuttals like this, Universal detailed the state's case against Hauptmann but refrained from endorsing it. Instead, by displaying the evidence itself, the newsreel ostensibly invited its viewers to make up their own minds. Using close-ups and slow panning shots of the items in question, Universal allowed its viewers to move their gaze across the image, implicitly asking them to inspect the evidence against Bruno Hauptmann. This was something radio and print media did not and could not do. Radio reports may have offered up-to-the-minute information, but they could only summarize the evidence presented in court. Newspaper coverage of the trial described the evidence in the case in elaborate detail, even printing witness testimony verbatim in their transcripts, but they did not publish the evidence itself. For example, the *New York Times* described Albert Osborn's testimony regarding the handwriting in the ransom notes on its front page and presented complete transcripts of his findings, but the only image accompanying this article was a picture of Osborn himself.[82] Only the newsreel invited its audience to look at the evidence for itself.

No piece of evidence was more crucial than the accused himself. Right from his arrest, the newsreels were fascinated by Hauptmann's face, voice, and demeanor. Throughout the legal proceedings, newsreels repeatedly showed close-ups of his face, as if his guilt or innocence might be read in his reaction to the testimony against him or simply in his face itself. In one striking shot from *Hearst Metrotone News*'s coverage of Hauptmann's first court appearance (before his extradition to New Jersey), the newsreel simply presented Hauptmann's face in close-up, illuminated by a succession of flashbulbs as a throng of photographers took his picture.[83] Although the voiceover announced that this was Hauptmann's first appearance before a judge, the close-up was also his first formal appearance before the cameras of the world and the newsreel audience. This tight shot of Hauptmann's face lasted several seconds, providing Hearst's viewers with plenty of time to study it for signs of guilt or innocence. Universal was more explicit in its invitation to examine Hauptmann's face. In the company's coverage of the same court appearance, Universal showed police sketches of a suspect that John "Jafsie" Condon, Lindbergh's friend and intermediary, had described as the man to whom he had given the ransom money. Comparing the sketch with shots of Hauptmann, Universal asked, "Note Hauptmann's picture. Do you see the resemblance? What do you think? Is that man guilty?"[84] Whether implicitly or explicitly, this is the question that Universal and its competitors asked each time they showed Hauptmann's face on screen.

The search for some sign of guilt or innocence in Hauptmann's face and mannerisms showed in the considerable media interest in his habit of smiling in the courtroom. A few days before Hauptmann was due to take the witness stand in his own defense, *Universal Newsreel* ran a short item titled, "Hauptmann Smiles as State Nears Completion of Case." In the story, Hauptmann was described as being "in almost a friendly mood" as the prosecution was wrapping up its case. In sound footage, Hauptmann is seen and heard responding to questions from reporters and—at the urging of someone behind the camera, who can be heard saying, "let's a have nice smile"—smiling.[85] In the days that followed, Hauptmann's smile came under considerable scrutiny, both in the courtroom and in the press. Once Hauptmann took the stand, his smile became an issue as Attorney General David T. Wilentz questioned whether or not he found the court's proceedings a humorous matter. Hauptmann responded by saying, "I can smile because I am innocent." Newspaper accounts of the cross-examination, however, noted how quickly these smiles turned to anger when confronted with inconsistencies in his story. These stories implied that Hauptmann's smiles revealed something more sinister. Alexander Woollcott, a columnist for the *Los Angeles Times*, described the "puzzling smiles" as "curious," "chill," and as "compounded in equal parts of complacency and contempt."[86]

For its part, Universal offered no comment on Hauptmann's smile. Instead, it ended its report by asking its audience a question. Referring to earlier testimony from Charles Lindbergh identifying Hauptmann's voice as the one he had heard call out to his friend John Condon when he paid the ransom, Universal asked, "Is that the voice Lindbergh heard over the cemetery wall the night the ransom was paid?"[87] This question is characteristic of the newsreel's coverage of the Hauptmann trial. Unlike newspaper reporters, whose descriptions of the trial included implicit interpretations of witnesses and evidence, the newsreel left such analysis up to its audience. While the cajoling of a smile from Hauptmann demonstrates that newsreelmen were not above manipulating people and events to manufacture controversial or sensational footage, Universal and its competitors realized that their unique appeal rested on apparently allowing audience members, as much as possible, the opportunity to see and hear the news for themselves and to draw their own conclusions.

The newsreel dramatically demonstrated its ability to grant its audience access (however mediated) to the news events of the day when Hauptmann finally took the stand in his own defense. Under the headline "Hear Hauptmann Testify at Last," Universal claimed to satisfy the burning desires of audiences to see and hear Hauptmann:

> With bated breath, millions and millions have anxiously awaited the sensational day in this terrific trial! Millions upon millions want to hear and see and know exactly what happened and how! "What does Bruno Hauptmann say? . . . How does he look? . . . What will be the jury's and public's reaction to his testimony?" For weeks every newspaper has front-paged and built up this tremendous real-life drama! Now Universal Newsreel takes it out of the imagination and flashes it right before your very ears and eyes![88]

Hearst Metrotone News was equally breathless:

> Actual cross-examination in greatest criminal trial recorded by sound cameras—the most gripping court duel ever presented in a newsreel . . . Questions and answers, word for word, recorded in this remarkable real-life document—the first of its kind ever presented on the screen.[89]

It is interesting that both these descriptions put such heavy emphasis on the realness of their offerings. The real in this case, however, was not a truth inherent to the filmic document itself but the opportunity to see the defendant testify in his own words, for the first time, on screen. Implicit in the Hearst description and explicit in Universal's is the promise that the newsreel would allow its audience to see and hear for itself as Hauptmann finally faced his accusers.

These films were unusual for the newsreel in that they featured very little commentary. With only a few words to identify the people on screen, they mostly allowed the "real-life document" to speak for itself. The footage was taken from a pool camera positioned in the courthouse and shared by the five major newsreel companies. Universal, which devoted its entire reel to the Hauptmann testimony, ran over eight minutes of this footage, showing Hauptmann on the stand with no voiceover commentary at all. After briefly showing scenes of Charles and Anne Lindbergh on the stand and the crucial testimony of John "Jafsie" Condon, who testified that Hauptmann was the man to whom he gave the ransom money, the rest of the reel featured Hauptmann himself answering questions from his own defense lawyer and then under cross-examination from Attorney General Wilentz (Figure 3). Having edited together a whole day of testimony, Universal had plenty of dramatic moments to choose from. They chose to highlight Hauptmann's repeated denials and key moments in the cross-examination when Wilentz focused on inconsistencies between his answers and his previous statements to police and during his grand jury testimony. In one particularly dramatic scene, a defensive Hauptmann can be heard saying to Wilentz, "Stop that!" as Wilentz pressed him on his answers to the grand jury:

> WILENTZ: "Didn't you lie under oath?"
>
> HAUPTMANN: "No."
>
> W: "Time and time again, didn't you?"
>
> H: "I did not."
>
> W: "When you were arrested with the ransom money, did the police ask you where you got it?"
>
> H: "They did."
>
> W: "When they asked you where you got that money, did you lie to them or did you tell the truth?"
>
> H: "I said not the truth."
>
> W: "You lied didn't you?"
>
> H: "I did, yes."[90]

Figure 3. Bruno Hauptmann on the stand under questioning from Attorney General Wilentz. Still from "Hauptmann Testifies at Last," *Universal Newsreel,* vol. 7, no. 324

Each of these moments was captured in simple static shots taken from the pool camera in the courtroom balcony. The camera showed the lawyers from behind but captured Hauptmann's face and movements as he sat nervously on the witness stand. With the camera situated high in the gallery, these shots mimicked the view of the courthouse audience itself. Indeed, between its footage of Hauptmann's testimony, Universal cut to brief shots of the courtroom spectators. In these scenes, we see curious onlookers craning their necks, apparently to get a better view of the defendant (although it is virtually certain these shots of the crowd were taken at a different time). As with similar techniques used during the newsreel's coverage of Roosevelt's inauguration, these cross-cutting crowd shots served to align the newsreel spectator's look with that of the crowd on screen. For those unable to be one of the lucky few to attend the trial itself, the newsreel offered mediated access to the event. But the newsreel did not just align its audience's gaze with the courtroom gallery; it also asked its viewers to weigh the evidence for themselves. With

Figure 4. "From the maze of testimony, twelve men and women must decide Hauptmann's fate. But millions . . . the entire world awaits the verdict!" Still from "Hauptmann Testifies at Last," *Universal Newsreel*, vol. 7, no. 324

no commentary to color the testimony one way or another, Universal allowed Hauptmann to speak for himself, silently asking the audience to consider the question, "Is he guilty?" It was up to the viewer to decide if he looked and sounded guilty or not (Figure 4). To push this point home, Universal ended its story on the courthouse drama with a shot of the jury followed by a close-up of Hauptmann's face and the voice-over comment, "From the maze of testimony, twelve men and women must decide Hauptmann's fate. But millions . . . the entire world awaits the verdict!"[91] By ostensibly letting the footage "speak for itself" and positioning the audience in the gallery, the newsreel placed the spectator next to, if not in, the jury box itself. Although the newsreel spectator was relieved of the solemn responsibility of determining Hauptmann's fate, Universal implicitly invited its audience to come to its own verdict.

Shortly after the films of Hauptmann on the stand were released, they—and the ability of the newsreel viewers to judge Hauptmann's guilt for themselves—became a problem in the courtroom. In a telegram to newsreel companies, New Jersey Attorney General David T. Wilentz wrote:

> In the name of the State of New Jersey and in the name of decency, it is requested that you order the immediate withdrawal of Hauptmann pictures taken during actual trial sessions. These sound pictures were secured by trickery and in defiance of the order of the court.[92]

Wilentz argued that the films had been taken in violation of Judge Tranchard's instruction to still photographers and newsreel cameramen that, while cameras would be allowed in the courtroom, no photographs were to be taken while court was in session. Despite this ruling, the newsreel pool set up a camera—encased in a box designed to deaden the sound of its motor—in the courtroom balcony, in full view of the judge and the sheriff. Operated by remote control, the camera, along with a directional microphone mounted on the wall, was presumably allowed on the understanding that it would not be filming while court was in session.[93] Judging by Universal's footage of John Condon, Charles Lindbergh, and Anne Lindbergh on the stand, in addition to Hauptmann himself, however, the camera must have been used throughout the course of the trial. Upon receipt of Wilentz's protest, *Fox Movietone* immediately withdrew its films of the Hauptmann testimony, with Hearst and Paramount eventually following suit. Only Universal and Pathé refused to recall the footage. R. H. Cochrane, vice president of Universal Pictures, wrote in a telegram to Wilentz that the whole trial had become a "great show":

> The Universal Company has violated no agreement with the court in using trial scenes in our newsreel. The truth of the matter is that the whole trial has been ballyhooed in some of the newspapers and over some of the radio stations day after day, while newsreels have been so decent and dignified that they have defaulted in their duty to the theatres they serve.[94]

For Cochrane, it was the newsreel's duty to show the trial footage. Moreover, because the footage was presented largely without comment, Cochrane could argue that it represented an antidote to the overwrought and sometimes inaccurate "ballyhoo" in print and on the radio.

Wilentz had some reason to be concerned about the footage. Edward J. Reilley, defense counsel, was reportedly preparing to move for a mistrial on the grounds that "his client was being persecuted and judged in advance of a verdict on the screens of the country."[95] Indeed, as we have seen, Universal's use of the footage was an invitation to judge Hauptmann, and the footage, although not completely damning, was certainly not flattering. As a result of the controversy, Judge Tranchard ordered all cameras removed from the courtroom, and it would be several decades before any U.S. judge allowed cameras in the courtroom again.[96] The controversy over the Hauptmann footage demonstrates the unique power of the newsreel's realism. It was not simply the power of the camera to capture reality that threatened the court. As Reilley's protests reveal, it was the ability of the newsreel to open up the courtroom to the general public and its ability to subject his client to public scrutiny that posed a problem. By offering its audience access to the court and inviting it to judge Hauptmann for itself, the newsreel transformed the trial into an unparalleled media event and the movie theater into a jury room.

Coverage of the Hauptmann trial was exceptional for the amount of time Universal and its competitors devoted to the story but not in their deployment of the newsreel system's particular notion of realism. Whether it was a great sporting achievement or the scale of a natural disaster, the newsreel offered its audiences a chance to see visual evidence of what they had heard on the radio or read about in the newspaper. While radio had the potential for real-time coverage and the press provided endless analysis, only the newsreel offered audiences the opportunity to "judge for themselves." Just as coverage of the kidnapping had provided audiences with the images and clues necessary to enlist them in the search for the Lindbergh baby, the trial coverage offered them the chance to be on the jury. Through the act of looking, American audiences engaged in a mediated participation in the case. While newspapers and radio broadcasts offered the expert analysis of lawyers, psychologists, and handwriting experts, the newsreel seemed to give its audiences access to the evidence they needed to come to their own conclusions. In doing so, the footage of the Hauptmann testimony simply made explicit what was so often implied in the newsreel's parade mode of representation. By repeatedly asking its audience to inspect the evidence on screen and to judge for itself, the newsreel moved the locus of the real away from the events in front of the camera and into the theater.

Conclusion: Guilty

By the time the jury reached a guilty verdict in the Hauptmann case, the newsreel companies were already well prepared. Several of them distributed alternate reels in advance of the jury's verdict, one in case of a guilty verdict and another in case of a finding of not guilty. Paramount even produced a third reel "in the event the jury found Hauptmann guilty with a recommendation of mercy." With the reels made in advance, news of verdict could be shown in theaters as soon as the verdict was announced. According to the *Motion Picture Daily*, the *Hearst Metrotone News* reel screened in 107 theaters of the Loew's circuit just five minutes after the verdict was announced.[97] Once again, the full power of the newsreel system of production and distribution was employed to allow its audience to participate in the media event.

As we have seen, the unprecedented access the newsreel offered its audience was key to the newsreel's unique realism. The newsreel system allowed Americans to participate in media events through the shared act of looking. By making the world visible—as evidence on screen—the newsreel invested looking with new power. Looking ostensibly allowed audiences to see for themselves and come to their own conclusions, and, like the Hauptmann jury, newsreel spectators were engaged in this process collectively. This is not to suggest that newsreels were objective or without the biases that many of its popular critics identified. Newsreel realism, however, did not rest on the idea of objective truth but rather on a populist notion that the audience could decide the truth for itself. The popular realism presented in the newsreel did not claim to provide the kind of synthesis that Grierson or Lukács would identify as key to realism. Instead, it offered its audiences the opportunity to perform such a synthesis on their own. As such, the newsreel had more in common with P. T. Barnum's operational aesthetic then it did with documentary film in the 1930s.[98] The newsreel did not purport to show audiences proof but rather invited them to inspect the evidence. In doing so, it bound the audience together as other media could not. Watching the news on screen was not like being there or even better than being there; watching in the theater was a way to participate in the media event itself. The great power and appeal of the newsreel's realism lay not in its images but in the invitation to look at them.

CHAPTER 3

"Heroes of the Lens"

Newsreel Cameramen, the Sino-Japanese War, and Looking as Action

In 1937, the Japanese invasion and occupation of China became the most filmed war in history. With dozens of cameramen representing the international newsreels in the region, American companies like Universal and MGM promised to provide the most sensational and graphic images of modern war. Thanks to the efforts of cameramen like George Krainukov, H. S. "Newsreel" Wong, and Norman Alley, they delivered. The news films taken during this conflict are some of the most powerful films made in the 1930s. This chapter, however, will focus less on the dramatic images these men recorded and sent back to North America than on the men themselves: on how they did their dangerous work, but more importantly, how they were represented in newsreels, in studio promotional materials, and in the wider culture. As the preceding chapters have demonstrated, the newsreel system and its parade mode invited the audience to experience the news—and participate in a mediated public sphere—through collective spectatorship. By investing looking with such importance, the newsreel made the news present in the theater and real for its viewers. As chapter one discussed, however, the appeal of the newsreel rested on the tension between the closeness of the image and the distance of the events on screen. Celebrity, glamour, danger, and the exotic proved to be crucial elements in maintaining this tension and highlighting the power of the newsreel to mediate the distance between the audience and the news.

In the 1930s, the figure of the newsreel cameraman and the tales of his heroic exploits became a key way for studios to promote their newsreels and their sensational scoops. Although the newsreel business involved an elaborate system of production, distribution, and exhibition, the cameraman was the public face of that system. Emerging as both a model of masculinity and a symbol of American power in the 1930s, the cameraman represented the newsreel's commitment to go out into the world and "capture the news," bring it back to the United States, and allow audiences to see for themselves. Using the figure of the cameraman—and his much lauded courage and skill—newsreel companies promoted their products as exciting and invited their audiences to join these heroes on their adventures around the world. In doing so, newsreels further invested looking with its own power. Embodied in the newsreel cameraman, looking did not signify passive observation but rather a modern, active, and powerful means to explore the world.

By the mid-1930s, the newsreel cameraman had become an iconic figure in the American popular imagination. He was the subject of books, films, pulp stories, and, by the end of the decade, comic books. Although the image of the cameraman as a glamorous adventurer had been well established, the outbreak of war in the Far East was a touchstone event. As the first truly modern war to be caught on film, and the first to feature the extensive use of air power, the Japanese invasion of China offered unprecedented images of spectacular explosions, urban devastation, and human tragedy. It also offered an unprecedented opportunity for newsreel cameramen to prove their bravery and skill. This chapter examines the figure of the cameraman in the newsreels made of the Sino–Japanese War—in particular the bombing and invasion of Shanghai and Nanking in the summer and fall of 1937—as well as a series of fictional representations of the cameraman in Asia that were made in the war's aftermath.

In popular representations, the cameraman played a double role, both as a heroic adventurer-explorer braving the dangerous war-torn locales of the Far East but also as a representative of the United States and the West in Asia. His whiteness, as well as his masculinity, was key. At a time when American public opinion opposed intervention in the Sino–Japanese conflict, the figure of the heroic cameraman addressed potential anxieties over the United States' policy of neutrality. Drawing on discourses of masculinity and orientalism, newsreel photographers could show on-the-ground images of the war while holding it at a safe distance for their viewers in the United States. In doing so, the newsreel cameramen mediated the relationship between West and East as well as the distance between film audience and film object. The play of distance embodied in these mediations—as well as the deployment of racial and gender categories—is vital to understanding the newsreel's power to bind local audiences to the reality of the media event. The white newsreel cameraman acted as the agent of the spectator's gaze, at once testifying to the authenticity of the image, authorizing a masculine and imperialist form of vision, and reinscribing the power of looking on screen.

"Heroes of the Lens": Newsreel Cameraman as Masculine Icon of the 1930s

The newsreel cameraman was a hero in the 1930s. In books, magazine articles, movies, and comic books, news photographers were shown braving natural and man-made dangers, dodging bullets, solving crimes, and always getting the shot in the process. Borrowing aspects from other popular heroes of the day—the detective, the cowboy, the explorer, and so on—the newsreel cameraman embodied a unique model of masculinity that combined daring and toughness with worldly sophistication. By representing these masculine traits, the newsreel cameraman's own authenticity emerged as a key way for newsreels to promote their films and assert their authority to represent the world.[1]

The extent to which the newsreel cameraman had entered into the popular imagination in the 1930s can be measured by the 1933 publication of the *Boys' Book of Newsreel Hunters* by Irving Crump.[2] According to its inside cover, this book joined others in the Books for Boys series that detailed the accomplishments and history of other iconic workers: firemen, policemen, forest rangers, airmen, arctic explorers, and coast guard members. In order to join this pantheon of masculine endeavor, newsreel cameramen from all of the major studios had demonstrated their skill and bravery in getting spectacular footage from around the world. But it wasn't just their own efforts that had made newsreel cameramen into icons; the newsreels themselves, in their promotional materials and voiceovers, regularly extolled the exploits of their cameramen to get the shot. The studios too had helped boost the newsreelman as a heroic figure by making films to either directly or indirectly promote their newsreels. Crump's book and others, as well as stories in the pulp press, suggest that these efforts propelled the newsreel cameraman to near mythic status in the 1930s.[3] As if to confirm this status, by the end of the decade, the newsreel photographer had become a comic book regular and, in some cases, literally a superhero.[4] These fictional representations often blurred with news reports and studio promotional material on actual newsreel photographers to help shape, as well as reaffirm, the myth of the news cameraman.

The mythic qualities of the newsreel cameraman were exceptional. He was the consummate professional—equally at home in the company of famous and powerful people as he was in the most primitive, exotic, and physically extreme locations. He was brave and willing to risk his life to get the shot—whether that meant balancing precariously hundreds of feet above the ground, tying himself to a diving submarine, or going into a war zone. Crump's book covered all these exploits in vivid detail. By looking at the popular myth of the newsreel cameraman, as it was cultivated by newsreel studios and reflected in popular culture, we can begin to see the power this figure had to authenticate the films he shot as well as the role he played in mediating between the audience and the world on screen.

Above all, the newsreel cameraman was represented as a man of adventure. Over and over again, newsreel companies added editorial commentary to their voiceovers and promotional materials pointing out the dangers endured by their cameramen. In a 1929 promotional film released by MGM to celebrate their new *MGM International News* series, the company put together a reel of its most spectacular footage, celebrating the newsreel cameraman's abilities to go wherever was necessary to get the shot. Showing a photographer carrying his camera out onto the beam of a skyscraper still under construction, the film proudly announced that "an *International Newsreel* man is not content with picturing the perils of others; to obtain a good shot, no risk is too great."[5] Indeed, sometimes the danger was such that the news was simply the shot itself. Under the headline, "Cameraman Risks Life To Film 'Sub' In Striking Speed Tests," Universal featured "exclusive pictures off the California Coast as Mervyn Freeman, *Universal Newsreel* staff photographer, [took] remarkable pictures of sensational diving maneuvers while lashed to the periscope of the Navy's largest submarine, Narwhal."[6] This episode was recounted again by Crump along with other hair-raising tales of parachute jumps, erupting volcanoes, and man-eating tigers. In a chapter titled "Stunt 'Shooters,'" Crump extolled the stunt cameraman as "the most daring of their profession":

> All cameramen display rare courage, for their career is one which constantly brings them shoulder to shoulder with dangers; but the men who undertake some of the stunt pictures that are brought out to thrill newsreel audiences display a brand of bravery that astounds the normal individual.[7]

The newsreel cameraman's bravery did not just satisfy the audience's demand for spectacular news footage; it also helped to legitimate the newsreel itself. By emphasizing cameramen's courage and skill in stunt shots, the newsreel demonstrated their desire to get the shot no matter what the risk. This commitment to their profession testified to the strength and quality of their character, which, in turn, worked to authenticate the rest of their footage.

The image of the daredevil cameraman was not restricted to the newsreel's own publicity materials; the newsreel hunters of fiction film regularly put their bravery to heroic use. In movies like *Ladies Crave Excitement* (1935), *Anything for a Thrill* (1937), and *Headline Shooter* (1933), newsreel cameramen captured kidnappers, confronted gangsters, solved mysteries, prevented crimes, and discovered murders.[8] Even a comedy like Buster Keaton's *The Cameraman* (1928) had Keaton's character transform from bumbling tintype photographer to daring newsreel man. By the end of the film, Keaton had braved Chinese gangsters, rescued the heroine from drowning, and caught the whole thing on film.[9] The newsreel cameraman's courage in the face of danger made him an ideal Hollywood hero.

Although the figure of the newsreel cameraman was principally a swashbuckling adventurer, he was also expected to be sophisticated and comfortable in glamorous and dignified company. As Crump pointed out, the cameraman needed:

> . . . the ability to feel at home and at ease in the presence of the world's notables and dignitaries of all kinds, and to be able to make accurate and intelligent records of such important events as

> the meetings of the League of Nations, the London Round Table Conference and similar world-important gatherings. Then there are the interviews that cameramen are expected to obtain. They must be able to approach such men as the Prince of Wales, John D. Rockefeller, George Bernard Shaw, Mahatma Gandhi, Babe Ruth and others of prominence, and feel sufficiently at ease with them to talk with them intelligently on almost any subject.[10]

The notion that it was up to the cameraman to secure footage of even the most aloof celebrity was an important part of the myth of the newsreelman. In addition to trick shots and slow-motion photography, MGM's 1929 promotional film for its *MGM International News* series highlighted the news photographer's access to celebrity and power. Stating in its intertitles that "no man is too great for the news camera's all embracing eye,"[11] the film showed footage of Pope Benedict XV, Woodrow Wilson, and Theodore Roosevelt. Living up to the challenge to make everyone subject to the newsreel's gaze—and to offer viewers access to even the rich and powerful—was important to newsreel companies. It was up to the cameraman to use his wits. Fox made this challenge the central dilemma of its 1928 film *News Parade,* starring Sally Phipps and Nick Stuart. Timed to help publicize Fox's new sound newsreel, the film told the story of "Newsreel Nick," a young cameraman who, after impressing his bosses by shooting an aerial stunt, is assigned to get pictures of eccentric and reclusive multimillionaire, Dillon Morgan. Naturally, after foiling a kidnapping attempt on Morgan's daughter, Nick is rewarded with exclusive footage of the wealthy man, not to mention the affections of his daughter. According to promotional materials from the studio, the film was made in consultation with *Fox News'* Director-in-Chief Truman Talley and cameraman Russell Muth, and the film was based on the real-life difficulties newsreel cameramen had in photographing J. P. Morgan, John D. Rockefeller, and other "shy Wall Street Magnates."[12] The ability of the newsreel cameraman to move in elite circles was important because the newsreel promised its audience access to celebrity and power through the screen. By stressing the unusual skill of the cameraman to get celebrity interviews, the newsreel further emphasized the difference and distance between their audience and the famous people on screen, as well as the power of the newsreel to mediate this distance.[13]

If the newsreel cameraman's wit and personality allowed him to close the figurative gap between the rich and powerful and the newsreel's audience, then his status as a brave explorer enabled him to bridge the literal distance between the audience and the exotic places shown on the newsreel screen. In the 1920s and 1930s, newsreel cameras were regularly sent on expeditions to the farthest reaches of the globe. Admiral Richard Byrd, who had already made expeditions to the Arctic and Antarctic, took two Paramount cameramen on his 1932 journey to the South Pole. A book about the trip, *Paramount Newsreel Men with Admiral Byrd in Little America,* detailed the difficulties of filming in the frigid temperatures of Antarctica, not to mention the problems of processing the footage and keeping expensive equipment from freezing up.[14] If it wasn't the newsreel joining explorers, then it was explorers joining the newsreel. Under the headline, "Famous Explorers go to Africa for Metrotone," Hearst proudly announced that the prominent explorer-filmmakers Martin and Osa Johnson would be the first to "shoot" jungle life with sound cameras. An editor's note below the story pointed out that:

> *Hearst Metrotone News* takes pride in announcing the first sound-camera expedition to the Dark Continent. Mr. Johnson and his intrepid wife are the foremost photographic authorities on African wild life. They return to the jungle with the most modern scientific equipment to record for you its life and danger in picture and sound.[15]

Martin and Osa Johnson were already well known for their popular ethnographic documentaries like *Jungle Adventures* (1921), *Headhunters of the South Seas* (1922), and *Simba: King of the Beasts* (1928). Combining the conventions of the travelogue with those of ethnography, these films presented indigenous cultures as primitive, strange, and savage.[16] The Johnsons, the newsreel camera, and the audience, in contrast, represented modernity, science, and civilization. This formulation of the newsreel cameraman as a symbol of heroic modernity penetrating the primitive and exotic corners of the world reiterated the distance—both literal and figurative—between the newsreel subject and its audience while giving viewers the chance to see the world in close-up. As we have seen, the tension between the onscreen presence of the absent image was central to the newsreel's appeal. The newsreel cameraman was, in turn, key to marking this tension. The cameraman embodied both the audience's mediated presence in the far-off location as well as the real absence of the dangerous and exotic images present on the screen.

In some ways, war zones were the ultimate exotic locales; they represented a similarly dangerous terrain for the cameraman to brave with his camera. Even as the world moved toward war at the end of the 1930s, the United States was apparently well insulated from the hostilities. The Italian invasion of Ethiopia, the Japanese incursions into China, and even the Spanish Civil War seemed remote, unlikely to threaten the American public watching the newsreel in local theaters. The newsreel cameraman and his penchant for the dangerous and exotic sent back spectacular footage of these distant wars but, in doing so, helped maintain these conflicts as faraway problems. No matter how close the cameraman got, no matter how much danger he faced, the audience was encouraged to view these events as spectacle. Little or no attempt was made to explain the causes or ramifications of these conflicts. A *Universal Newsreel* story about a Red Cross unit being bombed by the Italian air force in 1937, for example, was described this way:

> Exclusive, authentic pictures graphically show the flaming terror hurled against a Red Cross field unit near Nugelli by Italian airmen. Bombs and machine-gun fire kill and cripple Swedish doctors and their Ethiopian assistants. Scores of wounded soldiers die as the raiders ignore Red Cross flags.

This was typical of the newsreel's war coverage, stressing the spectacle of modern warfare and its apparent senselessness. In such an environment, where there were few heroes, just victims and perpetrators, the heroic newsreel cameraman stood apart. The promotional material for these films announced that they were "photographed by Howard Winner, Ace Universal Newsreel Cameraman . . . and among the most amazing ever made by a newsreel cameraman." The film itself included a shot of what audience members must have assumed was Winner turning the crank of his camera as the voiceover informed them that the "exclusive pictures were filmed at great personal peril."[17] Such scenes were echoed in fictional representations of the newsreel cameraman in war. War offered the cameraman the ultimate environment in which to prove his mettle while also allowing him—and his audience—to differentiate themselves and American civilization from the barbarism on screen.

Although modern warfare meant the combatants were equipped with the technology of the twentieth century, the cruelty and barbarism emphasized in the newsreel's coverage demonstrated their supposed primitive nature. This lack of sophistication was a theme in some fictionalized versions of the cameraman at war. In *I Cover the War* (1937), for example, John Wayne plays Bob Adams, a newsreel cameraman covering an Arab rebellion against the British somewhere in North Africa. Adams uses his camera to film exciting scenes, including exclusive footage of the rebel leader. He also uses his camera to dupe the natives. Using what is, to them, an apparently unfamiliar piece of technology, Adams tricks the rebels into letting him escape, whereupon he saves the British Army from attack. Although they had modern weapons, the rebels in *I Cover the War* remained primitive and technologically unsophisticated. The newsreelman's camera itself was a way to contrast the misuse of modern technology—barbaric warfare—with its responsible application. In the war zone, the newsreel system represented a civilized alternative to the senselessness of war, one in which technology was used for peaceful purposes and the only "shooting" was with the camera.

Prior to the outbreak of World War II, the most vivid example of the newsreel cameraman at war came during the conflict between Japan and China, which simmered for years before the full outbreak of hostilities in 1937. Even before the war, a series of international incidents attracted attention from newsreels. In 1932, Japan invaded Shanghai for the first time, providing cameramen with the perfect arena to prove themselves. As Crump details in *The Boy's Book of Newsreel Hunters*:

> The first international hostilities of a magnitude to be considered a real man's size war, in which newsreel with sound effects functioned, was the Japanese invasion of Shanghai; and to say that the cameramen operating there were successful in depicting the thrills and horrors of warfare is putting it mildly indeed . . . The startling views of bombardments, air raids, assaults, and counter attacks [make] it evident that every cameraman at the front risked his life, not once or twice but constantly, in his efforts to get amazing pictures.[18]

Crump's language is telling. By explicitly linking the war zone and the bravery needed to film its horrors to the notion of a "real man's size" conflict, he underlines the links between the cameraman, his masculinity, and the newsreel's authenticity. Not only was the cameraman a hero—brave, adventurous, glamorous—he was a real man. As we shall see, the masculinity of the newsreel cameraman—especially when contrasted with the feminized, Asian bodies on display in these war pictures—became a crucial axis along which the authority of the newsreel cameraman was constructed. This manly status made the footage shot by newsreel cameramen beyond reproach—the authenticity of the men testified to the authenticity of the films they made.

War as a Spectacle of Pity: Newsreel Cameramen and the Imperial Gaze

The image of the newsreel cameraman was well circulated by the time the hostilities broke out in Shanghai, but the dangers confronted by newsreel photographers in the Far East and how studios promoted them in films and their related promotional materials helped to confirm and reinscribe the qualities that defined the newsreel cameraman as an icon in popular culture: his bravery and sophistication, as well his status as an explorer, an adventurer, and a "real man." The cameramen drew on all these traits to make spectacular film documents of the war in Shanghai and Nanking. These films did not just reiterate the myth of the newsreel cameraman; they cast this hero anew in the context of an increasingly dangerous world. In doing so, they positioned the American public as a spectator of war. This spectatorship was not innocent, however. As we shall see, the new ways of looking at the world, through the lens of the newsreel camera, engaged what E. Ann Kaplan calls the "imperial gaze." This gaze did not simply observe war in the Far East; it dominated it and objectified it.[19] By deploying orientalist discourses of Asian passivity and femininity and by aligning American audiences with active, masculine cameramen, the newsreel records of the Sino–Japanese conflict distanced viewers from the events on screen even as they ostensibly brought them closer.[20] This distancing permitted audiences to experience war—no matter how shocking and graphic—as a kind of spectacle of pity: an incomprehensible tragedy, but one that remained separate from viewers' lives, not to mention American politics and foreign policy.

After several years of high tension in the Far East and a series of military skirmishes—or so-called "incidents"—the Sino–Japanese War began in earnest in the summer of 1937, when the Chinese, under the command of Chiang Kai-Shek, attempted to force Japanese military units out of Shanghai. By November of 1937, the Japanese had forced the retreat of Chinese forces, and the fight moved to Nanking, where the Japanese Imperial Army surrounded and ultimately captured the city. The Sino–Japanese War featured some of the most brutal and violent fighting the world had ever seen. This was one of the first true air wars, and the sometimes arbitrary results of bombing from the air were devastating. Civilian casualties were high in both Shanghai and Nanking. These deaths were by no means limited to "collateral damage," however. During their assault on Nanking, Japanese troops systematically targeted Chinese civilians, sexually assaulting and killing hundreds of thousands.[21] The massive scale of the physical destruction and the human consequences of the war made the Sino–Japanese conflict an irresistible spectacle for the newsreel. Despite the technical difficulties and physical dangers, American newsreel companies dedicated significant screen time to the war in China.

The exceptional violence of the Sino–Japanese conflict made for vivid newsreel images. From August 1937 to January 1938, each of the American newsreel companies carried regular reports on the fighting in the Far East. With cameramen based in Shanghai, MGM's *News of the Day* and *Universal Newsreel* devoted particularly significant portions of their reels to the conflict and heavily promoted their coverage. These reports focused on the scale of the destruction as well as the human devastation unfolding in China. Under the headline, "Sensational Pictures of War in China," MGM boasted that the "extraordinary films made by *News of the Day* cameramen under fire [were] the first adequately to portray the great war tragedy in the Orient!" The graphic scenes made "one minute after airplanes [bombed the] heart of Shanghai" showed a city in ruins, civilians running for their lives, and the bodies of numerous dead strewn about the streets. "You're looking at war in the raw," Paul Alley's voiceover told his American viewers.[22] Indeed, the images of destruction were so raw that Universal preceded its special issue devoted to the "Bombing of Shanghai" with a foreword warning the squeamish not to look.[23] Of course, this warning came after the hyperbolic language of Universal's promotional materials presented the "sensational scoop" of "the spectacular fear-fraught tragedy" as something that had to be seen. The lobby card accompanying the release described the lurid scenes this way:

> Bombs splintering through the Cathay Hotel! 1,000 civilians, including women and children, killed! Over 5,000 injured! Fear-crazed populace fleeing from scenes of carnage! Dead and wounded stacked up seven deep on the sidewalk! You SEE it happen before your very eyes![24]

While newsreels were seldom shy in sensationalizing their stories, even for Universal the number of exclamation points in this paragraph was impressive. In addition to underlining the spectacular nature of their coverage, this exclamatory style stressed the immediacy of the very disturbing images. Audiences could see the carnage right before their "very eyes." Despite—or because of—the graphic nature of its special issue, the *Motion Picture Daily* applauded Universal and its cameramen for a magnificent job of filming and editing its footage. Praising the company for showing "the crash of guns, the flight of terror-stricken refugees, the wrecked and the shambles of innocent civilians, headless, armless and torn apart by the explosion of Japanese bombs in the center of Shanghai,"[25] the trade journal noted that Universal had bravely refused to censor its coverage. Such commentary underlines the extent to which the spectacle of war—in all its graphic detail—was the principle attraction on offer in the newsreel coverage.

The focus on the war as spectacle was, among other things, a way of maintaining neutrality in the face of mounting global tensions. In 1937, isolationism dominated American political discourse. Few Americans wanted the country to be directly engaged in the crises in Europe or Asia. The newsreels' coverage of the Sino–Japanese War seemed to cater to such feelings.[26] The extremely graphic images of bombed-out cities and terrible human suffering made for spectacular film images, but the newsreels did little to contextualize the war in the Far East. They did not explain the causes of the war nor the larger issues involved. Instead, the war was portrayed as general evidence of "man's inhumanity" and the "frightfulness of modern war that spares no one."[27] Universal's scenes of Chinese civilian misery were so graphic that a group of Chinese Americans in San

Francisco contacted the company in the hopes of buying newsreel footage from the company to use in fundraising efforts to support the refugees. Although Universal offered to rent its newsreels to the group, Universal's editor, Charles Ford, refused to sell the footage, saying the company did not want to take sides in the conflict.[28] By staking out its neutrality in this way, Universal did more than reiterate journalistic objectivity; it aimed to empty the images of some of their political potential. American public opinion was divided on the war in the East, and studios were anxious not to appear to favor one side over the other.[29] Both MGM and Universal framed their coverage of the war in terms of its incomprehensible brutality and made a spectacle of its pitiful victims. This approach, with its special emphasis on civilian casualties and refugees, heaped scorn and pity on both sides of the war. Both Japanese and Chinese were equally culpable in what Universal characterized as "Oriental madness."[30]

By framing the "great war tragedy of the Orient" as a kind of spectacle of pity, both MGM and Universal fell into well-worn orientalist discourses that served both to feminize and infantilize the people of Asia. Building on Edward Said's theoretical insights, many scholars have described the sexualization and exoticization of a feminized Orient in Western art and film.[31] In his book *Orientals,* Robert Lee complicates these ideas in the American context. Since the nineteenth century, the Chinese in American popular culture had been characterized as troubling traditional gender boundaries and as a threat to the purity of the white family. According to Lee, in films like *The Cheat* (1915, Paramount) and *Broken Blossoms* (1919, United Artists), "the representation of the Oriental as both seductively childlike and threateningly sexual allowed for both sympathy and repulsion."[32] The newsreel coverage of the Sino–Japanese conflict rehearsed just such tropes. Although the war was framed as barbaric and vicious, the newsreel showed relatively few soldiers in action. Bombing raids by both sides and street fighting made shooting the actual battles extremely dangerous. Instead, cameramen for Universal and MGM shot the aftermath of these attacks, focusing on the effects of war on women and children by showing repeated images of refugees fleeing the combat. In its story about the ultimate fall of Shanghai, for example, Universal detailed the plight of the civilian refugees escaping the city after it was "put to the torch by Japanese shells and Chinese defenders."[33] Referring to the refugees as "homeless hordes," "pitiful wanderers," "human wrecks," and a "vast army of misery," Universal represented the Chinese people as nothing more than victims. This emphasis on victimhood and helplessness conformed to orientalist tropes of Asian passivity and a feminized East. No wonder then, that in its year end "News Parade" for 1937, *News of the Day* revisited the war in China in explicitly gendered terms. Showing footage of refugee women and children, the newsreel framed the war in terms of its female victims and a feminized victimhood: "For women particularly, 1937 brings home the frightfulness of modern war that spares no one . . . Always it is the innocent who suffer most from war's cruel lash."[34] It wasn't just literal shots of women that served to feminize the Asian victims of war. Repeated shots of dead bodies and the injured lying in the streets of Shanghai also rehearsed orientalist notions of the feminine Asian body. Shown dead and dying, the bodies of soldiers and civilians were presented in various ungainly and unnatural positions. Recalling nineteenth-century images of the languid female bodies in the orientalist fantasies of artists like Jean Auguste Dominque Ingres, these contorted bodies, stripped of agency and humanity, were the ultimate objectification of the human form.[35] In this context, even the bodies of soldiers became objects of "sympathy and repulsion."

No single image of the war in China captured this spectacle of pity better than the famous shot of a crying baby at Shanghai's South Station after a Japanese bombing raid had destroyed the transportation hub (Figure 5). The image became iconic after a still was picked up by the International News Service, reprinted in hundreds of newspapers across the country, and featured in a *Life Magazine* photo essay, but it was originally shot by H. S. "Newsreel" Wong for MGM's *News of the Day.*[36] Showing a lone crying baby seated on train platform surrounded by the still smoking ruins of the station, the image worked as a neat metaphor for the Far East conflict as imagined by the North American press. The *News of the Day* commentary accompanying the shot asked, "What could be a more damning indictment of war than these frightened, bewildered, agonized babies?"[37] By encapsulating the war in the image of a screaming baby, the shot revisited orientalist imagery of an infantilized Far East that needed the help and guidance of the more mature nations of the

Figure 5. H. S. "Newsreel" Wong's famous image of a baby crying after the bombing of Shanghai's South Station in August 1937.

West.[38] Indeed, the shot perfectly captured how the newsreel's coverage of the Sino–Japanese conflict represented Asia as the helpless victim of its own barbarism.

While the films of the bombing of Shanghai and Nanking focused on the misery brought on by war, they also allowed the newsreel to highlight the heroism of its own cameramen. In stark contrast to their graphic images of human devastation and Asian passivity, these reports described newsreelmen as active subjects on the battlefield. Newsreel reports were peppered with allusions to the danger encountered by the cameramen sent to China to film the war and the bravery that they showed in carrying out this task. *News of the Day* voiceovers regularly mentioned that their cameramen risked their lives capturing their footage, frequently noting, for example, that they shot the war "underfire" or just "75 yards away [from a] building swept by machine gun fire at the height of the assault."[39] These references helped create the sense of immediacy that was key to the newsreel's coverage of faraway events. Universal was even more effusive in its references to its cameramen in its reports, making these men central features of its coverage. The company's special issue on the bombing of Shanghai praised its cameramen and the lengths they went to in order to get the shot almost as much as their footage. A lobby card promoting the issue included photos of Universal cameramen George Krainukov and Howard Winner along with details of their efforts to get dramatic pictures of the war:

> George Krainukov: Wounded in the hand by a bomb fragment, Universal's intrepid cameraman stood up under fire and kept on grinding—so that YOUR screen might be enriched by the most spectacular scoop of the century! The whole New Universal organization is proud of you George!
>
> Howard Winner. Another Universal hero of the newsreel! While shells burst and bullets whistled by, he stood shoulder to shoulder with Krainukov, and together they shot nerve-tingling scenes . . .[40]

These descriptions were not simply the florid language of copywriters. The cameramen covering the war were indeed in extremely dangerous situations, and Krainukov's own notes are in many ways more vivid than the promotional material. On his cameraman's caption sheet (or dope sheet), where normally the cameraman would simply list mundane details like the shots taken, the names of specific people and places, and perhaps note some difficulties encountered in getting the shot, Krainukov described the risks he took to get footage of the bombing of Shanghai in September 1937:

> The air was screeching with wizzling shrapnel, roaring and diving bombers, bombs exploding, planes falling in flames. The top of the building roof on which I was taking pictures was swinging from the terrific detonation of the bomb's explosions. Truly it was hell on earth during these few minutes, when all my life was in my hands with my camera! It was to get the picture! Pieces of shrapnel and bomb fragments were falling all around us. My eye was glued to the view-finder. I could feel nothing but the roar of destruction all around me.[41]

It is not a coincidence that Krainukov's description of his experiences read like a pulp magazine. In some respects, the myth of newsreel hunter had come full circle. The cameramen saw themselves as heroes amid the turbulence of war. In light of how the war itself was presented in terms of its pitiful Asian victims, the reliance on the myth of the newsreel hero as masculine icon is telling. Not only did this image stress the heroism of the cameraman himself, but it also positioned the audience's own looking in terms of that same masculine rhetoric. While the war was represented in terms of its feminized and infantilized Asian victims, the newsreel spectator experienced the war through the active, masculine gaze of the cameraman hero.

The juxtaposition of the heroism of the newsreel cameraman to the spectacle of pity on screen during the Sino–Japanese conflict drew on a long orientalist tradition that framed colonial encounters in visual—as well as racialized and gendered—terms. As European colonies expanded, so did the desire and the possibility to explore these new territories and to bring back artifacts from strange and exotic places. Almost from its inception, photography provided the ideal means with which to document these journeys. The photograph was itself an artifact; as a trace of the "other," it was evidence of the exotic. Photographs of the pyramids at Giza, photographs of the natives in India, Guinea, and the Arctic—everywhere a camera could go, a photographer-explorer was ready to take it. The explorer went where others could not, and the photograph was evidence that he had done so. The way in which much of this travel and expedition photography of the nineteenth century served to essentialize and objectify foreign bodies and cultures has been well documented, but these images also worked to frame the photographer as a certain kind of active subject.[42] In these colonial images as well as in the newsreels of the 1930s, the cameraman acted as a kind of ambassador of civilization. Marking his modernity and superiority, the camera worked as a passport, authorizing the photographer to document the "other." As passive, traditional, and feminized, the object of the photographic gaze defined the bearer of the gaze as active, modern, and male.

This tradition of racialized and gendered vision persisted in Hollywood as well as ethnographic film. Indeed, Fatimah Tobing Rony argues that it is the process of racialization that defines the ethnographic film. "What distinguishes the genre of the ethnographic film," she writes, "is not the color of the people filmed, but how they are racialized . . . how, in other words, the viewer is made to see 'anthropology' and not history."[43]

The newsreel coverage of the war in China racialized the Chinese and Japanese in much the same way an ethnographic film might. By not providing its audience with the context of the Sino–Japanese War, the newsreel's coverage of the conflict failed to present it as history, focusing instead on a spectacle of pity that stressed a kind of anthropological interest in racial and cultural difference. Moreover, by contrasting the barbarism of the Asian war and the passivity of its victims with the heroism of its newsreel cameramen, Universal and others framed these racial differences in terms of gendered notions of looking. In her book *Looking for the Other: Feminism, Film, and the Imperial Gaze,* E. Ann Kaplan makes the link between the racialized vision of colonialism and ethnographic film and the gendered looking relations identified by feminist film theory. Using examples from Hollywood film—*Birth of a Nation* (1914), *King Kong* (1933), and *Tarzan, the Ape Man* (1932)—Kaplan describes how the "male gaze" and the "imperial gaze" are linked. She argues that in films like *King Kong,* the travels of male explorers to exotic locations are imagined "through the sexual metaphor of mastering and conquering the female body" and that "in some senses . . . the male primitive body is feminized (equated with the castrated body) to put it in the position of being mastered."[44] The newsreel coverage of the Sino–Japanese War enacted a similar metaphor as the masculine newsreelmen and their (phallic) cameras were contrasted with the feminized bodies of Chinese refugees, the injured, and the dead. Seen in this way, the newsreel cameraman's masculinity literally embodied both the racial and gender relations of the imperial gaze, and the newsreel images of the destruction of Shanghai and Nanking conformed to a long orientalist cinematic tradition in the West.

By incorporating orientalist themes in the newsreel, the image of the cameraman in the Far East did not simply reinscribe notions of race and gender; it also helped to distance the newsreel spectator from the violence on screen. As Kaplan points out, the imperial gaze is one that elides its own power:

> The gaze of the colonialist refuses to acknowledge its own power and privilege: it unconsciously represses knowledge of power hierarchies and its need to dominate, to control. Like the male gaze, it's an objectifying gaze, one that refuses mutual gazing, mutual subject-to-subject recognition.[45]

By casting the Sino–Japanese War as both incomprehensible and barbaric, the newsreel allowed its audience to engage in an imperial gaze that need not acknowledge the subjectivity of the war's victims or its perpetrators. By embodying this gaze in the hypermasculine figure of the newsreel cameraman, MGM and Universal indulged their audiences in a gendered and racialized form of looking that offered a privileged vantage point from which to observe the conflict. While the heroism of the cameraman offered a close-up view of the destruction, the imperial gaze maintained its distance and its difference by ignoring the causes and consequences of the war and objectifying the human suffering on screen. In doing so, newsreels mediated the public's relationship with the war in the Far East, permitting the audience to remain neutral and aloof while viewing the destruction of Shanghai and Nanking as an incomprehensible spectacle of pity.[46]

Panay Incident: Neutrality under Threat

The power of the newsreel cameraman to mediate the war for American audiences and to distance them from the crisis was exemplified—and to some extent tested—by the bombing of the U.S.S. *Panay.* On December 11, 1937, the *Panay* evacuated most of the remaining American citizens and several other foreigners from Nanking—including *Universal Newsreel*'s Norman Alley and *Fox Movietone*'s Eric Mayell. Japanese bombers shelled the gunboat as it sailed up the Yangtze with American flags in full view. The boat sank, several of the ship's passengers and crew died, and the rest were forced to flee overland. The incident sparked outrage in the United Sates, and it pushed the Sino–Japanese conflict to the top of the front page in American newspapers—after all, it could well have been viewed as an act of war by the U.S. government. Because of the presence of the newsreel cameramen, their own story became entwined with the fate of the *Panay.* Both Alley and Mayell were able to record many of the events, with Alley getting extensive footage of the bombing and the aftermath. Predictably, the films were an opportunity for studios to laud the bravery of their cameramen while offering newsreel audiences an extreme, close-up view of the incident. As we shall see, however, these films—and their cameramen stars—also captured a key moment in the American public's relationship to the conflict itself. The attack on the

Panay threatened American neutrality in the region, but there was little appetite in the United States for involving the country in war. The mediating figure of the newsreel cameraman and his heroism offered a way for the American public to engage with the news while maintaining neutrality.

The U.S.S. *Panay* was stationed in Nanking to evacuate the few remaining U.S. citizens in the city before Japanese forces began their final assault. On December 5, 1937, the U.S. Embassy in Nanking issued the following statement:

> The Embassy considers it inadvisable that Americans remain longer in Nanking. All Americans are urged to foregather at the Embassy West compound tomorrow morning, Monday, December 6, at 9:30 am, to proceed in a group to the Bund and embark on the "USS Panay."[47]

Most of the remaining Americans complied with the request, but some returned to the mainland during daylight hours, as the *Panay* remained in Nanking harbor until December 11. By that time, the Chinese resistance had dwindled, and the Japanese were ready to mount their final siege on the city. In addition to its crew, the *Panay* set sail with a dozen civilians on board, including employees of Standard Oil, a number of embassy officials, one independent businessman, and several members of the press, including Alley and Mayell. A third newsreel cameraman, *Paramount*'s Arthur Menken, elected to stay in Nanking to shoot the final stages of the siege, but Japanese forces arrested him days later, confiscating his film and his camera.[48] The *Panay,* under the protection of several large and prominently displayed American flags, steamed twelve miles upstream from Nanking and anchored overnight, but, by the morning, nearby shelling forced the gunboat to move a further fifteen miles upstream. The plan was to remain at anchor until what was assumed would be an easy victory by the Japanese made it safe to return to Nanking. This plan literally went up in smoke when, just after 1:30 p.m. on Sunday, December 12, six Japanese planes attacked the *Panay,* dropping bombs and strafing the ship with machine-gun fire. Several bombs hit the boat, and it sustained considerable damage. Just twenty minutes after the first bomb hit, the boat was taking on water; soon, the gunboat lost power, and the captain gave the order to abandon ship. The last lifeboat left the *Panay* just after three o'clock. The crew and civilians gathered on the river's edge and watched the *Panay* sink into the waters. After hiding in the reeds to avoid Japanese patrols until nightfall, the party—with dozens of injured men (three of whom would eventually succumb to their wounds)—made its way to the small town of Hohsien, where there was a small hospital. The survivors wired news of the *Panay*'s sinking to the U.S. Embassy in Hankow. It was the first ship of the U.S. Navy ever lost to enemy aircraft.[49]

The bombing of the *Panay* was instantly front-page news in the United States. The Japanese Navy accepted responsibility for the bombing and pledged to take immediate steps to find out how the attack had occurred. In a communiqué quoted in the *New York Times,* Japanese authorities regretted the incident "most deeply."[50] Washington condemned the bombing, and President Roosevelt requested formal redress from the Japanese, including full compensation and guarantees against "a repetition of any similar attacks in the future."[51] The incident could have been seen as cause for war, but few in the United States wanted to get directly involved in the Asian conflict. Nevertheless, the diplomatic crisis following the bombing occupied the nation's headlines for the next week and more. Indeed, interest in the *Panay* Incident was such that it overshadowed news of the Japanese attack on Nanking itself and of the massive civilian death toll there. F. Tillman Durdin, a *New York Times* reporter, was one of the few foreigners to witness the siege, but it took several days for his report to reach North America. When the *Times* finally reported the atrocities on Saturday, December 18, the diplomatic fallout from the *Panay* still got the higher billing in its front-page headline: "U.S. Naval Display Reported Likely Unless Japan Guarantees Our Rights; Butchery Marked Capture of Nanking."[52] There is no evidence to suggest that the bombing of the *Panay* was deliberately timed to distract international attention from the Japanese abuses, but because most of the last newsreel cameras and print reporters remaining in the city left Nanking on the *Panay,* the attack effectively limited news reporting of what happened in Nanking.

The presence of so many reporters on board the *Panay,* combined with the ensuing diplomacy, ensured that the story stayed in the public eye until December 30, 1937, when newsreel images of the attack finally made it to American screens. As the *New York Times* reported, "The *Panay* bombing was the camera man's paradise. The light was excellent: the attacks continued long enough for movie men to get setups, and the ship even sank slowly enough for them to save their films and in some cases their cameras."[53] Alley was shooting on the deck of the *Panay* when the first bombs fell, and he was able to shoot particularly vivid pictures of the Japanese planes attacking the *Panay* and of the gunboat's anti-aircraft guns returning fire. In all, Alley shot more than 4,500 feet of film; Mayell had just 1,500 feet, but both men secured footage showing the evacuation of Nanking, the aftermath of the attack on the *Panay,* the boat sinking into the Yangtze, and the crew's overland journey to reach help. It took some time for the films to reach audiences, however. After the *Panay* survivors were rescued, they were taken to Shanghai aboard the U.S.S. *Oahu.* From there, Alley and the films sailed to Manila and flew by China Clipper to San Francisco. After a twenty-four-hour delay in Honolulu, the films and Alley finally arrived in California on Tuesday, December 28, 1937.[54] Upon receiving the footage in the United States, Fox, Universal, and MGM *News of the Day,* which had a pooling agreement in place with Fox to use Mayell's footage, rushed to edit their films and get them to screens. Both Fox and MGM released their special issues on the *Panay* Incident as part of the regular newsreel series, screening their films in New York just before noon on Thursday, December 30. Choosing to release its film as a special twenty-two-minute short feature, separate from its regular newsreel, Universal's film did not show until later that night.[55]

Despite the delay in getting the *Panay* films to the American public, interest remained high. Fox, Universal, and MGM promoted their films heavily, and the *Motion Picture Daily* reported that "marquees and lobbies billed the films everywhere."[56] *Fox Movietone* took the unprecedented step of placing a quarter page ad promoting its newsreel in the *New York Times* and listing 225 theaters in the New York area where it could be seen: "SEE the first motion pictures of the bombing of the U.S.S. *Panay,* taken by a Movietone News Cameraman aboard the ill-fated American gunboat!"[57] Each of the three companies also placed several ads in the trade press aimed at getting exhibitors to choose its company's film. With the most footage, Universal promoted its release as "the only complete picture of the attack that shocked the world!" and offered exclusive scenes.[58] Without any exclusive material, both Fox and MGM advertised the fact that, unlike Universal's film, their newsreels were available "at no extra cost" to exhibitors.[59] All promised "thrilling" images shot from the deck of the *Panay.* Reviews of the *Panay* films seemed to confirm these claims. In its review of the *Movietone* and *News of the Day* releases, the *Motion Picture Daily* reassured exhibitors that the films would meet their expectations: "the shots are just as dramatic as the world-wide build-up in the press and can stand billing above or alongside the feature. As an audience draw they are better than the *Hindenburg* because of the tremendous advance publicity."[60] Likewise, the *New York Times* praised Universal's thorough coverage of the incident, claiming that it would allow "all sections of the American public . . . the opportunity to pass judgment on a peace-threatening incident."[61] Indeed, the response from exhibitors was enthusiastic, and all three studios with *Panay* footage were forced to release extra prints to cover the demand.[62] The Photoplay section of the *New York Times* was full of ads from various exhibitors announcing the first screenings of *Panay* films from one or the other of the studios. Whichever films they were offering, many of the ads reiterated the *Times*' suggestion that the films offered the chance to "see for yourself what actually happened."[63] Once again, it was the invitation to join together in collective spectatorship that formed the basis of the newsreel's realism and authority.

Many of the promotional efforts around the *Panay* films centered on the cameramen themselves. As with the earlier films of the bombing of Shanghai and Nanking, studios stressed the bravery of the men in the Far East. Both Fox and MGM noted that their films had been made from the deck of the ill-fated gunboat, while Universal gave Alley top billing in its special release, calling it "Norman Alley's Bombing of the *Panay.*" Indeed, some of Universal's ads featured a prominent picture of Alley behind his camera wearing a military style helmet and chomping on a cigar.[64] In these ads, Alley was the epitome of the manly newsreel hero. Universal had good reason to focus so much on Alley. In the days after the bombing and Alley's return to the United States, he had become something of a celebrity. In an interview with CBS radio while Alley was still in Shanghai, the cameraman paid tribute to the heroism of the crew but made sure to mention he "shot the works" despite being injured himself.[65] Once back in the United States, Alley met with reporters at the

Warwick Hotel in New York and posed for photographs with one of the *Panay*'s life preservers.[66] Alley's fame was magnified when he and his films were summoned to Washington to be examined by the Navy and the State Department as evidence in their investigation of the incident.[67] Alley's status as witness to the *Panay* bombing gave legitimacy to his footage upon which Universal was keen to capitalize. Unlike Mayell, who remained in the Far East to cover the war, Alley returned to the United States, a triumphant newsreel hunter with trophy in hand.

While the heroism of Norman Alley and Eric Mayell served to authenticate the films they shot, the *Panay* films also helped to bolster the reputation of the cameramen themselves. Using scenes of the men behind their cameras and colorful voiceover commentary, studios boasted of the prowess of their newsreel photographers. MGM's announcer, John Paul King, introduced the special issue of *News of the Day* from behind a desk by highlighting the dangers faced by Eric Mayell:

> I'm speaking for the newsreel cameraman who made the pictures you're about to see . . . Bear in mind that the cameraman more than once was forced to jump for his life to escape the Japanese missiles. That in the midst of death, he thought first of the traditions of his craft, provides one more remarkable instance of the courage and devotion that have made the newsreel cameraman the pride of the motion picture world.[68]

Although he did not mention Mayell by name (perhaps because he was a Fox cameraman), King's commentary pressed home the relationship between the newsreel cameraman's heroism and his compelling images. Universal went even further to make this link. The studio opened its special release with shots of Alley himself photographing the destruction in Nanking: "Despite the deadly peril Norman Alley takes his stand in the besieged city. Recording the ruin of war amid the constant rain of steel and high explosives that takes hundreds of lives and lights grisly fires throughout the capital." By emphasizing the bravery of their cameramen, MGM and Universal framed the *Panay* Incident as a human triumph over tragedy and its survivors as heroes, not victims.

These depictions of the newsreel hero once again marked the imperial gaze of the cameraman and newsreel spectator. In both the Universal

Figure 6. "Despite the peril, Norman Alley takes his stand in the besieged city." Still from "Bombing of the Panay," *Universal Newsreel,* December 30, 1937.

and MGM films, descriptions of the heroic cameraman were contrasted with scenes of the spectacle of pity. In Universal's "Bombing of the Panay," shots of Norman Alley were juxtaposed with his own footage of dead bodies and helpless civilians as the commentator Graham McNamee declared, "horror piles upon horror and one pitiful scene surpasses another."[69] Amid the ruins, Alley literally stood apart. Even as the war raged around him, he was made distant by virtue of his camera (Figure 6). Like the newsreel audience itself, Alley was separated from the action by the apparatus of the newsreel and by the act of looking. This difference and distance was crucial. It positioned the cameraman and spectator close to the action but above the fray. Calm and confident in the face of danger, the cameraman observed the destruction while ostensibly remaining neutral. Represented in this way, the heroic cameraman also embodied the United States' policy of neutrality in the Far East and helped dramatize the threat posed to that neutrality by the attack on the *Panay.*

The newsreel cameraman was not just an abstract surrogate for the

American public, however. In their *Panay* newsreels, both Universal and *News of the Day* tied the newsreel audience to the cameraman's point of view in an unprecedented way. Using first-person plural, the voice-over commentary in both films positioned the audience on the Yangtze River alongside the newsreelman. "And now on December 12," intoned *News of the Day*'s John Paul King, "we are standing on the Panay's deck about 15 miles from Nanking as these scenes are made." King continued to narrate the attack and the evacuation of the *Panay* in first-person plural, declaring, "we should be safe" once Mayell, the crew, and the rest of the passengers had finally made the river's edge.[70] Universal had apparently planned to have Norman Alley narrate its *Panay* release himself but ultimately opted to have regular commentator, Graham McNamee, tell most of the story in the third person.[71] Nevertheless, McNamee occasionally switched into first-person plural, reminding the audience members that they were seeing events from Alley's point of view. For example, viewers joined Alley shooting from the stern of a lifeboat as the sinking *Panay* receded into the background: "And now we go ashore with Norman Alley on one of the last boats to leave the ill-fated ship . . . Alley exposes himself, to film the final moments of the gallant warship."[72] This use of the first person placed the newsreel audience in the midst of the action. In doing so, both the MGM and Universal *Panay* films explicitly aligned the spectator with the point of view of the heroic cameramen. As we have seen, this position normally allowed newsreel audiences to see the war in close-up but still hold its dangers at a distance. The attack on the *Panay* and its newsreel cameramen passengers, however, put the distancing power of the newsreel to the test. The incident posed a significant threat to the cameramen and the American neutrality they embodied. By so closely aligning its audience with their cameramen aboard the *Panay*, both MGM and Universal dramatically brought home that threat to their audiences while maintaining a safe distance from the politics and danger represented by the sinking of the *Panay*.

President Roosevelt and his administration demanded stiff compensation from the Japanese for the sinking of the *Panay*, but ultimately the United States chose not to involve itself more directly in the Sino–Japanese conflict.[73] Nevertheless, amid growing tensions in Europe and the Far East, the incident made it clear that it would be increasingly difficult for the United States to isolate itself from war's effects. *Universal Newsreel*'s Graham McNamee captured this growing sense in his closing commentary on the war in the Far East: "An undeclared war it's true, but one that has outraged all humanity by its ruthlessness and its horror; an undeclared war that spares neither men, women, or children, that has little regard for treaties or neutrality."[74] Although the U.S government continued its neutral stance in the face of the "mistake" by the Japanese bombers, the incident was a turning point for U.S. sentiment and policy on the war in Asia. Public opinion polls showed that Americans increasingly sympathized with the Chinese and regarded the Japanese as the perpetrators.[75] Despite this sentiment, most Americans did not want the United States to intervene in the conflict, and as many as 70 percent still wanted the withdrawal of American military units from China.[76] It is impossible to attribute these shifts in public opinion to the newsreel alone, but given the pivotal role of the *Panay* Incident and the visual power of the footage, the newsreel did provide a crucial site for the American public to engage with the war through collective spectatorship. As war began to threaten the United States, the mediating power of the newsreel to hold the chaos of the world at bay also threatened to break down. In the 1930s, the newsreel in general and the newsreel cameraman in particular had offered a way for American audiences to see the war in Asia in close-up while maintaining a safe distance. By aligning the newsreel audience with their heroic cameramen during the *Panay* attack, both *Universal Newsreel* and *News of the Day* dramatized the threat to this mediating power. The United States' impartial observer status embodied by the newsreel photographer was now under threat from a war that had "little regard for neutrality."

Looking as Action: Chris Hunter and Speed Martin Save the Day and Get the Shot

In the wake of the Sino–Japanese War and the *Panay* Incident, the newsreel hero cemented his pop-culture cachet and took on new relevance in an increasingly troubled world. 1937 and 1938 saw a series of Hollywood films set in the tumultuous Far East, several of which featured newsreel cameramen as prominent characters. Most of the films, like *Exiled to Shanghai* (1937), *Mr. Moto Takes a Chance* (1938), and *International*

Settlement (1938), were low-budget B movies, but at least one major motion picture was made with certified Hollywood royalty. *Too Hot to Handle,* starring Clark Gable and Myrna Loy, told the story of a love triangle between a daring aviator (Loy) and two newsreel cameramen (Gable and Walter Pidgeon) who compete for her affections.[77] Gable's character, Chris Hunter, was everything one might expect from a newsreel hero: he was willing to do whatever it took to get the shot, and he got the girl. Along with these Hollywood representations of the cameraman in the Far East, the late 1930s saw the emergence of the newsreelman as comic book hero. DC's *More Fun Comics* featured a hero with superhuman speed named Johnny Quick, whose secret identity was Johnny Chambers, newsreel cameraman; Michael "Mickey" O'Neill, a newsreel cameraman for the Panacon Film Company, appeared in Centaur's *Amazing Mystery Funnies,* beginning in July 1939; and Speed Martin, an ace cameraman traveling the world for *United Newsreel,* was a regular feature in *The Funnies,* published by Dell in the early 1940s.[78] Martin's adventures often took place against the backdrop of war in Europe and the Far East, and, like Chris Hunter, he conformed to all of the well-established conventions of the newsreel hero.

Both Hunter and Martin, however, show that the newsreel cameraman had, by the end of the 1930s, become something more than just an adventure seeker in the popular imagination. As the world moved toward and ultimately went to war, a spirit of isolationism still prevailed in the United States.[79] As envoys of American neutrality and "common sense" in the increasingly chaotic and bloody world of the Far East, these newsreel cameramen offered a way for American audiences to consume these dramatic conflicts while implicitly negotiating a neutral yet heroic role for the United States. In both *Too Hot to Handle* and the Speed Martin stories, the newsreel cameraman was transformed from impartial observer to decisive actor. Despite this involvement, these men retained a distance from the conflict itself and, in so doing, helped to reassure American audiences about their position in global affairs. In these fictional representations, the newsreel cameraman embodied looking itself as a form of action.

The story of *Too Hot to Handle,* which requires a good deal of suspension of disbelief, revisits many of the tropes of the newsreel cameraman discussed above. Chris Hunter is brave, sophisticated, and adventurous, and he proves it by shooting dramatic newsreel footage. The movie opens on a scene in China. Hunter—after deliberately firing an anti-aircraft gun to attract attention—films a diving Japanese airplane as it swoops over him, strafing the area with machine-gun fire. As his fellow reporters dive for cover, Hunter braves the worst, standing in the open to get the shot of the plane and, once it passes overhead, blowing it a kiss and thanking its pilot for the great shot. When the film moves back to the United States, Hunter has another opportunity to prove his skills and daring behind the camera when pilot and love interest, Alma Harding (Myrna Loy), hears a distress call on her home shortwave radio. Harding and Hunter set out by plane to film the burning munitions boat stranded in the Atlantic. To get the shot, Hunter must climb out onto the wing of the plane in a deep fog. With Harding's expert flying skills and Hunter's acrobatics, the couple gets a sensational scoop of the boat exploding. Finally, the climax of the film recalls the cameraman as explorer. Hunter must journey into the impenetrable Amazon jungle where natives are holding Harding's brother captive. Using his film projector to fool the natives into thinking he is some kind of god, Hunter is able to save Harding's brother and get the shot of the siblings' tearful reunion on film. Once again, film—and the newsreel specifically—is used to draw a sharp contrast between the spectacle of primitive otherness and the modern spectator embodied in the figure of the cameraman himself.

Too Hot to Handle is not a straightforward paean to the newsreel, however. Both Hunter and his rival, Bill Dennis (Pidgeon), stage events in order to create more spectacular footage for the newsreel. In addition to the opening scene where Hunter himself fires the anti-aircraft gun in order to get the close-up of the Japanese plane, he is also shown blatantly staging a scene of devastation on the ground. After his film of the diving Japanese aircraft is ruined, Hunter employs a Chinese family and a toy airplane in order to reenact the scene—this time with a close-up of a frightened little girl clutching her puppy. Likewise, in the climactic scene in which Alma is reunited with her brother, Hunter dresses as a witch doctor in order to better stage manage the scene for his cameras hidden in the bushes. Despite his bravery and skill, Hunter is no saint—his goal is to get the shot, and he'll do whatever it takes to get it, including faking it.

Scenes of newsreel manipulation suggest that audiences were not naïve about newsreel realism. As noted in the previous chapter, by the end of the 1930s, audiences and critics were well aware of the stories of newsreel hoaxes and otherwise manipulated news stories. Instead of denying the newsreel's penchant for manipulating events to make them more sensational, *Too Hot to Handle* made this part of the cameraman's mystique. Although Hunter is not above trickery in order to get the best footage, he is only doing so because he will do anything to get his shot. This commitment is what makes him a great cameraman. As he says with a grin when his fellow reporters become suspicious of his Chinese war footage, "who's to say that there isn't a girl like that somewhere in China." Quips like this deliberately blur the line between audience expectations and naive newsreel realism. These lines are blurred again when, upon hearing of Hunter's stunt and the accolades he received in the United States for the scoop, Bill Dennis—a cameraman with a competing newsreel—conspires to create a newsworthy event and make sure Hunter doesn't get the story. Calling on the help of his old friend and pilot Alma Harding, Dennis stages an emergency delivery of a vaccine to prevent a typhoid epidemic in Shanghai. Dennis and his buddies plan to film Harding as she lands her plane and unloads the fake medicine. The plan backfires on Dennis, however, as Hunter is tipped off and, with his camera precariously mounted on the top of his news truck, manages to get close-up shots of the plane's landing. When the plane swerves out of control and crashes, Hunter saves Harding from the burning wreckage while his soundman films the entire rescue. Not only does Hunter get the story, he gets a scoop. As with several other scenes of newsreel manipulation in *Too Hot to Handle,* although the news event was staged, the danger to Harding and to Hunter was real, and the newsreelman's daring and courage could not be faked. Thus, despite his flaws, the newsreel cameraman depicted in *Too Hot to Handle* was an authentic hero. Not only was he willing to risk his life to get the shot, but he was also willing to put down his camera to save the day. These qualities made Hunter the perfect agent for newsreel realism—a realism that was not about simply representing the events of the world but about offering the viewer mediated access to those events. By involving himself in the news, Hunter offered his audience unprecedented access. Whether it was in the war zone of the Far East or the jungles of Brazil, Chris Hunter was more than just an observer of the action. As the active protagonist of the film, Hunter transformed looking itself into a heroic endeavor.

The notion of the newsreel cameraman as more than just an observer was taken to another level when the newsreelman began appearing as a comic book hero at the end of the 1930s. After the beginning of hostilities in the Far East and especially the outbreak of war in Europe, American isolationism was increasingly difficult to justify. Quite apart from questions of foreign policy, on a more visceral level, the United States' neutrality seemed to evoke cowardice. How could the American public (and government) literally sit by and watch as the ruthless armies of the Axis invaded Europe and Asia? The comic book newsreel hero offered a way to assuage these worries. By transforming the agent of the newsreel audience's gaze into a dynamic hero, these cartoon newsreelmen represented looking itself as a force for good. Indeed, in the hands of these heroes, the camera was more than a tool for looking; it was a tool for action.

The Dell Comics character Speed Martin first appeared in *The Funnies* in the fall of 1940.[80] In a series of stories by Vic Bloom, Speed Martin, newsreel cameraman, went on assignments around the world accompanied by his trusty sidekick, Mickey. Invariably the pair would discover criminal conspiracies or the nefarious activities of "foreign powers" and, in foiling these misdeeds, secure sensational footage for the *United Newsreel* (Figure 7). Perhaps in deference to American neutrality, in 1941 Dell referred only to a "foreign power" when U.S. interests were targeted; when Britain or its empire was threatened, the comic readily identified the villains as German or Japanese. In several episodes, Mickey and Speed were joined by the American newspaper reporter, Judy Jackson. Judy was Speed's pretty love interest; she was intrepid enough to get into plenty of trouble but helpless enough to require frequent rescue. Speed, on the other hand, was the prototypical newsreel hero: he was manly, daring, and suave. Each episode featuring Judy ended with her melting in Speed's arms and Mickey cracking wise with lines like, "Looks like this trio is gonna be a duet . . . but soon! Guess I'll find myself a nice exciting game of solitaire."[81] When Speed wasn't saving Judy, he and Mickey proved their bravery and daring by getting sensational shots for the newsreel. Scenes of Speed and his sidekick getting one last shot before abandoning

Figure 7. The Dell Comics character Speed Martin first appeared in *The Funnies* in the fall of 1940.

a sinking ship off the coast of Ireland or shooting an exploding chemical factory rehearsed the well-worn image of the newsreel cameraman as daredevil. When, in one episode, his boss tries to give Speed and Mickey a less dangerous assignment, they are appalled: "WHAT! Us film bathing cuties? Hey we're action men!"[82] But Speed Martin's heroism went beyond typical newsreel machismo and bravery. As newsreel cameramen, Speed and Mickey often found themselves in global conflict zones. Despite their role as reporters, they were never just impartial observers. Invariably the duo became active participants in these world events. At a time when the United States was neutral, these newsreelmen could take to the front lines in place of the United States' military heroes, who would emerge in the coming years.

As a comic book hero, the newsreel cameraman personified looking as both active and noble. Indeed, although Speed was always out to get a great shot for the newsreel, he and Mickey never put the scoop ahead of doing the right thing. In one episode, a captured Czech officer in the German Army reveals plans for a German chemical attack on England. Speed tells Mickey and Judy, "We've got to get this to the British Intelligence immediately." When Judy asks if she couldn't cable the story to her editor in the States first, Mickey responds emphatically, "Story?! This is *war* sister."[83] As a result of his tip, the British launch a raid on the German forces in occupied France, and Speed is able to get sensational footage of the landing party blowing up the German chemical plant. In the final frame of the comic, Speed is thanked by Captain Harrington

Park of the British Intelligence for his "invaluable service to the Empire!!" Speed responds with a thank you of his own: "We're glad we could help you Captain!! And we're obliged to your men for the hottest film scoop of the war!"[84] For Speed Martin, getting the story and saving the day were rarely at odds.

By portraying Speed Martin as a noble hero who fought against the Axis even before the United States entered the war, the comic helped to equate newsreel looking with heroic action. Speed's camera and the footage he shot with it regularly became the key to defeating "foreign powers" intent on harming the United States and the Allies. In the episode mentioned above, it was the possibility that Speed's pictures of the Czech officer might be shown in the newsreel and thereby endanger his family that induced him to divulge the location of the German gas plant. In another episode, set on a British merchant ship, Speed's camera recorded crucial evidence identifying a German spy on board.[85] As with Gable's character in *Too Hot to Handle,* Speed's camera was often more a tool for action than it was a device for looking. Indeed, in at least one episode, the camera literally became a weapon (Figure 8). When an agent for a "foreign power" attacks Speed, Mickey stops shooting the action and puts his camera to a more practical use: He hits the goon over the head with the camera, saying "sweet dreams baldy!"[86] With the bad guy unconscious and Mickey back behind the camera, Speed says, "The British officers will make this guy talk!! Then we ACT!" In this sequence and elsewhere throughout the series, both Mickey and Speed move easily between shooting the action and shaping events. By blurring the line between action and looking, heroes like "'Speed' Martin, Newsreel Cameraman" helped assuage anxieties about American neutrality.

As with Hollywood portrayals of the newsreel hero, the Far East offered the comic the ideal location to prove Speed's courage. As the site of conflict, it was a natural location for a newsreel cameraman to ply his trade and for Speed to uncover international espionage. In one episode, Judy Jackson stumbles upon a plot by a mysterious but charming Japanese businessman, Mr. Toto. Toto, who is in fact an agent working for a "European power," plans to load ships with explosives and explode them in "Singapore harbor," destroying the British coastal defenses. According to the plan, the British would blame the Japanese for the attack and declare war, drawing their attention and resources away from the

Figure 8. For Speed Martin, the camera was often more a tool for action than it was a device for looking. *The Funnies*, 54 (April 1941).

European theater. Toto doesn't count on Speed Martin. After Toto takes Judy prisoner, Speed discovers his plan and alerts the British forces to the danger before rescuing Judy. Mickey, meanwhile, gets sensational footage of Toto's boats being shelled by the British coastal defenses (Figure 9). Once again, Mickey and Speed secure a scoop for the newsreel while making the news themselves. In this respect, the episode recalled the *Panay* Incident when cameramen like Eric Mayell and Norman Alley

Figure 9. Mickey films Toto's boats shelled by British forces before they can reach Singapore. *The Funnies*, 54 (April 1941).

became an important part of the story they were covering. As with the bombing of the *Panay*, Toto's plan threatened to draw neutral parties into the war in the Far East. While Mayell and Alley embodied American neutrality under threat in Asia, however, the fictional Speed Martin reframed that neutrality, as well as newsreel looking, as both active and noble.

At a time when the United States was reluctant to involve itself militarily in the crises in Europe and Asia, the fictional newsreel cameraman became the ideal hero. As a journalist, the newsreelman was the embodiment of American neutrality, but as an active protagonist willing to use his camera in order to foil criminal activity, he was able to intervene to ensure the triumph of good over evil. In offering Americans a kind of heroic neutrality, the newsreel cameraman helped audiences come to terms with their own ambivalent position. He allowed them to see world events close-up while still holding them at a safe distance; more importantly, he embodied their looking as heroic action.

Conclusion

The newsreel cameraman played a key role in promoting and authenticating newsreel images of the war in the Far East. The popular culture image of a hypermasculine daredevil, willing to do whatever it takes to get the shot, helped legitimate the footage that these heroic figures captured in dangerous and exotic locations. By embodying both a masculine and imperial gaze, the cameraman offered a privileged perspective from which American audiences could view the rest of the world. Moreover, when that privileged position came under threat during the *Panay* Incident and the United States' neutrality in the Far East was tested, the heroic figure of the newsreel cameraman helped to assuage the public's anxieties. Newsreel heroes in films like *Too Hot to Handle* and comic books like "'Speed' Martin, Newsreel Cameraman" framed looking itself as an active and heroic endeavor. As agents of the audience's gaze, these heroes defined newsreel spectatorship as a way of participating in world events. This sense of participation was carried over into the newsreel theater itself, where the individual looking of the newsreel cameraman became the collective spectatorship of audiences who turned the newsreel into a kind of public forum.

CHAPTER 4

"Come Along. We're Going to the Trans-Lux to Hiss Roosevelt"

Modernity, Virtual Travel, and the Newsreel Cinema as Public Forum

In 1936, the *New Yorker* featured a cartoon by renowned illustrator Peter Arno depicting two well-heeled couples calling to their friends through the open window of a New York townhouse. The caption read: "Come along. We're going to the Trans-Lux to hiss Roosevelt."[1] This iconic image has come to epitomize the opposition of wealthy Americans to the president and his New Deal, but it also offers a glimpse of the newsreel audience in the 1930s. The Trans-Lux was one of several theaters in New York exclusively dedicated to showing newsreels and other short films. These newsreel cinemas began appearing in the United States in the early 1930s, and by the end of the decade, they could be found in cities across the country. Apparently, the *New Yorker* cartoon was inspired by the experience of caption writer Richard McCallister, who worked with Arno at the time. McCallister recalled hearing hissing while visiting a newsreel theater: "I thought it must be one of the radiators. Then I looked around, and I realized people were hissing the President."[2] In fact, derisive hissing and booing, as well as cheering and applause, were not uncommon occurrences in the newsreel theaters of the time. Audiences frequently used the space of the newsreel theater to express themselves to the personalities on screen as well as to their fellow patrons. Introduced as a way of capitalizing on the burgeoning popularity of news films, these cinemas often featured architecture and interior design that, much like the figure of the newsreel cameraman, emphasized the global reach of the news camera as well as the audience's shared modernity and common Americanness. But, as Arno's cartoon suggests, audiences regularly ruptured any apparent consensus with their vocal opinions of the images and personalities on screen. The newsreel parade and its emphasis on the experience of watching the news requires that we look more carefully at how Americans viewed these images. A closer look at the tensions between the forces at work in the newsreel cinema—of consensus and debate, hegemony and negotiation—provides a clearer understanding of the circumstances under which newsreels were received and understood in the years before the United States' entry into World War II. In a world that technology and the mass media had made at once closer and farther away than ever before, the newsreel cinema became a place to engage with both the reality on screen and those sharing the space of the theater itself. This engagement underscores the collective nature of newsreel spectatorship and how the news parade embodied an emergent public sphere mediated by the screen and the shared experience of looking.

The first newsreel cinema in the United States opened in 1929 in Times Square. Fox Films launched the Embassy Newsreel Theatre as a way of promoting *Fox Movietone News* and showcasing its still new sound technology to exhibitors. Times Square made for an ideal place for this experiment. Located in the heart of New York's entertainment district, Embassy took advantage of the passing crowds. For just twenty-five cents admission, audiences enjoyed an hour-long program of Fox newsreels and other short films running continuously from ten in the morning to midnight. With only six hundred seats, the theater relied on high turnover to make the venture profitable. And profitable it was: the theater opened to standing room–only crowds and achieved audiences of nearly seven thousand per day in its first week.[3] The success of the Embassy prompted a number of imitators. Over the next decade, approximately thirty newsreel theaters opened in cities across the country.[4] By the early 1940s, there were three small chains of newsreel houses as well as several independently run operations. Newsreel Theatres, Inc., which took over the Embassy in 1935, operated four newsreel cinemas in New York and another in Newark, New Jersey. The Trans-Lux Movies Corporation owned newsreel theaters in New York, Philadelphia, and Washington. The Telenews chain opened cinemas in Chicago, Dallas, Los Angeles, San Francisco, Oakland, Seattle, Portland, Cleveland, and Detroit. Newsreel theaters were also opened in Louisville, Cincinnati, and Boston.[5] Like the Embassy, these theaters were relatively small—usually less than five hundred seats and sometimes as few as one hundred—and offered a continuous program that allowed patrons to enter at any time. Typical programs ran for an hour or ninety minutes and included a selection of newsreel items and several short films, such as travelogues, comedy shorts, and cartoons (Disney's *Three Little Pigs* played for a record eight weeks at one theater).[6] Unlike the original Embassy Theatre, the vast majority of newsreel cinemas were not affiliated with any of the major studios and showed footage from several different companies each week. In fact, one of the main selling points of these theaters was that they offered the "best of" the week's newsreels—showing the most interesting and visually engaging coverage from Pathé, Fox, Paramount, Universal, and MGM.

Although most Americans watched newsreels in traditional movie theaters before the feature film or between the feature and the B-movie, newsreel cinemas offer a unique insight into how Americans saw the news and the world during this period. Unlike typical first- and second-run theaters, where the newsreel was just one small part of a larger program, at the newsreel cinema, the news was the main attraction. The spread of these specialized cinemas in the 1930s mirrored a corresponding rise in the newsreel's proliferation. The consolidation of the newsreel within the Hollywood studio system meant an increase in promotion for the newsreel, and its inclusion in the studio's complete line of films meant even wider distribution. During the 1930s, the newsreel was an integral part of the movie program at virtually every American cinema. Given the ubiquity of the newsreel and the wealth of newsworthy events in the lead up to the Second World War, it is hardly surprising that newsreel cinemas found a profitable niche in the moving picture business.

The history of newsreel reception and exhibition is elusive. As with most histories of moviegoing, evidence of the reception of individual films is rare. While the history of film exhibition is more easily traced using trade journals and theater records, this too is difficult with respect to newsreels, as they formed a relatively insignificant part of the average exhibitor's business. Thus the emergence of the dedicated newsreel cinema in the 1930s meant increased coverage in the trade papers and the founding of a series of small theaters whose success depended on cultivating an audience for the newsreel. This has left a rich, if diffuse, record of the newsreel's exhibition and reception in the 1930s and 1940s. By drawing together evidence of the companies that exhibited newsreels, the spaces in which they were shown, and the people who watched them, we can begin to piece together an understanding of where news was seen and how audiences, exhibitors, and studios used these spaces to work out the meanings of the images on screen. Although newsreel cinemas represented only a small minority of the screens where Americans saw the news, they offer a glimpse at what it meant to watch the news during this period.

This chapter will examine the conditions of newsreel reception from three different but related perspectives. First, an institutional history of the Trans-Lux Corporation will show how it marketed its theaters as the ultimate in modern moviegoing. The rise of the company, its technological innovations, and its forays into the moving picture industry helped transform newsreel spectatorship into an experience that spoke of modernity and luxury in the machine age. Next, a broader analysis of cinemas from across the country will examine the newsreel theater as a physical space and consider how this structured the viewing experience. Building on the newsreel's associations with modernity, architects interpreted the newsreel theater as part of a new global information environment, playing up the role of the camera in bringing the world closer than ever before to American audiences. At the same time, these designers helped transform the newsreel experience into one of virtual travel and the theater itself into a kind of vehicle for reaching distant and exotic places. Finally, an analysis of the lively newsreel audience alluded to in Arno's cartoon will show that the newsreel theater was a public place where the news was not simply seen but also commented on and interacted with. In these vibrant spaces, audiences reworked the newsreel's associations with modernity and mobility and used them to inform their own experience of the newsreel theater as public and plural. Although evidence of newsreel exhibition and reception remains diffuse, by working from these multiple perspectives, we can begin to examine the history of the newsreel cinema in the United States and understand these venues not as monolithic entities but as contested spaces. In the newsreel theater, audiences, film studios, exhibitors, and architects negotiated the meaning of news and what it meant to be a watcher of the news in the modern United States. Together, they created a forum where audiences could engage with both the news and one another. Theaters such as the Trans-Lux were places where Americans could hiss each other as well as Roosevelt. They were shared spaces in which audiences did not simply consume the news as an image on screen but instead reveled in the collective experience of seeing and debating the news in public.

Examining the Audience: Reception and Spectatorship

Since the 1970s, questions of film spectatorship and reception have become at least as important to film studies as the movies themselves. Both theorists and historians of cinema have begun to look beyond film texts and their creators to how films address the viewer and to how audiences encounter moving pictures. Despite these shared concerns, scholars have differed sharply over the proper ways to address these questions. In the 1970s, film theorists drew on the traditions of psychoanalysis, semiotics, and Marxism to think through the position of the film spectator. Much of this theorizing rested on post-structural theories of the subject that argued that subjectivity was discursively constructed rather than an *a priori* condition of consciousness. Film theorists took up this insight to argue that both the structure of the film text and the so-called filmic apparatus worked to position the subject in specifically ideological ways. In his seminal article "Ideological Effects of the Basic Cinematographic Apparatus," Jean-Louis Baudry drew on the writing of psychoanalyst Jacques Lacan and Marxist thinker Louis Althusser to argue that the cinematic apparatus—which, for Baudry, included the camera and editing process, as well as the projector, the darkened theater, and the spectator—was a "support and instrument of ideology."[7] In other words, the very technological structure of the moving picture and its projection positioned the spectator as an ideologically implicated and complicit subject. In the years that followed, a number of influential film theorists took up Baudry's basic position to show how classical Hollywood film in particular worked to position the viewing subject as complicit with the camera and, as feminist film critics pointed out, its implicitly masculine gaze.[8]

A group of influential film historians have also shifted scholarly attention away from accounts of cinematic auteurs and their films. Instead of a theoretical interest in cinematic spectatorship, however, authors such as Robert C. Allen and Douglas Gomery have examined historical questions about film exhibitors and their audiences.[9] These historians of American moviegoing tend to privilege the particular and often focus on certain geographical locations, time periods, or specific theaters and segments of the audience.[10] Implicitly, and sometimes explicitly, these histories appear to challenge the notion of "the film subject" of film theory. Film historians have particularly criticized Baudry's characterization of the cinematic apparatus and its reliance on a narrowly defined cinematic experience characterized by the "darkness of the movie theater, the relative passivity of the situation, [and] the forced immobility of the cine-subject."[11] Instead, these historians have pointed to the multitude of ways in which films were viewed in the past. For example, studies of the boisterous atmospheres in the early nickelodeons and the rural audiences of itinerant film exhibitors have shown that many early film audiences were anything but passive and that they watched movies in a variety of spaces—and in varying degrees of darkness.[12] Nor were audiences homogenous. As Richard Maltby points out in his essay "Sticks, Hicks, and Flaps: Classical Hollywood's Generic Conception of its Audiences," while production studios tended to view their audiences as undifferentiated and unified, in the early sound era, film distributors and exhibitors already recognized different "taste publics" that could be classified into a "series of overlapping binary distinctions between 'class' and 'mass,' 'sophisticated' and 'unsophisticated,' 'Broadway' and 'Main Street'" as well as distinguishing between viewers within these audiences by age and gender.[13] Unlike the unified subject described by film theorists of the 1970s, what emerges from much of this scholarship are both multiple histories of American moviegoing and a picture of active audiences who often contested and sometimes resisted the ideologies present in film.

It is easy to set these two traditions of film studies in opposition, but their different perspectives are not wholly incompatible. Critics who have used empirical studies simply to point out the historical exceptions to the ideal spectator described by Baudry and others miss the point.[14] Apparatus theory was never intended as an empirical account of material audiences. Instead, it offers a way of thinking about the relationship between films and their audiences that takes into account the ideological effects of the cinema. As Judith Mayne argues, many of the criticisms leveled against notions of the "cinematic apparatus" confuse the "subject" of film theory with the "individual."[15] The individual is not a subject but rather responds to numerous discursively produced subject positions. Nevertheless, film theory has often failed to make this distinction clear enough. Moreover, 1970s film theory paid careful attention to the subject positions created by the film text and some of the institutions of the classical Hollywood cinema, but it often ignored the sometimes competing discourses of the exhibitors, critics, and fans. By taking these into account, we might better locate our analyses as theoretically useful but historically contingent.

Similarly, histories of moviegoing need not reject theoretical notions of spectatorship. Indeed, as Miriam Hansen demonstrates in her excellent account of silent film spectatorship, *Babel and Babylon: Spectatorship in American Silent Film,* the two tendencies of film studies can be profitably combined. While Hansen acknowledges criticism of theoretical concepts of spectatorship and recognizes the need to historicize accounts of reception, she rightly points out that, "by the same token, however, a reception-oriented film history cannot be written without a theoretical framework that conceptualizes the possible relations between films and viewers."[16] What is necessary in the history of moviegoing is a recognition that audiences of the past experienced several competing ideologies. Even if the film text and the cinematic apparatus are seen as ideologically coherent, audience members were subject to, and subjects of, numerous other interpellating discourses: their class, gender, and race, but also the theatrical space itself and the public with whom they shared that space. As Hansen points out, "what's missing in any theory that conceptualizes the spectator as a function—or effect—of a closed, albeit flexible system . . . is a place for the public dimension of cinematic reception."[17] This public dimension, she argues, is where the social determinations of spectatorship come together with the textual to create autonomous and unexpected dynamics.

By looking at the specific space of the newsreel theater, this chapter attempts to mediate between the discursively constructed subject positions of the newsreels and the social audiences who viewed them. As we have seen in chapter one, the news parade imagined newsreel spectatorship as collective in nature. The news parade offered audiences the opportunity to join with the virtual crowd on screen, but, in the space of the theater itself, audience members were also part of a real crowd. The newsreel theater was thus both an ideologically charged space that positioned the newsreel spectator as a subject in particular ways and an empirical place where audience members encountered the news and each other. It is only by looking at the newsreel cinema from both of these perspectives that we can understand the contested nature of the news in the 1930s. In addition to the companies that produced the news, exhibitors, architects, designers, and audiences actively shaped how Americans saw and engaged with the world through the newsreel.

Trans-Lux: The "Modern Theatre"

Although the success of the Embassy Theatre in Times Square proved the viability of the "all news" concept, it was some time before the idea was applied elsewhere. Courtland Smith, a former editor at *Fox News* and the person behind the Embassy, believed that a chain of newsreel theaters would be profitable. After all, the Embassy had cost just $19,000 to convert into a specialty theater, and it made $150,000 in one year.[18] But Smith discovered that there were only thirty-eight theaters in the United States that were cheap, small, and well-situated enough to be converted into viable newsreel houses. Without the same conditions, it would be difficult to replicate the same high turnover that had made the Embassy so successful. But a new player in the business of motion picture exhibition promised to solve this problem. The Trans-Lux Daylight Screen Corporation had perfected a rear projection system for use in motion picture theaters. This unique technology did away with the need for raised projection booths, meaning that extremely small theaters—those with fewer than two hundred seats—could be constructed in rented stores or office spaces. Without special real estate needs, these theaters could be located wherever it was deemed profitable, and, because of the relatively small capital investment, they could be relocated if necessary.

Smith was convinced of the technology's potential and joined Trans-Lux in 1931 with a view to creating a chain of small newsreel cinemas. The company had apparently already identified 125 possible locations in the New York area alone.[19] Although the company never lived up to these early expectations, Trans-Lux succeeded in establishing a small chain of as many as seven theaters in New York, Boston, Philadelphia, and Washington, D.C.[20] In doing so, the company became synonymous with news exhibition and helped define newsreel spectatorship in the United States. Using technological innovation and a new business model, the Trans-Lux Corporation transformed the newsreel cinema into a profitable enterprise and a symbol of information, modernity, and efficiency in the machine age.

Percy Furber founded the Trans-Lux Corporation a decade earlier.[21] Furber set out to solve a problem for his friend Newell Hillis. Hillis, a minister from Brooklyn, conducted a lecture series called "Better America" using a stereopticon slide projector. Hillis hated that he had to dim the lights for his lectures; he wanted his audience to see him. Furber, assisted by Arthur Payne, an engineer who had worked with Thomas Edison, developed a system of rear projection that could be used in a lighted room. Incorporating a specially designed projector and a wide-angle lens, the key to their invention was a seamless silk screen that allowed the image to pass through it. After several failed experiments, the company began producing its unique screens in 1923 under the name Trans-Lux Daylight Picture Screen Corporation.[22] Although Hillis used the screen and others were sold for lecture use to churches and schools, Furber recognized that these markets offered little possibility for growth and profit.

The Trans-Lux screen did not begin to take off until Furber turned to the rapidly rising stock market—not for capital, but for customers. After visiting the New York Stock Exchange and witnessing the crowds of people jostling one another to get a look at the ticker tape, Furber realized that projecting an enlarged version of the stock quotations could eliminate this pushing and shoving and provide all brokers with equal access to the information. In 1924, Trans-Lux installed the first so-called "Movie Ticker" at the New York Stock Exchange. This machine projected stock quotes from a specially designed transparent ticker tape onto overhead screens. Despite initial skepticism from the financial world, the invention proved extremely successful. Through an agreement with the Western Union Telegraph Company, the machines became a ubiquitous feature of financial offices. By 1929, Trans-Lux had sold the Movie Ticker to 1,489 exchanges and brokerages across the United States and Canada.[23] Such was their success that, in an official history of the Trans-Lux Corporation written in 1929, the company claimed credit for the massive growth in the stock market in the 1920s:

> The wholesome effect that the perfection of the Trans-Lux Movie Ticker has had on the world of finance, and the invaluable service it is rendering in financial centers throughout the country, is easily gained by a casual review of the tremendous growth of trading since the year of its trial installation . . . The heavy volume of trading that marked 1925 and the years following would have been humanly impossible had brokers and participating public been dependent solely on the ticker tape of Russell Sage's day.[24]

It is far-fetched to credit the Trans-Lux ticker with the exponential growth of trading at the New York Stock Exchange—from 237,276,927 total shares traded in 1923 to 919,661,825 in 1928—but the company did make information more accessible and surely helped to quicken the pace of financial transactions.

As the company grew, it introduced several new products to enhance its services to the financial sector. The "Private Office Movie Ticker" was essentially a smaller version of the regular Movie Ticker, and the "Movie News Ticker" used similar technology to project newswire stories from the Dow Jones or New York news bureaus. These new devices certainly changed the way American brokers viewed financial information. Stock quotations and financial news were now a constant presence in an executive's office. Instead of sporadically consulting the ticker tape in the corner, financial professionals and their customers could watch a steady procession of numbers and news as they streamed by on Trans-Lux's backlit screens. The company's official biographer called the machine "a needful device for modern offices geared to high efficiency, the Trans-Lux Private Office Movie Ticker is conserving valuable minutes and saving physical and nervous energies even more precious."[25] In the context of the brokerage, stock watching took on a form of mediated spectatorship that resembled motion pictures more than the stock exchange. While these early tickers only gave their specialized audiences numbers and words, the notion of constantly streaming information that offered the instant availability of the financial world anticipated some of the key aspects of newsreel spectatorship.[26]

The October 1929 stock market crash once again left Trans-Lux looking for new markets for its rear projection technology. Fortunately, the company had already begun investigating the possibilities of entering the motion picture business. In the company's annual report for 1928, Trans-Lux looked forward to the potential for growth in the entertainment industry, pointing out to stockholders that "in the United State alone there are over 23,000 theaters, and new ones are being built at the rate of 1,200 every year."[27] The company hoped to convince exhibitors of the benefits of its rear projection units and to sell them to existing theaters. After successful installations at the Roxy Theatre and RKO's Assembly Theatre in New York City, the company turned its attention to creating its own chain of theaters to demonstrate the potential of its technology. It was at this stage that Courtland Smith, then working as operations manager for RKO's theaters, came on board, bringing with him a sizeable investment from RKO in the newly formed Trans-Lux Movies Corporation.

The first Trans-Lux theater was opened on March 13, 1931, in a converted store at the corner of Madison Avenue and Fifty-Eighth Street in Manhattan. With just 158 seats, the cinema was an experiment in the principle of high-turnover theater operation as well as rear projection. Well positioned to take advantage of crowds of shoppers and office workers, the theater yielded higher than expected early returns and, with its low overhead, proved profitable. Building on this early success, Trans-Lux opened a new Twin Cinema at Forty-Ninth Street and Broadway several months later in order to capitalize on the crowds of New York's Entertainment District. The double theater had two small auditoriums of 161 and 210 seats. In one theater, there was an hour-long program of newsreels, and in the other, there was a program of short subjects including comedies, cartoons, and musical shorts. Both programs ran continuously, and, despite the small size of the theaters, the Broadway location took in over ten thousand paid admissions in its first weekend.[28] With its small theaters built in converted storefronts and continuous program of short subjects, the Trans-Lux business model recalled the nickelodeons of the early days of cinema. Nevertheless, with its first two locations in place, Trans-Lux hoped to prove the viability of its new (old) concept in motion picture exhibition and to attract new investment to facilitate expansion.

In brochures designed to entice investors, the company boasted of the technological advantages of the Trans-Lux rear projection system. Rear projection, they argued, was safer because the projection room, where the majority of theater fires started, could be separated from patrons by an asbestos curtain in case of fire, reducing panic and giving audiences a chance to leave the theater quickly and safely.[29] The company also claimed that rear projection reduced eyestrain caused by the flicker of conventional projection because, by projecting movies from behind their special screen, "there [was] no eye-irritating projection beams of light to look through."[30] Finally, rear projection did not require a darkened theater to be effective. This meant that windows could be opened to allow for air circulation, and the auditorium could be lit during shows, allowing patrons to read their programs easily and find their seats without tripping over others. For theater managers, the lighted theater meant less "rowdyism" and more potential juvenile patrons because "people behave themselves when they are in plain view,"[31] and "a lighted theatre is not conducive to that sex freedom against which parents and teachers rightly object."[32]

Technology was not Trans-Lux's only innovation. As the first Trans-Lux theaters in New York demonstrated, rear projection screens allowed for a new business model for motion picture exhibition. Not only would the company's cinemas provide news film and short subjects to audiences in a timely and efficient manner, it would do so with minimal capital investment and low overhead: Trans-Lux boasted that its miniature units could operate for less than $500 a day, even in expensive districts. This was considerably less than the $1,000 to $5,000 daily overhead that more elaborate theaters incurred.[33] In addition to the lower real estate costs resulting from the small space required for rear projection, Trans-Lux theaters needed fewer staff than traditional cinemas. Because the daylight screen allowed for a lighted theater, ushers were unnecessary.

Instead, patrons saw only one employee, the seller in the ticket booth, before entering the theater through a turnstile and seating themselves. Combining the virtues of the high-turnover short subject program pioneered by the Embassy Theatre with the advantages of rear projection, Trans-Lux hoped its low cost and niche position in the market would prove successful. According to its promotional material, "every community in the country [was] a potential center for a Trans-Lux Modern Theatre. These theatres [did] not compete with regular movie houses. They [filled] a niche all their own—supplying the universal demand for short features and well-edited newsreels."[34]

Corporate optimism aside, Trans-Lux failed to find a large demand for its new projection system. Indeed, not every Trans-Lux theater flourished. After the success of its Manhattan locations, the company opened two theaters in Brooklyn that failed to turn a profit. Despite busy locations on Flatbush Avenue and Fulton Street, the theaters were closed after only a couple of years. According to the company's annual report, "the residents of Brooklyn [showed] that they were not interested in 'Newsreels and Shorts.'"[35] This was the last time the company attempted to introduce its newsreel concept to suburban locations. Instead, the company chose modest expansion in some of the most cosmopolitan locations in the country. Over the next few years, Trans-Lux successfully opened several new theaters in uptown Manhattan as well as downtown Boston, Philadelphia, and Washington, D.C.

Capitalizing on their cosmopolitan locations, the hallmark of these Trans-Lux theaters was their modernity. For the Trans-Lux Corporation and its audiences, the newsreel theater was the ultimate in modern movie exhibition. All Trans-Lux theaters featured the slogan, "The Modern Theatre," and the company's advertising proclaimed, "the theatres of tomorrow are here today."[36] Although this was partially advertising hubris, Trans-Lux's cinemas did offer their patrons a uniquely modern experience. Not only did Trans-Lux cinemas offer immediate access to the world through their newsreels, they did so in a way that was seemingly emblematic of the new machine age. Trans-Lux's minimal staff, small theaters, and continuous program created a sense that the Trans-Lux was a kind of automatic cinema. One observer and newsreel man called this model the "coin-in-the-slot newsreel theatre."[37] Unlike the elaborate experience of grand movie palaces, Trans-Lux offered an efficient moviegoing experience for both manager and patron. While the company's business model ensured low overhead and minimal staff for theater owners, for the busy denizens of New York and Trans-Lux's other metropolitan locations, the newsreel program provided a movie experience that could be easily accommodated between appointments. For commuters, shoppers, and busy workers, the Trans-Lux was designed for the pace of modern city life.

By adapting rear projection technology from the lecture circuit, to the stock market, and ultimately to motion picture exhibition, Trans-Lux developed new avenues for the distribution of information. The shift from stock tickers to newsreel cinemas reveals more than a simple technological compatibility. Both the stock ticker and the newsreel were part of a new modern information environment, one that had not yet reached the simultaneity and scope of the television and satellite ages of the late twentieth century but nevertheless featured a continuous flow of information—stock quotes and spectacular images. It is no coincidence that, following World War II, Trans-Lux developed the scrolling news signage that would eventually dominate Times Square. The movie ticker and the newsreel cinema shared more than technology; they were both mediated responses to a new modernity and catalysts for new ways of seeing the world. Moreover, these technologies came to symbolize the modern world they professed to make more knowable. As more and more newsreel theaters opened across the country in the 1930s, architects and designers picked up on these themes, and newsreel cinemas became both machines and shrines dedicated to making the modern world visible.

Streamline Moderne: The Architecture of Newsreel Theaters and Virtual Travel

Architecture played an integral role in the moviegoing experience in the 1930s. Changes in the motion picture business and the onset of the Depression meant that the era of the moving picture palace came to an end. New modern and identifiably American architectural styles replaced the sumptuous revivalist architecture that had marked earlier decades. While "old-world" architectural allusions to the grand buildings of Europe and the "exotic" motifs of Asia had legitimated moviegoing for middle-class audiences in the 1920s, economic necessity made the huge and elaborate palaces untenable in the 1930s. Instead, established theater architects such as Thomas W. Lamb and John Eberson, as well as a new generation of American architects, including S. Charles Lee, turned to art deco and distinctively modern lines to create luxurious—if less expensive—cinematic spaces.

That architects and exhibitors embraced this new aesthetic was no coincidence. Art deco design was not simply a way of framing Hollywood films; it became symbolic of Hollywood glamour itself and a regular fixture of the most visually opulent movies of the 1930s. Indeed, historians of architecture and film have argued that the cinema was a key means through which the vocabulary of art deco was popularized.[38] Films such as *The Grand Hotel, 42nd Street,* and the musicals of Fred Astaire and Ginger Rogers helped introduce American audiences to modernist aesthetics and the opulence and luxury of art deco in particular. In her work on Hollywood and art deco, Ghislaine Wood describes how, amid the trying economic times of the 1930s:

> Hollywood wove a magical web with tales of luxury, youth and beauty, upward mobility, individualism, sexual liberation and rampant consumerism. The backdrops for this exploration of contemporary dreams and aspirations were fantastic Deco-styled hotels, night-clubs, ocean liners, offices, apartments, and skyscrapers.[39]

It is no surprise, then, that architects chose to incorporate these new aesthetics into the design and construction of new moving picture palaces. Unlike the elaborately themed theaters of the 1920s that created fantasy worlds borrowed from past architectural styles (rococo, neoclassicism, etc.) or exotic motifs (arabesque, orientalist), the art deco theaters of the 1930s offered a different kind of fantasy—one based on the same affluence, modernity, and technological sophistication on display in Hollywood movies.

Despite the natural affinity between such lavish Hollywood sets and the art deco architecture of movie exhibition, the traditional notion of the theatrical space facilitating escapism doesn't seem to fit in the case of the newsreel cinema. After all, patrons who attended the newsreel theater presumably went not to escape the real world but to find it—at least in its mediated form. Given this, what styles and motifs did the architects of newsreel cinemas employ? And what can these decisions tell us about the newsreel-going experience of the 1930s? As we shall see, the architecture of the newsreel cinemas constructed in this period did take up the vocabulary of art deco. Indeed, in many ways this style proved the perfect idiom for this new kind of motion picture exhibition. Yet rather than offering an escape from reality, architects for Trans-Lux and others drew on new motifs to evoke the modernity and speed of communication in the industrial age as well as to offer patrons a virtual vehicle in which to travel to faraway places and a privileged vantage point from which to safely view the world.

In order to maintain its image as the ultimate "modern theatre," Trans-Lux adopted architectural elements in each of its cinemas that spoke to the newsreel's place in the machine age. The exterior facades and interior decor of the chain's theaters were a distinctive blend of art deco and the closely related streamline moderne design style that came to prominence in the United States in the 1930s. More commonly described by contemporaneous observers as functional, modernist, modernesque, or simply modern, architectural historians now distinguish American art deco from the more popular and populist streamline moderne.[40] While art deco typically used straight lines, angular forms, and verticality, streamline design emphasized the horizontal, aerodynamic curves of high-speed modern transportation like the automobile, the airplane, and the zeppelin. Art deco favored ornamentation and geometric motifs often borrowed from nature. Streamline chose simple, smooth lines that spoke of scientific efficiency and hygiene. And while art deco employed expensive, or expensive-looking, materials, streamline moderne used mass-produced, easy to install components. Moreover, one architectural historian has suggested that, while art deco used materials and forms that suggested permanence, "the Streamline Moderne structure with its 'flash-and-gleam beauty,' implied a built-in impermanence akin to the need to replace one's automobile every year due to Detroit's annual ritual of restyling."[41] This made streamline moderne perfect for remodeling projects and quick overhauls. As most Trans-Lux theaters were built by converting existing office and retail space, the use of relatively inexpensive decorative materials helped in affecting these transformations.

Trans-Lux architect Thomas W. Lamb used aluminum and black

Figure 10. Facade of the Trans-Lux Twin Cinema at Broadway and Forty-Ninth Street.

vitrolite (a type of opaque glass), as well as custom lighting, to create a "Trans-Lux look" that made the company's theaters instantly recognizable.[42] Figure 10 shows a detail of the aluminum facade on the Twin Cinema at Forty-Ninth Street and Broadway in New York City. Constructed in 1931, this typical art deco motif used geometric and naturalistic forms to evoke the luxury of more expensive European and American design while incorporating materials that were both a product and a symbol of the machine age. Geometric shapes were repeated in the interior, where Lamb chose round doorways, mirrors, furniture and even circular rooms. The lounge shown in Figure 11 illustrates the repetition of these circular forms and how Lamb created a sense of the ultramodern. Producing the illusion of luxury and modernity at minimum cost was central to Trans-Lux's brand identity. With locations in downtown business districts and relatively affluent neighborhoods, such as New York's Upper Eastside, luxury became a key component of Trans-Lux's promotional materials. A 1942 program for the Broadway and Forty-Ninth Street theater spelled out its name with the following claim: "The Real

Figure 11. Circular lounge in the basement of the Trans-Lux Theatre at Madison Avenue and Eighty-Fifth Street, designed by Thomas W. Lamb in 1937.

Acme of Newsreel Screen fare in Luxurious Ultra modern Xcellence."[43] The same program described the theater as "scientifically air conditioned" and as offering "90 minutes streamlined entertainment." These claims suggest the degree to which modernist design, technological innovation, and a new kind of movie experience came together to bolster Trans-Lux's reputation as "The Modern Theatre." With sleek black exteriors and curvilinear forms, the chain's distinctive look reflected the streamlined efficiencies of the Trans-Lux system.

By the mid-1930s, Trans-Lux was no longer alone in the world of newsreel exhibition, nor was it the only theater to adopt streamline elements into its designs. For these new newsreel cinemas, art deco, and streamline moderne in particular, was the ideal architectural style to express the newsreel's association with movement and speed. As we have seen in previous chapters, the newsreel's own rhetoric about itself stressed its ability to bring the news to its audience faster than ever before. Exhibitors joined the studios in a race to get footage of big news events to the screen before their competitors. With their all-news format, these theaters could screen news specials as soon as the studios released them; and, given the proximity of the newsreel offices, theaters in New York City, like Embassy and Trans-Lux, offered their audiences exclusive first looks at the most recent newsreel editions. Streamline architecture and design helped emphasize these associations. As David Gebhard points out in *The National Trust Guide to Art Deco in America*:

> The style evinced an intense fascination with speed—speed of transportation and communication. Its visual vocabulary (the curve, the tear drop, the uninterrupted horizontal line) was derived largely from the form of high-speed modern transportation machines: the airplane, the automobile, the ocean liner.[44]

Thus, as newsreel theaters took up the streamlined aesthetic in their architecture and design, they aligned themselves with technologies of transportation. Promotional materials, like postcards promoting the theater at Grand Central Terminal, articulated these links. The promise of the theater to show "news when it's news" was symbolized both by a stylized image of a high-speed train and by the design aesthetic it embodied.[45] References such as this not only alluded to the means by which the news was gathered and distributed; they spoke to how newsreel spectatorship itself was linked to travel and mobility. As we shall see, a trip to the newsreel theater became a journey, both literal and metaphorical.

For many newsreel audiences, a visit to the newsreel theater started in the train station. In the 1930s, several all-news cinemas opened in or near major transportation hubs to take advantage of the critical mass of patrons provided by rail and bus stations. Newsreel cinemas were opened inside Boston's South Station in 1936, New York's Grand Central Station in 1937, and across the street from New York's Pennsylvania Station in 1938. According to the *Motion Picture Herald,* the theater in Grand Central hoped "to draw most of its patronage from commuters, among others, who missed their train and [had] time to kill before the next one."[46] The continuous program was perfect for these busy travelers waiting for trains because it allowed them to enter and exit at any time. Part entertainment, part waiting room, the newsreel theater offered a comfortable, air-conditioned space to spend time between connections. Likewise, the Penn Newsreel Theatre also catered to commuters. Illuminated clocks within the auditorium reminded patrons when it was time to catch their train, while the theater posted train schedules and installed service booths to allow Long Island commuters to check parcels.[47] In Boston, the South Station Theatre even offered a call service to remind commuters of their train departures.[48] Unlike traditional movie houses, patrons of these theaters were never completely taken out of their commuter lives. Instead, they were encouraged to make the newsreel part of their journey.

One of the first newsreel theaters built outside of New York City most clearly demonstrated the newsreel's deep associations with both literal and metaphorical travel. Built in 1933 by New York architects Alfred Fellheimer and Steward Wagner, the Cincinnati Union Terminal literally linked that city to the world as it consolidated the seven different private rail lines and five different stations that had previously serviced the area. The building itself was a striking example of American art deco architecture (Figure 12).[49] Its dramatic curves and enormous domed foyer were daringly modern for their time and place. The design of the terminal, and especially its prominent mosaics conceived by Winold Reiss, spoke of the city's desire to connect with the rest of the country. A series of murals

Figure 12. Cincinnati Union Terminal.

Figure 13. Newsreel Theatre at the Cincinnati Union Terminal.

Figure 14. Newsreel Theatre at the Cincinnati Union Terminal.

above the ticket booths and other amenities in the main concourse of the terminal depicted both the people who had built the city and the modes of transportation that had brought them to Ohio. These murals, featuring canoes, riverboats, wagon trains, and airplanes, as well as locomotives, reflected Cincinnatians' view of their city as a kind of American crossroads: a city linking the United States, East and West, North and South. The inclusion of a newsreel theater in this landmark construction was a product of this impulse. The cinema offered instant access to the world through the screen, and its presence in the station reflected the city's aspirations toward the modernity and cosmopolitanism of larger American cities to the north and east. At the laying of the terminal's cornerstone, Alfred Fellheimer remarked on the station's importance as more than a simple transportation hub:

> In addition to the use of the station facilities as a means of access to and departure from the trains, the city of Cincinnati and the traveling public demanded something more. Civic feeling and personal pride in the city of Cincinnati had also to be considered. In responding to these requirements, whatever of architecture the design may exhibit has been created. And whatever effect the result may have in creating a sympathetic attachment of the public to its station, has been augmented by the incorporation therein of every reasonable facility, such as a representative restaurant, superior shops, and a news reel theater, thereby further stimulating the public interest as well as serving its convenience and necessity. It is therefore to be hoped that the station, designed primarily as an adjunct of transportation, will soon become a real part of the organic activities of the city itself.[50]

As a monument to civic pride, the architect imagined the train station becoming an "organic" part of Cincinnati while articulating the city's identity in terms of its role in transportation and transcontinental travel.

The architects and the muralist, Pierre Bourdelle, continued the motifs of travel and mobility in the newsreel theater itself. Here, typical art deco elements such as the black and white marble wainscoting, curved detailing on the seats and proscenium, and aluminum trim were embellished with a series of carved linoleum panels that alluded to modern technology and transportation.[51] According to a review in the *Cincinnati Star-Times,* Bourdelle deliberately chose themes to fit the space:

> He views mural decoration, not from the point of view of subject matter, but as an architectural problem which must be functional with the room. And yet he chooses subject matter that is appropriate to the setting. In the moving picture theater he gives glimpses of important modern inventions—an airplane, a zeppelin, a phonograph—just as a newsreel gives them to us, and he ties them together with an unrolled movie film.[52]

Two other murals, no longer extant (Figures 15 and 16), show the further elaboration of Bourdelle's designs. While the bare-breasted mermaids on either side of the screen and the aquatic scene planned for the curtain itself at first seem to depart from the modernist imagery of transportation, such nautical allusions recall the illustrations featured on maps and charts, thus suggesting the romance of travel in a bygone era, not to mention the voyeuristic aspects of watching the news. But it is the mural on the east wall where Bourdelle brought together many of the themes under discussion here. Not only did he work the technology of transportation into this carving, but, using art deco geometrical forms, he abstracted these into a kind of panorama of the nation. The mural (Figure 16) shows the airplane, the ocean liner, and the zeppelin amidst a modernist landscape that also includes urban and rural settings—symbolized by the office tower and church on rolling hills respectively. As the *Star-Times* suggested, the newsreel showcased modern technologies, but, in doing so, it also mimicked their effects. Bourdelle's mural implied that the newsreel—like technologies of transportation—brought the world to its audience and that the newsreel theater, like the terminal itself, connected the residents of Cincinnati to the world beyond.

The parallels between cinematic spectatorship and rail travel were not new with the newsreel theater. Indeed, scholars have noted the interconnected histories of both technologies since the first introduction of moving pictures at the end of the nineteenth century. Wolfgang Schivelbusch argues in his book *The Railway Journey: Trains and Travel in the Nineteenth Century* that the railroad initiated a perspectival shift that culminated in the motion picture. Like the train, which could annihilate

Figure 15. South elevation of Newsreel Theatre at Cincinnati Union Terminal. Drawings by Fellheimer and Wagner, architects.

Figure 16. West elevation of Newsreel Theatre at Cincinnati Union Terminal. Drawings by Fellheimer and Wagner, architects.

both time and space by dramatically cutting the duration of travel to distant locales, film juxtaposed radically disparate images and places. "In the filmic perception," Schivelbusch argues, "the new reality of annihilated in-between spaces finds its clearest expression: the film brings things closer to the viewer as well as closer together."[53] While cinema may have brought the world closer to audiences by eliminating distance, films of faraway places and of travel itself also worked to emphasize distance and geographic difference. From the earliest experiments in filmmaking, the reproduction of the tourist experience was one of the key pleasures of the movies. Films of exotic places—both real and imagined—allowed audiences to go on virtual journeys.[54] As Noël Burch suggests in his work on early cinema, "the myth of the globe trotter first took root among the bourgeoisie, but the cinema helped extend it as a fantasy through other strata."[55] One of the most vivid examples of this virtual travel was the Hale's Tour. First presented at the St. Louis Exposition in 1904, Hale's Tours became extremely popular throughout the country; by 1908 there were at least five hundred operating in the United States.[56] The Hale's Tour consisted of one or two railway carriages, where audiences typically watched a ten-minute film shot from the point of view of the front or rear of a moving train. The carriages were often rocked from side to side, with the sound of clattering wheels and steam whistles added to simulate the experience of train travel. Films depicted journeys through scenic parts of North America, strange and foreign lands, and even urban cityscapes.[57]

Although the newsreel cinemas of the 1930s did not attempt to affect the same physical simulation of travel in the Hale's Tour, they certainly borrowed from this tradition of film as a simulated voyage and the theater as a virtual vehicle. Newsreel images were gathered from around the world and often listed on programs with prominent datelines, suggesting a travel itinerary. Moreover, the frequent addition of travelogues to the programs of all-news cinemas gave audiences a chance to travel the globe virtually. Newsreel producers and exhibitors capitalized on these associations. Images of globes, maps, zeppelins, airplanes, and trains dominated the promotional materials for newsreels and newsreel theaters, while slogans like the Newsreel Theatre's "World around, in sight and sound"[58] helped to reinforce the link between new technologies of transportation and new modes of vision.

Given the long-standing connection between travel and newsreel spectatorship, it is little wonder that these themes would be taken up by architects and newsreel theater designers. The interior murals at the Cincinnati Union Terminal show how newsreel spectatorship was linked to new ways of viewing the local in relation to the modern nation. Architect S. Charles Lee took the travel theme one step further, designing newsreel cinemas that symbolically offered patrons a new perspective on the world. Lee, based in Los Angeles, designed approximately 250 theaters between 1920 and 1950. His unique take on the streamline moderne aesthetic became a touchstone for movie house architecture on the West

Coast. In her book about Lee and theatrical architecture, *The Show Starts on the Sidewalk: An Architectural History of the Movie Theatre, Starring S. Charles Lee,* Maggie Valentine states that Lee believed that theaters "should be attractive showplaces for the product, but not interfere with the illusion."[59] Moreover, he felt that dramatic facades and exterior ornamentation could lure in pedestrian passersby by stimulating what he called the "escape psychology."[60] Valentine argues that Lee represented "the avant-garde of popular taste"[61] and that, by employing an accessible form of modernist architecture, he created spaces that were dramatic but not intimidating. She writes:

> The best of his theatres created a sense of wonder and exploration that embraced users who were willing to pay repeatedly for the experience. There was an accessible monumentality to a Lee building; it was theatrical and imposing but inviting nonetheless. The manipulation of space created a nurturing environment that imparted to the ticket buyer a sense of power and elegance.[62]

Lee's newsreel theater designs not only created a "sense of power" for the ticket buyer but also, by tying this power to travel and a kind of global vision, a privileged vantage point from which spectators might view the world.

By the beginning of World War II, Lee had built his career on creating landmark theater designs in Southern California. But the war meant that building materials and labor were in short supply. After the War Production Board limited the availability of steel and other materials for nonessential use, Lee kept his business alive by working on remodeling projects. Among these were a number of newsreel theaters, including remodeled facades for the Globe Theatre in Los Angeles and the Oakland Newsreel Theatre. Featuring prominent three-dimensional globes, these designs advertised what was on display inside: the world itself. These projects were far less ambitious than many of Lee's pre-War designs, but the proposed Town Theatre (Figure 17) shows that Lee imagined the newsreel cinema in equally monumental terms. This theater, according to Lee's notes, was "planned to care for a change in theatre patronage. It [was] meant to speak up to the people to come in and see what [was] inside, and [was] planned for a locality where the newsreel [had] become

Figure 17. Sketch of proposed Town Theatre, S. Charles Lee, Architect.

an important attraction."[63] In these designs, Lee took on the relationship between motion pictures and travel and aligned the newsreel with the tourist experience. In doing so, Lee's designs draw our attention to how the newsreel theater was regarded as a place to see the world. At a time when war loomed, the virtual travel on offer in these theaters enabled audiences to take in the world from the comfort of their seats. By his own admission, Lee's theaters were "showplaces for the product" inside. These globes suggest that Lee understood that, in the newsreel theater, the product was the world itself. Lee's designs literally put that world on display. If the newsreel made the world visible, then Lee's newsreel theaters presented it as accessible and consumable.

Lee's use of the globe motif reflected more than a straightforward advertisement for the newsreel and the access it offered. These globes articulated a particular relationship between the world on screen and the American newsreel audience. Looking at it today, the size of the globe remains the most impressive feature of the Town Theatre. The sphere dominates the image, dwarfing the people below. This contrast in scale is impressive. Lee's design dramatized the power of the newsreel theater to fuse the local with what we would now call the global.[64] The magnitude of world events was set dramatically against the neighborhood and its inhabitants. By designing the theater in this way, Lee simultaneously emphasized the enormity of the world, the power of the newsreel to represent it, and the privileged position of the American spectator. From the safety of their neighborhood, newsreel viewers could not only see the world but contain it and possess it through vision. Film scholars have long aligned cinematic spectatorship with possession of the image on screen.[65] As we have seen in earlier chapters, the newsreel itself worked to imagine the whole world as visible. By symbolically presenting the world for spectators' consumption, Lee's designs offered audiences the power of vision on a global scale.

The centrality of the audience remains implicit in Lee's newsreel theaters and in others that underlined the themes of travel and transportation. The architecture and interior design of these newsreel cinemas assured patrons of their privileged vantage point. In providing its audience with this powerful perspective, the newsreel theater reinforced the otherness of the world on screen. In the auditorium of the Trans-Lux theater at Madison Avenue and Eighty-Fifth Street, for example, wall sconces featuring world maps and murals depicting newsreel subjects from around the world emphasized the newsreel's ability to take its audience on a virtual tour of the globe. With modernist renditions of exotic places, tourism, and Hollywood glamour, these murals underlined the sense of difference between the viewing audience and the images on screen. In doing so, they beg the question as to how audiences were to relate to world events that were both "real" and "other." Unlike Hollywood feature films and the theaters that showed them, the newsreel cinema did not offer its customers a fantasy escape. Instead, it projected a reality that was at once close-up and available for inspection while still remaining foreign and comfortably distant. Through their allusions to travel and modern transportation, the newsreel theaters made any journey into the world of news a temporary visit: audiences could pass through war-torn Europe and Asia before stops in Washington and New York for political speeches or beauty contests. While war and terrible natural disasters happened on the screen, viewers shared the comforts of the modern cinema and the knowledge that, just outside the doors, there was shopping to do and a train to catch. In the context of the increasingly troubled world of the 1930s, this mode of spectatorship offered Americans a shared perspective on global events—one that was both fascinated and aloof. At the newsreel theater, audiences could be both a part of the world and apart from it.

"Public Forums of the Screen"

In order to better understand how Americans viewed the newsreel in the period leading up to World War II, we must now turn to the audience itself. Chains like Trans-Lux presented the news as both modern and technologically sophisticated, and architects like Thomas Lamb and S. Charles Lee embodied the newsreel's associations with travel and speed in the streamlined aesthetic of the age. Although these sources are helpful in understanding how the newsreel was represented and, to some extent, what it represented in American culture in the 1930s, they can't tell us much about how particular historical audiences watched the news. It is notoriously difficult to get at this problem, but Peter Arno's *New Yorker* cartoon hints that newsreel audiences were not simply passive consumers. There is considerable evidence that Arno's New York sophisticates were not alone and that hissing—not to mention cheering, jeering, laughing, and booing—at the newsreel theater was an important part of watching the news. While the theater may have offered audiences a vantage point from which to view the world at a safe distance, the patrons of these theaters often chose to engage loudly with the images on screen. As we shall see, audiences refused simply to watch the world from their seats. They felt the need to comment on the images before them. In doing so, these vocal audiences transformed the theatrical space into a kind of public forum where they could engage with the world and each other.

The question of the vociferous audience forces a reconsideration—at least, in part—of the theoretical models of film spectatorship founded on the notion of the darkened cinema and the isolated subject. As we have seen, newsreel spectatorship was not simply a matter of the film and its viewer. Architects and designers, as well as newsreel chains, imagined their audiences in ways that positioned the viewing subject even before the film began. But, as we shall see, the audience itself reconfigured these conditions of reception. These reconfigurations are not just matters of individual viewership but a collective experience, part of what Miriam Hansen calls the "public dimension of cinematic reception":

> This public dimension is distinct from both textual and social determinations of spectatorship because it entails the very moment in which reception can gain a momentum of its own, can give rise to formations not necessarily anticipated in the context of production.[66]

The audience responses in newsreel theaters were just such moments. When audiences booed or cheered the images on screen, they demonstrated that cinematic reception involved far more than the experience designed by film exhibitors and producers. As such, these negative responses can help us complicate notions of newsreel spectatorship and better understand the relationship between news films and their audiences.

Although sporadic, newspaper reports and commentary chart some of the audience responses to newsreels in the 1930s. Applause was a regular occurrence in movie theaters and thus rarely warranted media comment, but negative audience reactions appear in the accounts of controversial film screenings and during times of public debate. By the middle of the decade, by far the most popular targets for the so-called "boo birds" were Mussolini and Hitler, but Joseph Stalin, Joachim von Ribentrop, Emperor Hirohito, and other foreign figures also reportedly faced disdain. Patrons voiced their displeasure for various American politicians as well. Election campaigns in particular seem to have sparked partisan expressions. Audiences commonly booed and hissed images of President Roosevelt and his various Republican opponents—President Hoover and candidates Alfred Landon and Wendell Wilkie—while mayoral candidates in New York and Chicago also reportedly prompted jeers. These negative noises were usually met with equally vocal cheering from candidates' supporters. Other figures feeling the ire of newsreel audiences included Congress of Industrial Organizations president John Lewis and prominent government functionaries like George Wickersham, chairman of President Hoover's commission investigating prohibition, and Roosevelt's powerful postmaster general, James Farley.[67]

Such was the frequency of this opinionated interjection that journalists sometimes turned to the theater as a kind of microcosm of public opinion. In her syndicated column, "A Woman's New York," Alice Hughes described going to her favorite newsreel theater "whenever in doubt as to how the public [felt] about this or that." She noted, for example, how the hissing at President Roosevelt and the First Lady had changed to "sincere applause" following his reelection in 1936. Hughes also recognized differences according to neighborhood. In her preferred theater—a Trans-Lux on Madison Avenue—John Lewis was hissed, but on Broadway at the Embassy Theatre, he won "rounds of applause."[68] This kind of neighborhood-specific response surely reflected class differences as well as ethnic and political affiliations. When scandal hit New York's City Hall in 1932 and Tammany Mayor James Walker was forced to resign, the *New York Times* surveyed neighborhood theaters to gauge public support for the ousted Mayor, and for Judge Samuel Seabury, the man who led the investigation into municipal corruption. According to the survey, Walker still garnered applause from audiences on the Lower East Side and in Harlem while getting booed and hissed heartily in theaters in Upper Manhattan, the Bronx, and Greenwich Village.[69] Although reports such as this one offered little conclusive evidence to the journalist, let alone the modern day historian, of public opinion in the 1930s, they do indicate the prevalence of vocal engagement with the newsreel. Moreover, this evidence suggests that boisterous audience responses were not limited to economically or socially marginalized groups. Booing and hissing newsreel villains apparently crossed class lines and other affiliations.

Not everyone embraced these lively newsreel audiences. Although some journalists saw the booing and hissing in theaters as a reflection of public opinion, others questioned the sincerity of this audience dissention. For some satirists, such lusty outbursts were less than discriminating. In a 1936 cartoon that caricatured the neighborhood movie house and its various types, W. E. Hill described the newsreel hisser as fickle in the extreme: "[He] hisses Hitler, Mussolini, Hoover or Roosevelt on occasion. Depends on the mood."[70] Similarly, in his humorous "Interview with a Hisser" for the *Washington Post,* H. I. Phillips questioned whether "Hisser Number One" really had the strength of his sibilant convictions.

> "Who were you hissing just now Landon or Roosevelt?" we asked.
>
> "Oh, I hissed both of 'em. I'm impartial and want to play fair with both."
>
> "But I notice some weeks the hissing is more pronounced for the Republican candidate than the Democratic and vice versa."
>
> "That's the trouble. Most hissers are not dependable. A good many have no independence. They wait until the hissing starts and then they join in if they thinks it's violent enough. The movie houses are full of these follow-the-leader hissers. Then there's the furtive type of hisser who looks all around to see if he recognizes anybody near him before hissing. I'm a straight from the heart hisser and I'll hiss anybody in any theater at any time, especially in an election year . . . I once hissed Woodrow Wilson, Gen. Foch and 700 feet of Lloyd George all in one newsreel."[71]

Other critics went further. By the end of the 1930s, journalists, theater managers, and others questioned the propriety of any booing or hissing. One letter writer complained to the *New York Times* that "the behavior of audiences in our motion-picture theatres [sank] to a low level indeed when the Presidential candidates [appeared] in the daily newsreels." The author lamented the prevalence of "boos, hisses, catcalls and Bronx cheers" and called for the public to show more respect. He argued, "The real American way of voicing approval [was] applause and cheers and disapproval [was] voiced by making no sound at all."[72] Paul S. Purdy, a theater manager in Winsted, Connecticut, agreed. During the 1940 election campaign, he went on stage to ask his patrons to be more respectful to the presidential candidates: "Clap all you want, but please don't boo," he said. "One of them will be elected President."[73] That same year, *Los Angeles Times* columnist Jimmie Fidler denounced the practice of booing the president in unequivocal terms. He wrote, "As I sat in theaters and heard those boos I felt a sick hollow sensation in the pit of my stomach which I recognized as shame that some of my fellow citizens had so far lost their sense of honor as to commit such an unsporting, un-American act."[74] Denunciations such as this remind us that the question of proper theater etiquette was by no means settled in the years before World War II. Was the rowdy newsreel audience disrespectful and fundamentally un-American, or was the public debate embodied in such behavior a quintessentially American manifestation of the democratic tradition in the age of mass media? Whatever it was, the booing of public figures made sure that the newsreel experience was not simply a dull summary of world events but an occasion for public engagement with the news and the men and women who made it.

Ironically, at least one of the major studios sought to discourage this kind of engagement. As early as 1931, Fox sent an order to its theater managers instructing them to censor controversial subject matter in the newsreels:

> It is our business to show entertainment—and nothing else but entertainment—on our screens. It happens, however, that at times subjects included in the newsreels are of such a character that they stir up resentment of one kind or another . . . It is up to you, however, to see to it that nothing is presented to your audiences that can in any manner cause demonstrations or irritation inside of your theatres. Therefore you are not only authorized, but you are herewith very pointedly instructed to delete all subjects of a controversial nature on prohibition, pro or con; all subjects which can be construed as Bolshevist propaganda; all political speeches which take sides on matters of public interest; shots showing bread lines; and economic discussions on which the country or your particular patronage is divided.[75]

Such a blanket prohibition is striking. The memo also specifically mentioned instances where various personalities had been both booed and applauded by audiences. Again, Fox argued vehemently against encouraging such behavior: "Do not make the mistake of believing that a demonstration for or against a subject makes that subject entertaining. We don't say that such matters are not interesting, but the danger is that they are liable to become too interesting."[76] Exhibitors, it seems, sought to ensure that their theaters provide a relaxing environment for entertainment alone. In an article titled "The Exhibitor's Screen—How Shall it be Used?," Martin Quigley, editor-in-chief of the *Motion Picture Herald,* the main trade paper for movie exhibitors, argued, "the motion picture theatre is and should remain devoted to the mission of providing entertainment . . . [The industry] has no intention whatsoever of allowing its theatres to be converted into bedlams of turmoil and dissension."[77] He denounced filmmakers who deliberately generated controversy in their films and argued, "It is quite all right to have the villain on the screen hissed. But it is not all right to foment a condition in a theatre in which members of the audience hiss each other."[78] For Quigley, the cinema provided a respite from the world, and it was the job of the exhibitor to make the theater as inoffensive as possible in order not to alienate the audience.

In stark contrast to the vehement positions of Quigley and Fox, the managers and owners of several newsreel theaters proved ready to embrace debate. Indeed, far from worrying about alienating their audience, these exhibitors saw their role as encouraging discussion of the news. Courtland Smith, head of the Trans-Lux theater chain and onetime newsreel editor for both Fox and Pathé, told reporters he believed the American public was interested in controversy, and he regularly visited theaters to gauge the audience's reactions to specific stories and personalities.[79] French Githens, president of the Newsreel Theatres chain, was emphatic about the policy of his theaters:

> We will show without fear or favor news which comes to us from any recognized American producer, no matter how controversial the subject matter may be. We show all the news impartially, take no sides and play no favorites. In short, our embassy newsreel theatres are the public forums of the screen.[80]

Even when a group of prominent patrons, including Irving Berlin, complained about German newsreels being played at the Embassy Theatre in 1940, Githens didn't waver. Instead of removing the offensive footage from his program, he added a foreword to the newsreel, noting that several British-made war films had shown recently at the theater and that "The film which you are about to see is a picture of the other side of war. We present it purely for its historical news value. We will be glad to receive your written comments on this type of film. See any attendant."[81] Unlike traditional movie theaters, where the newsreel was a footnote to the main program, newsreel houses relied on the news—and on the controversies it could ignite—to attract their audience. Conventional exhibitors saw their theaters as offering an escape from the world and naturally worried that when audiences reacted negatively to controversial subjects, they adulterated that fantasy with the real world of politics. Githens recognized that the newsreel theater was different. Rather than offering an escape from the world, the "public forum of the screen" was a place where audiences could see the world and engage with it, albeit in a mediated way.

Although Githens and other newsreel exhibitors sought to exploit the desire of spectators to comment on the news, boisterous audiences would not be confined to these designated venues. It may have been discouraged, but even in the most prestigious of motion picture theaters, newsreel audiences cheered and jeered the heroes and villains of the screen. A remarkable document of one such screening offers tremendous insight into how Americans watched the news. On August 13, 1941, the producers of the documentary series *The March of Time* made a sound recording of a screening of their film "Peace by Hitler" as it premiered at the Radio City Music Hall in New York.[82] *The March of Time* series was a news magazine. Unlike conventional newsreels, each twenty-minute episode featured one or two stories treated as short documentaries. *The March of Time* was no stranger to controversy. In 1938, the news feature "Inside Nazi Germany" ignited criticism from all sides.[83] The film was denounced as both pro-Nazi and anti-German propaganda and was even removed from theaters by the Warner Bros. chain. When the film showed at the Embassy Theatre, "there were a few 'Heils' for Hitler and an opposing and equivalent number of 'Pfui,'" and some fist-waving audience members had to be separated.[84] Perhaps the extreme responses from both critics and audiences to "Inside Nazi Germany" were the reason that the producers of *The March of Time* wanted a record of how audiences received their latest film on Hitler. Whatever the purpose, this unique recording captures the audience as it responds to the film and the personalities it portrayed.

As captured by the recording, the audience greeted *The March of Time* with polite applause. The film opened by relating the current situation in England where citizens were dealing with the threat of German bombing raids and the privations of rationing. Audience members enthusiastically applauded images of British tanks and the country's air force, apparently indicating support for the people of Britain as they endured these hardships. More applause greeted images of American troops and equipment sent to help the British war effort along with the narrator's declaration that the "tide of the battle [was] turning." Next, the film summarized events leading up to war in Europe, including an accounting of Hitler's broken promises and of his various peace treaties with European nations. The audience was quiet during this grim outline of Nazi betrayal, but a ripple of laughter did pass through the crowd when a German spokesman referred to Roosevelt as "bloodthirsty." The film's intended irony was not lost on those at Radio City. The audience's reaction became more complicated when the film turned to the issue of American war preparations and the isolationist stance of people like Charles Lindbergh and Senator Burton K. Wheeler. At this point, boos and applause competed with one another as the audience divided over the question of U.S. participation in the war. Roosevelt received applause from some as he announced support for the European allies, but, in the next scene, others in the audience expressed their approval of an anti-war speech by Wheeler and a shot of a campaign postcard signed by the senator, which read, "Write today to President Roosevelt at the White House, in Washington, that you are against our entry into the European war." This applause continued when Charles Lindbergh, the famous aviator and member of the America First Committee, appeared on screen. But this expression of approval was met with boos from other parts of the audience. Lindbergh had been perhaps the United States' most prominent isolationist in the early 1940s; he campaigned against Roosevelt's Lend-Lease Act, and by 1941 his opponents labeled him a Nazi sympathizer. Clearly, he polarized the public at Radio City Music Hall.

While the specifics of who was applauded and who was derided is interesting from the point of view of American public opinion at a crucial historical moment, this recording is illuminating in other ways. It reveals an audience that was willing to take on the public figures on screen as well as the film itself. This audience did not simply accept *The March of Time*'s perspective on world events. While most viewers apparently agreed with the film's disdain for the idea of making peace with Hitler, some, at least, were just as opposed to the United States' entry into war. More importantly, this recording reveals an audience willing to engage with one another. The timing of the responses suggests that people were not just reacting to the images on screen. Booing in the New York theater seemed to be directed as much at those audience members who had applauded Lindbergh as it was against the man himself. In this context, watching the news was not an isolating experience, but one that brought viewers into dialogue with those around them. While newspaper accounts and other evidence hint at this dynamic, this recording confirms that news spectatorship before World War II provided a venue for public debate. Ironically, "Peace by Hitler" ended with a thinly veiled call to support the "Crusade for Freedom" and the "V for Victory" campaign. The film's narrator informed the audience and the world that "the American people are not divided." But the screening at Radio City Music Hall suggested otherwise. Indeed, the consensus that *The March of Time* imagined was very much up for debate. Newsreels and films such as "Peace by Hitler" did not necessarily foster unanimity but rather, as French Githens had hoped, a "public forum of the screen."

The public dimension of film reception revealed by the Radio City recording is crucial to understanding newsreel spectatorship before World War II. Audiences were not passive consumers of the news. Nevertheless, the noisy newsreel spectator should not simply be interpreted as subversive or inherently progressive. It is tempting to view vocal engagement with the screen as counter-hegemonic—as opposed to passive responses that are generally seen as ideologically complicit—but such a binary view of reception fails fully to understand the complex dynamics of public reception. In her book *Perverse Spectators: The Practices of Film Reception,* Janet Staiger rightly warns against universal ideological evaluations. "Talk is not always progressive in the public sphere," she argues. "Talk can be quite incendiary. It can, however, also be binding and supportive."[85] Above all, Staiger is aware that cinematic reception is not simply a personal response but a social one in which audiences "use the text as the object through which to construct networks of attachment, discovery, and sometimes, authority and power."[86] While some audience reactions might indeed be viewed as contesting hegemonic representations of the news, taken together these outbursts are best understood as examples of audience members engaging each other through the news. Moreover, audiences who booed the newsreel did so not simply to reject the images or personalities on screen but to negotiate their own roles as spectators and Americans. When war came to the United States after the bombing of Pearl Harbor, exhibitors and audiences collaborated to curtail the opportunities for such negotiation as theaters became places where patrons showed their support for the war effort through bond drives and the cheering of American troops on screen.[87] In this new atmosphere, there was little space for political dissent by the newsreel audience. Indeed, two Japanese patrons were apparently arrested after fellow audience members reported hearing them hissing Roosevelt at a Los Angeles theater.[88] During wartime, the news was no longer up for debate, especially for those racially marked as un-American.[89] Such restrictions only serve to highlight the contested nature of newsreel reception before World War II. While definitions of appropriate news spectatorship and Americanness could be challenged in the 1930s, by 1942 such opportunities were more limited. The news remained a means for Americans to actively forge "networks of attachment," but whereas audiences had once used the newsreel, and the newsreel theater in particular, as a space for debate, the "public forum of the screen" had become a venue to demonstrate patriotism and to police the unanimity of support.

Conclusion

Newsreel spectatorship was a contested arena in the United States before World War II. Contrary to some analyses, the newsreel was not a simple instrument of propaganda or even the manufacturer of consensus. In the 1930s, at least, newsreel spectatorship offered audiences an opportunity to view the world from a new perspective. Newsreel theaters flattered their audiences with architectural and other references to technology, travel, and modernity. In doing so, these theaters offered their patrons a virtual journey around the world of current events. These allusions to travel stressed the shared identity of the audience as American—while the events on screen were made closer through the lens of the news camera, they remained separate and distinctly other. In a world that seemed to be getting progressively more dangerous, the newsreel cinema allowed audiences to watch that world while keeping it safely at bay. This distance, however, did not make audiences indifferent to current events. Instead, newsreel audiences felt fully able to watch the news and voice their opinions about it. Indeed, the privileged perspective of modernity on offer in the newsreel cinema may well have made such commentary possible. In a world made smaller by technologies of communication and travel, the newsreel gave audiences virtual access to faraway people and places. Given the power to see the world, it is not surprising that American moviegoers transformed the newsreel theater into a public forum of the screen. These responses remind us that despite the global vision and shared identity of the virtual crowd on offer in the newsreel, the shared public dimension of newsreel reception was distinctly local and transpired in actual spaces. As a public forum of the screen, the newsreel cinema reflected a tension between competing notions of news consumption, between the mass-mediated crowd of the news parade and the vocal debates of the actual crowd in the theater. It is precisely in the tension between the real places of newsreel reception and the imagined space of newsreel spectatorship that one can see the mediated public sphere of the screen come fully into focus.

While the vocal responses of audiences at the newsreel theater demonstrate the extent to which the screen offered the opportunity to participate in a mediated public sphere, there were limits to this participation. The example above of the Japanese audience members arrested for allegedly hissing Roosevelt shows that not all Americans shared equally in the privileges of looking. Moreover, the nature of the imperial gaze described in chapter 3 ensured that Asian Americans, African Americans, and other racial and ethnic minorities would find it difficult to join in the newsreel's collective spectatorship in any straightforward way.[90] Indeed, in an increasingly visual public sphere, many marginalized Americans struggled to make themselves seen at all. It is exactly this struggle for visibility that we turn to in chapter 5.

CHAPTER 5

Double Vision

World War II, Racial Uplift, and Politics of Visibility in *All-American News*

Launched in November 1942, *All-American News* was a weekly newsreel entirely devoted to the activities and accomplishments of African Americans. The weekly series' first offering featured a selection of subjects typical of the issues to follow in the next decade, including "Marion Anderson's christening of the new ship *Booker T. Washington*, the colored WAACs [Women's Auxiliary Army Corps], Satchel Paige's latest pitching and many other interesting events."[1] By combining coverage of African American celebrities with the details of "the race's" contributions to the war effort, the film's producers hoped race pride would make their upstart production a success. At a time when the newsreels produced by the major Hollywood studios all but ignored black America, *All-American* filled a crucial niche in the American moving picture industry. Just as importantly, this new offering held out a promise to African Americans that the achievements and contributions of their community would finally be represented and acknowledged on film. The news parade and its unique mode of realism, emphasizing the experience of watching the news, had made such onscreen recognition important. Reality was increasingly defined in terms of mediated looking and the newsreel's invitation to examine the visual evidence. In this context, *All-American News* offered African Americans the opportunity to be represented—in the sense of being depicted but also in the sense of having a delegate to speak for their concerns. In the racial politics of the 1940s, this dual representational power of the newsreel seemed to present a potent weapon in the battle for the uplift of the race and an opportunity to participate in the new mediated public sphere of the screen. For the film's producers, its audience, and its critics, *All-American* had the potential to be far more than a simple chronicler of African American achievement. Indeed, many saw the visual power of the newsreel as a crucial tool in achieving recognition and respect—by displaying evidence of black accomplishment but also by educating African American audiences. As we shall see, the newsreel adopted a specifically pedagogical address aimed at promoting the values of hard work, discipline, and self-improvement. By looking at how *All-American* deployed this pedagogical address and the rhetoric of uplift in the context of wartime race relations and a Jim Crow motion picture industry, we will see how the newsreel contested racial inequality while accommodating segregation. Images of achievement implicitly refuted racist portrayals of African Americans on film and encouraged its viewers to advance the race through their own talents and diligence. Nevertheless, *All-American News* largely ignored the issue of racism itself, and critics and audiences began to question a politics of visibility that put the onus for change on the newsreel's African American viewers rather than white America.

This chapter focuses on the content of thirty-nine issues of *All-American News* released between 1944 and 1945 (practically all that remains of the newsreel's decade-long weekly output).[2] These films reveal a company and its audience negotiating the politics of visibility and the rhetoric of racial uplift during the Second World War. These negotiations took place in the context of the United States' deeply segregated film industry as well as the contradictory demands of what W. E. B. Du Bois called double consciousness: "that sense of always looking at one self through the eyes of others."[3] For its African American audiences, *All-American News* represented both the possibility and the limits of the mediated public sphere. Just as mainstream newsreel viewers did not sit quietly, *All-American*'s audiences talked back to the screen in a variety of ways. In the tension between *All-American News*' pedagogical address and the responses from audiences and critics, a kind of counterpublic emerged in response to the mainstream news parade. As Michael Warner points out, "a counterpublic maintains at some level, conscious or not, an awareness of its subordinate status. The cultural horizon against which it marks itself off is not just a general or wider public but a dominant one."[4]

While the newsreel itself avoided directly addressing American racism, viewers were able to recognize and call out these omissions. In doing so, *All-American*'s counterpublic acknowledged and contested the subordinate position of African Americans within the United States' visual public sphere.

All-American, Racial Uplift, and Double Victory

Before turning to the newsreel's content and reception, it is first necessary to situate it more fully in the context of World War II discourses of racial uplift and Double Victory, as well as the United States' segregated film industry. *All-American News* was founded by Emmanuel Glucksman, a film producer and veteran of the motion picture and theatrical entertainment businesses.[5] Glucksman was a so-called "white angel," regularly employing African American talent behind the camera as well as in front of it. Charles Wilson was the voice of *All-American*, providing commentary in most of the reel's stories, and William Alexander—who himself went on to produce films for African American audiences, including a documentary series called the *By-Line Newsreel*—worked as a cameraman, director, on-camera interviewer, and, for a time, *All-American*'s Washington bureau chief.[6] Glucksman also received important advice and support from Claude Barnett, the head of the Associated Negro Press, a wire service for black newspapers and magazines modeled on the Associated Press. This combination of white money and black talent was a common arrangement in the race movie market of the late 1930s and 1940s. The Depression and the added costs of sound had all but eliminated the black independent film producers of the silent era.[7] In the years following the launch of *All-American*, Glucksman also used this model to produce several feature films in addition to the newsreel. With titles like *Killer Diller* and *Hi-De-Ho*, these black-cast films were essentially variety shows with loose plots tying together musical numbers and vaudeville acts by well-known performers such as Moms Mabley and Cab Calloway. Although these films gained moderate success, the newsreel remained at the core of Glucksman's business well into the 1950s.[8]

Like other race movies of the 1930s and 1940s, *All-American*'s audience was almost exclusively African American. The primary market for *All-American*'s films, including its newsreel, was the black movie theater circuit—which included the segregated theaters of the South and black neighborhood houses in cities like New York, Chicago, and Philadelphia. It's difficult to know exactly how widely the newsreel was exhibited, but in November 1943, Glucksman boasted that four million people saw his product each week. He told the *American Cinematographer* that *All-American* was "seen regularly in 365 of the 452 civilian negro theatres" and added that the films were distributed to seventy military camps throughout the country.[9] With the help of Claude Barnett, Glucksman also distributed prints of the newsreel to several black colleges in the United States and even to Africa—screening the newsreel in Liberia and Nigeria.[10] After the end of the Second World War, Glucksman looked for ways to distribute the newsreel even more widely. One idea was to distribute a version of the newsreel to television stations around the country. This plan held out the promise that white audiences as well as black might see the newsreel. In a letter to Barnett, Glucksman stressed the importance of television in reaching audiences beyond the race theater circuit:

> As you no doubt know, it is very difficult for us to put the accomplishments of the Negro race before the white theatre goers but, with television reaching the most influential class of people of all races, we feel a subject [devoted to African American achievement] would be one of the most potent presentations put into the American parlor. . . .
>
> You, who are so very much interested in visual education, will realize what a presentation of this kind once a week would mean nationally. I am sure you are aware as much as I am how little people know about the accomplishments and achievements of the American Negro and what a program of this kind would do while a family is sitting around the television set relaxed in their own home.[11]

Although Glucksman's plan to produce a weekly *All-American* news program for television did not materialize, he did partner with Barnett to produce a series of documentaries sponsored by Liggett and Myers, the makers of Chesterfield Cigarettes. The six-part Negro America series featured episodes on "The Negro in . . ." education, sports, entertainment, science, industry, and national affairs.[12] Using footage from *All-American News* as well as original interviews and scenes, the series aimed to highlight black achievement in various areas of American life. Having secured sponsorship for the films, Glucksman also made prints available at low cost to "interested social and fraternal organizations, trade unions, colleges and educational groups."[13] By reaching a wider audience—in particular one that included white Americans—Barnett and Glucksman hoped that the series might extend *All-American*'s ability to educate viewers about African American achievements.

The power and potential of the newsreel to educate viewers was an integral part of *All-American*'s appeal from the outset. The African American press praised the new offering and expressed hope that the series would help build black morale during the war effort while demonstrating to the rest of the country the contributions already being made by African Americans. Somewhat hyperbolically, a writer for the Scott Newspaper Syndicate called it "probably the most significant motion picture news item for negroes since the invention of the motion picture camera,"[14] while Ted Watson, a columnist for the *Atlanta Daily World*, articulated the high expectations placed upon *All-American News* in his review of the first edition:

> In this gigantic feature every colored American was justly portrayed, no smudge, nothing derogatory to the race; simply a resume of the news in which the Negro shows his real worth. It is the belief of this writer that the All-American Negro newsreel will acquaint the white race with the modern colored American, and if kept on a clean basis will tend to mold national unity.[15]

Watson's enthusiastic response reflects the largely negative way African Americans were portrayed in the Hollywood films of the era and the hope that more positive filmic representations of the race would help to combat racism in American society. It also reflects a faith in the visual potency of the newsreel; by making the African American community visible, the newsreel had the potential to shape as well as reflect the reality of "national unity."

All-American was not the first to link African American wartime morale to racial progress. Prompted by a letter to the editor from James G. Thompson of Wichita, Kansas, the *Pittsburgh Courier* introduced the notion of a "Double Victory"—or "Double V" for short—in February 1942. Adapting the "V is for Victory" campaign slogan, the *Courier* suggested that African Americans should rally to support the war effort while fighting for civil rights on the home front. Introduced, in part, to counter suggestions that the newspaper was unpatriotic due to its criticisms of Jim Crow society in general and a segregated military in particular, the slogan was enthusiastically embraced by its readership, African American personalities, and eventually other members of the black press. In an editorial celebrating the early success of the Double V campaign, the newspaper called on its readers to fight for democracy by waging "a two-pronged attack against our enslavers at home and those abroad who will enslave us. WE HAVE A STAKE IN THIS FIGHT . . . WE ARE AMERICANS, TOO!"[16] By offering visual evidence of the contributions African Americans were making to the war effort, *All-American* echoed these sympathies. As one reviewer wrote in the *Pittsburgh Courier*, "Now we can 'see' the news as we read it in *The Pittsburgh Courier* [and] other publications of the Negro Press . . . *[All-American News]* is another 'Double V' advancement!"[17] At a time when the NAACP and others explicitly linked motion pictures to the struggle for equal rights and respect for the black community, *All-American* seemed to offer both a powerful educational tool as well as a way to boost black morale. Despite the early optimism about *All-American*'s potential to educate white audiences, however, its limited viewership outside the African American community would lead some to criticize the series and question its role in achieving the Double V.

In addition to its role in the wartime struggle for recognition, *All-American*'s pedagogical address must also be seen in light of the general rhetoric of racial uplift. In the 1940s, the notion of racial uplift already had a long history in the political discourse of the African American community, and it encompassed a complex set of popular and intellectual meanings as charted by historians like Edward Wheeler, Evelyn Brooks Higginbotham, and Kevin Gaines.[18] Although popular calls for racial uplift could be deployed in more or less democratic appeals for economic, political, and even spiritual betterment, these authors detail how middle-class African Americans and others took up the discourses of temperance, chastity, and social purity as a means to achieve a measure of social mobility and respect. Gaines points out that these discourses often had as much to do with class as they did race. For the black middle classes, respectability and individual achievement refuted notions of innate racial inferiority in favor of a philosophy of cultural difference and social evolution. Nevertheless, as black members of the middle class stressed the adoption of bourgeois mores as key to racial uplift, they "implicitly faulted African Americans for their lowly status, echoing judgmental dominant characterizations of 'the Negro problem.'"[19] As we shall see, however, *All-American*'s pedagogical address blurred the lines between the social struggle for racial progress and the bourgeois values of self-help and respectability.

Although *All-American* was a part of these wartime debates over racial uplift and the Double V, the visual potency of the newsreel form made the series unusual. What Higginbotham calls the "politics of respectability" was deeply invested in countering racist stereotypes of African Americans.[20] For *All-American* and others, the politics of vision, visibility, and appearance were key to achieving this goal. *All-American*'s newsreel representations fell within the traditions of what Allyson Nadia Field calls "uplift cinema." They "were not direct assaults on racism and social inequities. Rather, they were indirect, perhaps even coded, attacks on inequalities through the representation of black respectability, promise, and advancement, along with images to counter the prevalent on-screen racism."[21] Given its ostensibly documentary authority, the newsreel was uniquely placed to counter negative images of African Americans in the media. At times, *All-American* would explicitly instruct its audience in the importance of appearance and good conduct. More often, by showing the patriotic actions of both prominent and "regular" black Americans, the newsreel simply displayed a model for respectability while urging its viewers to do their part for the war effort. As important as these efforts to encourage patriotism were, many hoped that *All-American* would provide something more than a boost to black morale. They hoped that the newsreel would not only help promote wartime contributions but ensure that the black community was *seen* to be making these contributions. As we shall see, the visibility of the African American war effort became a key axis along which the struggle for Double Victory was fought.

A Jim Crow Cinema

American cinema was a segregated world in 1942. African Americans were marginalized behind the camera, on screen, and in movie theater audiences. But segregation did not prevent African Americans from being eager participants in the production and consumption of American films.

Despite their marginalization in Hollywood, blacks were involved in almost every aspect of the motion picture industry: as consumers of and performers in mainstream film and, in the "race movie" business, as writers, directors, cinematographers, and producers as well. Indeed, at the outset of World War II, the relationship between the movies and the black community had become an important economic, social, and political issue. Academic publications like the *Journal of Negro Education* repeatedly discussed the educational uses of motion pictures as well as the effects of movies on race relations and black morale.[22] African Americans were also a growing market for moviemakers, as independent "race movie" producers capitalized on the segregation of movie theaters to find a willing, if not always eager, audience. But by the early 1940s, a growing number of African Americans became dissatisfied with race movies, and groups like the NAACP pushed for better roles for black actors in mainstream Hollywood films. This push branded race movies as Jim Crow films. Instead of supporting films with all-black casts, the NAACP looked for (and in some cases won) support in Hollywood and Washington for improving the representation of blacks in mainstream film. New Deal liberalism and the wartime push for national solidarity finally made racial integration on screen a possibility. But even while the war paved the way for better roles for black actors, the reality of war—on screen and off—remained segregated. The U.S. military was not officially integrated until 1948, and newsreels produced by Hollywood's Big Five all but ignored the contributions of black regiments and of African Americans on the home front. Just as it had created the conditions for the race moviemakers of the 1930s, segregation provided the possibility and the demand for an all-black newsreel in the 1940s. The fact of segregation gave *All-American* both a captive audience and plenty of racially homogenous footage. Thus, even while Hollywood fiction film moved toward a degree of racial integration and the representation of blacks on screen improved, the reality of the war for African Americans—filmic and otherwise—remained a Jim Crow affair.

When *All-American* made its debut, it found a home in the legally segregated theaters of the South and the culturally and geographically segregated black neighborhood cinemas of the North. Large centers in the North and South supported these "negro theatres," and, as black

Americans migrated from the rural South to these cities, their numbers grew rapidly.[23] According to the *Motion Picture Herald*, the number of black movie houses in the United States rose from 232 in 1937 to 430 in 1942 and then to 684 in 1947.[24] As a result, in major urban centers, African Americans often enjoyed a relatively wide selection of movie houses. For example, according to the *Negro Handbook 1944*, by that year, thirteen of the sixty-five cinemas in Washington, D.C., were "Negro theatres."[25] But despite the growing number of all-black cinemas, black Americans remained underserved—one contemporary estimate put the numbers of black cinemas at one for every 21,000 people.[26] Most African Americans in 1942 still watched movies from the balconies of white theaters. By law in the South and by custom in the North, black moviegoers were relegated to the cramped quarters of the "peanut galleries," where patrons would suffer the heat, few if any refreshments were available, and sometimes only a restricted view of the screen itself was possible. When they weren't segregated spatially—and sometimes even when they were—many southern theaters chose to segregate their audiences by time. Midnight screenings for black audiences became common in the 1930s and 1940s.[27] These late-night offerings added to the so-called "race circuit" for black-cast films and would have provided another outlet for Glucksman's newsreels.

The production of films for black audiences had always been a precarious business proposition. While black independent producers had found some success in the silent era, they were all but wiped out by the Depression and the rising cost of moviemaking brought on by the advent of the "talkies." Even the most accomplished of these producers, Oscar Micheaux, filed for bankruptcy in 1928. Despite the relative popularity of movies such as *The Brute* (1920) and *Body and Soul* (1925)—featuring Paul Robeson in his screen debut—Micheaux could not overcome the marginal nature of the enterprise. The limited number of theaters willing to show black productions, the ad hoc distribution networks needed to reach them, and the lower ticket prices they charged made it impossible for Micheaux's production company to stay afloat.

The void left by the collapse of the black independents was quickly filled by a host of white entrepreneurs seeking to capitalize on the African American market. Indeed, Micheaux continued to make films in the 1930s and 1940s, but did so with the financial backing of so-called white angels.[28] These independent producers, like Jed Buell, Alfred J. Sack, Leo and Harry Popkin, and Bert and Jack Goldberg, made low-budget films throughout the 1930s. These films usually stuck to conventional Hollywood genres but distinguished themselves by exclusively using black actors. Westerns, like Jed Buells's *Harlem Rides the Range* (1938) and *Bronze Buckeroo* (1938), and musical detective flicks, like the Goldbergs' *Mystery in Swing* (1938), were typical titles designed to appeal to black audiences. But while these films offered much needed work to black actors, as well as provided audiences a chance to see people like themselves represented on screen, they were far from a "black cinema" and did little to confront racism and inequality. In fact, these films were often curiously devoid of racial content. As historian of black film Thomas Cripps points out, "to 'inject race' would have spoiled the premise of all-black casts, caused 'trouble' in southern markets, and closed off 'extra juice' from white patrons."[29] Instead, the films took place in surreal all-black worlds where everyone, from the lowest criminal to the judge who convicted him, was black.

Hollywood did make some efforts to cater to African American audiences—and to capitalize on the late-1920s vogue for all things black—with crossover films such as Fox's *Hearts in Dixie* (1929) and MGM's all-black musical *Hallelujah!* (1929). But disappointing box office results discouraged any further such forays, and for the most part African Americans in Hollywood were limited to the peripheral roles of porters and maids. This is not to say that there were not some black actors who found success in Hollywood. Actors like Clarence Muse and Hattie McDaniels, who won an Academy Award for her role in *Gone With the Wind,* made careers of playing the stereotyped roles that Hollywood reserved for African Americans. But others, like Paul Robeson, were unwilling to conform to the ideal of the "Hollywood Negro." During the 1930s, Robeson mostly preformed in European film productions, and in 1942, after returning to Hollywood to play a minister in *The Tales of Manhattan,* he was so disgusted with the American film industry that he vowed never to work in the town again. "I thought I could change the picture as we went along," Robeson explained to reporters. "And I made some headway. But in the end it turned out to be the same old thing: the Negro solving his problem by singing his way to glory. This is very offensive to my people.

It makes the Negro childlike and innocent and it is the old plantation tradition."[30]

But as war spread from Europe to the Pacific, attitudes in and about Hollywood began to change. The rhetoric of war called on Americans to unite and fight for democracy. Government propaganda denounced Hitler's notions of racial superiority as abhorrent and, in doing so, brought the United States' own racial problems into focus. The Double Victory campaign of the *Pittsburgh Courier* and similar arguments seized on official pronouncements against fascism and sought to apply them to the situation of African Americans in the United States. In addition to the federal government, Hollywood and the motion picture industry became prime targets for these campaigns as groups like the NAACP pushed for more and better representation for African Americans on film.[31]

For the push for Double Victory to succeed, it would be crucial to maintain black morale while seeking to change white perceptions of the race. Motion pictures would play an important role in these efforts. In a 1944 article, "Educational Programs for the Improvement of Race Relations," L. D. Reddick argued that organizations dedicated to the improvement of relations between the races would fail if they did not "realize the decisive influence of [the] agencies of mass communication in determining public attitudes."[32] Reddick, a researcher at the New York Public Library, reported that out of one hundred "important films shown in the United States which have included Negro themes or Negro characters of more than passing significance . . . 75 of them must be classified as anti-Negro, 13 as neutral—with equally favorable and unfavorable scenes—and only 12 as definitely pro-Negro."[33] He called on the black community to pressure Hollywood and the U.S. government to improve the kinds of roles for African Americans on screen. Despite Reddick's dismal statistics, there did seem to be some cause for optimism. According to a poll published in the *Negro Digest* in 1943, a majority of white Americans rejected the stereotyped Hollywood portrayal of Negroes. Some 93 percent of blacks and 53 percent of whites responded negatively when asked the question, "Is Hollywood fair to Negroes in its films?"[34]

The NAACP attempted to use this apparent change in attitude and the government's own wartime rhetoric to pressure Hollywood into better representing African Americans on screen. In 1942, the organization held its annual meeting in Los Angeles, and then executive secretary Walter White spoke at a special luncheon hosted by Walter Wagner and Darryl F. Zanuck of Twentieth Century Fox and attended by over seventy well-placed representatives of the film industry. White told the gathering that African Americans did not want to be treated as "superhuman heroes" but simply as normal human beings. White said the "restriction of Negroes to roles with rolling eyes, chattering teeth, always scared of ghosts, or to portrayals of none-too bright servants perpetuates a stereotype which is doing the Negro infinite harm" and contributing to "low morale."[35] In a second trip to California the following year, White explicitly tied the country's war aims to film portrayals of African Americans:

> If we liberate our own minds of half-truths and misconceptions and use our media to build a world free of racial and religious hatred, a world free of vicious and fictitious notions of the superiority of one race over another, a world free of imperialism and colonialism, we can then help immeasurably to insure a durable peace.[36]

By linking race harmony on screen to victory in the world war, the NAACP and others implicitly rejected all-black race movies in favor of a more tolerant Hollywood. The low production values and limited distribution of race movies meant that they would never have the universal power of Hollywood fare. More importantly, the films, with their all-black casts, did not depict the integrated United States of American propaganda. In a *Journal of Negro Education* article detailing how the federal government should boost African American morale during the war, Mary Morton rejected the creation of "all-Negro films" in favor of integrated motion pictures. "Negroes must be portrayed as self-respecting citizens integrated into a cross-section of American life," she argued. "Their likeness to other Americans—not their real or imagined differences—must be emphasized if harmful stereotypes of long standing are to be destroyed."[37] For Morton and White, motion pictures represented not an opportunity for black cultural expression but a medium through which the rest of the United States could come to appreciate and acknowledge the place of African Americans in the nation. As Thomas Cripps has pointed out, race movies had become an anachronism amid the push for an integrated cinema: "After all, how could a segregated movie serve the cause of a war that slowly took on among its aims the self-determination of all peoples and the integration of the blacks into the fabric of American life?"[38] But while the NAACP and others pushed for integration in the fictional films of Hollywood, similar pressure could not be so easily applied to the production of nonfiction motion pictures.

The fact that much of the United States' war effort remained segregated made it difficult for factual films to represent an integrated war effort. While fictional scenarios could be imagined where black and white Americans found themselves together, the armed forces remained segregated until 1948, and much of American society was similarly divided. As Thomas Doherty points out, most of the wartime movies that showed blacks and whites interacting on screen did so in exotic locales far removed from the realities of segregation at home: "*Casablanca, Bataan, Sahara*—the titles bespeak the geographical displacement of a national dilemma too close to home to address on native soil."[39] Unable to manufacture integrated settings, newsreels and other documentary films were left to cover the segregated reality of war. The Department of Defense and the Office of War Information (OWI) did produce a few documentaries showing black and white Americans working together, but these could only go so far. OWI films such as *Manpower* and *Colleges at War* featured only token mention of the role of the black community in the war effort, while movies focusing on the contributions of African Americans, like *The Negro Soldier* and *Negro Colleges in War Time,* had virtually all-black casts, making them poor models of integration and limiting their commercial distribution to white audiences.[40]

Meanwhile, mainstream newsreels simply ignored African Americans. The Hollywood Writers' War Board pointed out in 1944 that, out of the previous year's newsreels, they had found only three items featuring African American troops: "one showing a Negro soldier guarding a hen coop, another concerning a jitterbug contest in Australia. Only the third was of a serious nature, depicting the 99th Pursuit Squadron."[41] There was considerable, ongoing pressure on newsreels to exclude material relating to the African American war effort from their releases. Exhibitors and municipal censors in the South routinely cut out material from fiction and nonfiction films showing blacks in situations of "social equality" with whites. According to *Variety,* "local censors [would] eliminate such scenes, regardless of the effect on the artistic side or the continuity of the film."[42] Such editing not only made the onscreen product "patched up" and "confusing" but also made the print unusable for further circulation. With only eight to ten minutes per newsreel, the effects of censorship could often be felt more dramatically than in a feature-length drama. It is perhaps not surprising, then, that Hollywood newsreel producers were unwilling to risk the artistic and economic damage of carrying African American material.

Given the exclusion of African American subjects from mainstream newsreels, demand remained for nonfiction race movies, and directors had some social, cultural, and economic space with which to operate. The war had created a great appetite for news films throughout the country, and the race circuit was no different. In addition to Glucksman, several other race movie producers began to invest in nonfiction films targeted at the African American market. In October 1942, Ted Toddy, President of Toddy Pictures and a partner in the Dixie National Pictures Company, announced plans for a *Negro Newsreel of Victory* that would "go down in history as one of the most effective means of enlightening the public of today and posterity of the major and minor roles played by the Negro during these perilous times."[43] The series never materialized, but Toddy did produce *Fighting Americans,* a "documentary showing scenes of air cadet activities at Tuskegee Army Air Field in Alabama and black WACs at Fort Devens in Massachusetts."[44] The Goldberg brothers also got in on the act, producing a documentary, called *We've Come a Long, Long Way,* about Negro contributions to the United States' various wars. The film, narrated by the black preacher Elder Solomon Lightfoot Micheaux was billed to African American audiences as a "picture to make you proud, to make you cheer."[45]

But the NAACP and most of the black press were not cheering. When *We've Come a Long, Long Way* was released in 1944, it was called "disgusting and insulting." A member of the NAACP who saw the film told the *Chicago Defender* that the film was poorly made, using old documentary and newsreel footage, "and that the main message of the film seemed to be a warning to American Negroes that they are much better off now than they would be under Hitler."[46] This attitude reflected the growing hostility toward race movies and the segregated United States they implicitly endorsed. This hostility was made worse by the release of *We've Come a Long, Long Way* coinciding with the release of the OWI film *The Negro Soldier.* Produced by the famous Hollywood producer Frank Capra, *The Negro Soldier* also dealt with the contributions black Americans had made to the United States' armed forces throughout history (although, significantly, it did not mention black participation in the Civil War). And while the government film was not exactly integrated—it featured an all-black cast—its high quality, professionalism, and OWI origins held out the possibility of it being shown to white audiences, and its message was one of progress, not satisfaction with the status quo. Poet Langston Hughes went so far as to call the film "the most remarkable Negro film ever flashed on an American screen,"[47] and the black press urged readers to lobby their local theaters to show the film despite its unconventional forty-minute run time. The praise heaped on *The Negro Soldier* is perhaps testament to the rarity, in 1944, of a high-quality documentary dealing sympathetically with black issues. Although there were plenty of reasons for this paucity, race movies like *All-American News* found it difficult to escape the suggestion that they did little more than profit from the exclusion of African American subjects from mainstream movies.

All-American was particularly susceptible to such charges, given its close relationship with the Office of War Information. Along with the Big Five studio newsreel companies, the OWI gave *All-American* full access to the Army's Signal Corps footage of the war effort. This footage was crucial for *All-American.* Beyond providing engaging and high-quality pictures, the Signal Corps films allowed the newsreel to cover international and war stories with an African American angle on the company's limited budget. It is unlikely *All-American* would have been able to sustain itself in the precarious motion picture industry without the support it received from the OWI. But almost from the outset, some questioned *All-American*'s relationship with the OWI. Truman K. Gibson Jr., Assistant Civilian Aide to the Secretary of War and a member of Roosevelt's so-called "black cabinet," wrote a letter to Claude Barnett expressing his concern about *All-American*'s use of the Signal Corps footage. He felt that *All-American*'s access to material dealing with African American subjects was exclusive and was thus preventing footage from being used by the other newsreels. "You will see," he wrote to Barnett, "the maliciousness of the *All-American* when you realize that it means a total exclusion of Negro material to white audiences."[48] Gibson attributed this situation to the influence of Milton Starr, a wealthy white businessman who also wrote an influential report on "Negro Morale" for the OWI.[49] Shortly after this letter, Harry McAlpin of the *Chicago Defender* repeated these allegations, citing a source in the War Department:

> The All-American News Reel, which is all-Negro in its news subjects and all-white in its management and advice, has been admitted to the major newsreel pool through the efforts of Milton Starr, millionaire, movie-chain owner and $1-a-year consultant on Negro affairs to the Office of War Information.
>
> The membership of the All-American News Reel in the major pool includes an arrangement whereby all Negro news subjects are the exclusive prerogative of All-American. The other major newsreel companies are forbidden by the arrangement to touch any such subjects.[50]

For McAlpin, like Gibson, the involvement of Starr, someone involved in and profiting from the Jim Crow motion picture industry, suggested that *All-American* and the OWI were conspiring to ensure newsreel coverage of the war remained segregated.

The OWI denied the existence of any exclusivity deal, and it seems unlikely that a formal policy would have been necessary given the reluctance of the major newsreel companies to upset their southern exhibitors.[51] Nevertheless, Claude Barnett felt the need to defend *All-American* against charges of Jim Crowism in an article in the *Journal of Negro Education*. Barnett called the response from "colored theatre-goers . . . enthusiastic" and argued that the newsreel provided an important service to African American audiences by helping to improve black morale. Moreover, he suggested that the reluctance of the mainstream newsreels had nothing to do with *All-American*:

> opponents [of All-American] contend that owners of the newsreel have conspired to keep Negro news pictures out of the general reels, and call it a Jim Crow opiate for the colored public. The facts are that the general reels seldom, if ever, show pictures of Negroes

> unless they are "funny." This again shows deference to the South for white audiences in that section will not countenance news shots of Negroes unless they are derogatory. General reels that have been sent there have returned mutilated with Negro sequences clipped by individual operators, thus causing a financial loss to the newsreel company.[52]

Despite Barnett's denials, worries over the relationship between the OWI and *All-American* remained, reflecting the growing feeling that race movies, including *All-American,* were not serving the best interests of the African American community.

In January of 1944, representations of the African American war effort in newsreels became headline news in the black press. Front-page stories in *Atlanta Daily World* and *New York Amsterdam News* accused the government and Hollywood of a "blackout" and of "cutting" scenes of African American soldiers from the major newsreels.[53] Specifically, the press charged the major newsreel companies with deliberately omitting scenes showing President Roosevelt reviewing black troops in his recent trip overseas. The omission was discovered after these scenes subsequently appeared in *All-American News.* According to the *New York Amsterdam News,* in their zeal to delete the African American troops, the newsreels "sacrificed the best shot of the president and General Eisenhower chatting in the jeep, merely because a Negro furnished the background."[54] The NAACP and others vigorously protested this apparently Jim Crow policy. In a letter to the major studios the organization wrote:

> Our people point out that there are about 700,000 American Negroes in various branches of the armed services. They feel that the failure to include them in newsreels places them at a disadvantage in the eyes of their 122,000,000 fellow Americans and will contribute to the idea that they have not done their share to win the victory.
>
> In our opinion this is a serious blow at the morale of Negro Americans and justifies them in feeling that their sacrifices are being disparaged, discounted, and concealed.[55]

Meanwhile, the editors of *Crisis* saw a deliberate "scheme" designed to denigrate the contribution of African Americans to the war effort.

> All this means that the movie going public, estimated at more than 75 million people weekly, sees no films of Negro soldiers, but does see many films of white soldiers. Inevitably white people get the impression Negroes are doing little if anything to win the victory.
>
> Negroes do not deserve this treatment of their efforts. They are buying bonds, working in war plants, sacrificing, fighting and dying along with other Americans. Their wounded soldiers are in Army and Navy hospitals here and abroad. This scheme to keep from white America the news that the minority is doing its part in the war is a dastardly trick, as mean as any perpetuated against the race.[56]

These protests show how critical the NAACP and others viewed visibility to achieving the goals of the Double V campaign. How could the war effort be used to push for civil rights gains if African American sacrifices were being concealed from the eyes of the American public?

Both major studio newsreel companies and the War Department denied there was any policy excluding African Americans from their films. Walton Ament, editor at *Pathé News,* said that the newsreel pool did not discriminate against black soldiers. He told the press that there was "no effort made along the line by the War Department or the newsreel cutters to make deletions except those based on pure pictorial judgment." He added that, "since the percentage of Negroes in the armed forces is comparatively small no specific effort is made to show Jews, Poles, Negroes and other racial groups."[57] Of course, Jewish and Polish soldiers were not forced to serve in segregated units, and Jewish and Polish moviegoers did not have to sit in the peanut gallery of their local theater. Like Ament, Major General A. D. Surles of the War Department denied any policy restricting the distribution of African American subjects, insisting that the department provided all companies with the same footage each week. In a letter responding to the concerns of the NAACP, Surles wrote: "Beyond including, wherever available, footage which shows Negro troops in action, the War Department can exercise no supervision over the editorial choices of the newsreel companies."[58]

Despite these denials, this episode once again raised the question of *All-American*'s complicity in keeping newsreels segregated. The NAACP's assistant secretary, Roy Wilkins, pointed out that, while *All-American* provided a valuable service, it could not achieve the proper recognition of African Americans in white society. "Of course," said Wilkins, "it is beneficial for Negroes who go to all-colored houses to see pictures of their men, but it is just as necessary that white Americans also see pictures of our fighting men."[59] In his "Watchtower" column for the *New York Amsterdam News,* Wilkins argued that any benefit *All-American* offered in maintaining African American morale and encouraging further contributions to the war effort was overshadowed if it prevented white Americans from seeing these contributions:

> If these Americans do not know the truth, Negroes will have just that much harder time after the war in holding their places and winning new ground as citizens . . . If All-American Newsreel is making profits at the expense of the future status of Negroes as Americans, then All-American should be forced out of business.[60]

For Wilkins and the NAACP, white acknowledgment of African American sacrifices was crucial to the struggle for equality. The motion picture industry, and the newsreel in particular, could play a key role in ensuring this visibility, but not if the news itself was segregated.

All-American was not forced out of business, but following the public outcry, mainstream newsreels made some concessions to placate their critics. A story on the all-black 99th Pursuit Squadron appeared in RKO-Pathé's newsreel and Paramount carried shots of Negro members of the Women's Auxiliary Corps parading on Staten Island. This was seen as a sign of progress for the NAACP and the black press that had pushed the issue. New York's left-wing *People's Voice* called the Pathé item "a major victory in the battle waged by the Negro for fair and representative treatment of the Negro soldier's contribution to the war."[61] But the victory was fleeting. Mainstream newsreels did not dramatically change the way they covered the war, and there remained a place for an all-black newsreel in the segregated world of American motion pictures.

Although the NAACP and others grew increasingly hostile toward *All-American* and its race movie cousins, the fact remained that the newsreel offered African American audiences a chance to see footage they would not see anywhere else. While mainstream newsreels portrayed the war as a near lily-white affair, *All-American* offered its viewers a very different image of war's reality. Even if *All-American News* failed to reach white Americans, its supporters believed the series could be a strong instrument of visual education for its black audience. Moreover, despite being circumscribed by the system within which it operated, the newsreel provided an important, if conflicted and contested, venue for the message of racial uplift. As we shall see, *All-American*'s pedagogical address worked to disrupt as well as confirm the racial status quo. For all its faults, the segregated nature of *All-American News* meant that it represented a reality that the integrationist films supported by the NAACP elided. In this way, its point of view was radically different from anything else available to audiences, black or white. *All-American* may have been a Jim Crow company offering a Jim Crow product for exhibition in Jim Crow cinemas, but for the vast majority of African Americans in the 1940s, Jim Crow was their reality.

All-American's Pedagogical Address

All-American announced its pedagogical intent right from its opening title sequence. The sequence featured a fanfare of horns playing a march, accompanied by the company's logo—an eye with a globe as its pupil. The globe dissolved to reveal the stars and stripes, followed by a succession of scenes typical of the series, including various African American military personnel on parade and several sports scenes featuring black athletes (Figure 18). The music, globe, and shots of marching and sporting events were all typical features of the major studio newsreels in the United States in the 1930s and 1940s, but a voiceover declaring, "*All-American News* brings you our people's contribution to America and freedom," along with the prominent display of black faces, clearly marked the newsreel's difference. The slogan directly addressed the spectator and pointed to the film's efforts to represent the African American community as patriotic and industrious. These representations were deployed as both evidence of accomplishment and as instructive examples for its audience. The visual nature of the didactic elements to come was underlined by the use of the eye motif. The superimposition of footage within that eye further highlighted how the visual qualities of the newsreel itself were crucial to the pedagogical aims of *All-American*. Trajectories of looking literally framed the content of the film. By taking up the newsreel's visual rhetoric

Figure 18. *All-American News* opening sequence. Still from *All-American News,* 123 (1945).

of display and evidence, *All-American* hoped to promote race pride and offer a model for behavior and self-improvement to its African American audience while ostensibly providing white viewers with evidence of the black community's participation in the war effort. But, as we shall see, the politics of visibility were by no means straightforward. In the context of the Jim Crow United States, the struggle for racial uplift was as much about maintaining appearances as it was about white recognition. *All-American*'s pedagogical mode—which combined the visual rhetoric of the newsreel with a unique deployment of the direct address—reveals a company and a community negotiating the complex and sometimes contradictory politics of race and visibility during World War II.

The slogan in *All-American*'s title sequence—with its use of the second-person pronoun and its emphasis on the word "our"—defined the newsreel's distinctive point of view. By referring to "our people's contribution to America and freedom," *All-American* clearly identified itself with the black community. In doing so, the slogan implied the newsreel would provide a corrective to its mainstream cousins and framed the stories to come as instructional as well as informational. *All-American*'s use of the second person "you" was more equivocal. The second-person address was not unique to *All-American,* but its deployment by the newsreel took on added resonance given its segregated audience. While mainstream newsreels used direct address as a way to draw the audience in and collapse the distance between the action on screen and the audience in the theater, *All-American*'s use of the second person also posed an important question in the context the newsreel's pedagogical mode: to whom was the newsreel's instruction directed? As we have seen, despite the efforts of Glucksman and Barnett, *All-American*'s audience was overwhelmingly African American. Nevertheless, the title sequence was ambiguous. The phrasing, "bringing you our people's contribution to America and freedom," left open the possibility that *All-American* also aimed to address a white American spectator. After all, the almost complete absence of black faces from the major studio newsreels made the notion of "bringing" the news of the African American war effort to white audiences an important element of the Double Victory campaign. Indeed, it was *All-American*'s potential to do just this that garnered the newsreel many of its early positive reviews from the black press. So, while some of the newsreel's items explicitly addressed an African American audience, the newsreel's slogan worked both ways. This ambiguity allowed *All-American* to identify its pedagogical mode with the politics of visibility as well as the philosophy of racial uplift, allowing audiences to feel as though they were participating in both aspects of the Double Victory—boosting black morale and working toward greater respect from white America.

The potential doubleness of the second-person address in *All-American*'s title sequence draws attention to the equally undetermined identity of the disembodied eye that frames the footage of these "contributions to America and freedom." Whose eye was this? No doubt, it implicitly belonged to the newsreel's black audience, who was able to witness the accomplishments of the race on screen for the first time. But it might also be understood as standing in for the critical eye of white America. In this sense, the eye recalls the state of African American self-surveillance that W. E. B. Du Bois famously described as double-consciousness. In *The Souls of Black Folk,* Du Bois refers to that "sense of always looking at one's self through the eyes of others, of measuring one's soul by the tape of a world that looks on in amused contempt and pity."[62] This visual metaphor, describing the conflicted nature of African American identity at the turn of the century, was echoed in *All-American*'s pedagogical address. While its evidence of achievement and patriotism could inspire race pride, the newsreel's examples carried with them an implicit, and sometimes explicit, exhortation to its African American audience to understand the importance of maintaining appearances. In this context, the newsreel's cameras provided a lens for African Americans to see themselves through the eyes of white America. Jane Gaines has pointed out in her work on the race movies of the 1920s and 1930s that Du Bois's analysis takes on new meaning when thinking about race in the context of black film spectatorship. "Suddenly," she writes, "one of the foundational statements in race theory appears as film theory, addressing the question of the execution of power through the trajectory of the eye."[63] But, while Gaines argues that race movies offered black audiences a chance to look at themselves through something other than the "distorted lens" of white America, *All-American*'s pedagogical address could not fully escape the dilemma described by Du Bois. Even as the newsreel sought to inspire race pride and overcome the distortions of mainstream representations of African Americans, it reinscribed the self-surveillance logic of double-consciousness.

All-American's pedagogy was most evident when the newsreel addressed the viewer directly and offered explicit instruction. While mainstream newsreels frequently used the second person in their voiceover commentary, it was rare that someone shown on screen employed such a direct address—when it did occur, it was usually in the form of a speech by a public figure. In the films of *All-American,* however, officials, instructors, and authority figures regularly spoke straight to the camera and the viewing audience. Instruction on filing proper tax returns, information on the benefits available through the Veteran's Administration, and repeated exhortations to maintain good conduct were among the straightforwardly didactic messages to be found in *All-American News.*

In 1944 and 1945, good conduct was a frequent feature of *All-American*'s pedagogy. The newsreel carried several stories on the importance of proper etiquette and courtesy, and, in 1944, it joined with the *Pittsburgh Courier* to promote the newspaper's "Better Conduct crusade."[64]

The campaign featured prominent citizens such as Bishop John A. Gregg, who lectured *All-American*'s audience on the value of manners and refinement, as well as the perils of "vulgarity," including "loud talk"[65] that might make others uncomfortable. These lessons in good conduct neatly encapsulated the black middle-class philosophy of racial uplift and the politics of respectability. According to Evelyn Brooks Higginbotham, in order to counter racist stereotypes, "respectability demanded that every individual in the black community assume responsibility for behavioral self-regulation and self-improvement along moral, educational, and economic lines."[66] A vivid example of this notion of self-regulation came in issue 123 of the *All-American News,* when Dorothy Rogers and the teenagers of Parkway Community Center modeled good conduct for the newsreel cameras (Figure 19).[67] Speaking directly to the audience, Rogers introduced the item by saying, "We are so often judged by the little things in life. If we stop to think we realize that it is as easy, often easier, to do things the right way instead of the wrong way." What followed was a series of vignettes illustrating proper manners as well as what not to do in social situations. After showing a pair of teenagers dancing sloppily—he with his hat on and she chewing gum demonstratively—the camera turned to a young man politely asking his date to dance and leading her to the dance floor. Rogers's accompanying commentary explicitly linked self-respect to respectability. She told the audience, "this young couple having respect for themselves and for each other command like respect from everyone," adding, "now don't you suppose they're having a good time, and yet they're not offensive to good taste." Although Rogers did not reference white Americans as those who might judge the black teenagers on screen (as well as those in the newsreel audience), she didn't have to. Implicit in the notions of good conduct presented in these frankly didactic segments was the assumption that, for the race as well as for individual African Americans, self-respect and respectability went hand in hand. In this context, how whites perceived African Americans became crucially important. Indeed, Rogers concluded the item by saying, "this has been a good chance to see ourselves as others see us. To which group do you belong? Let's make good conduct a habit, a good habit from now on." Rogers's invitation to viewers to "see ourselves as others see us" implicitly aligned the gaze of the camera with the gaze of white

Figure 19. "This has been a good chance to see ourselves as others see us." Dorothy Rogers addresses the audience directly. Still from *All-American News*, 123 (1945).

America. As a visual medium, *All-American News* could counter racist stereotypes by celebrating black achievement, but it also offered a lens through which African Americans could look at themselves. In doing so, it vividly recalled the self-surveillance raised by Du Bois in his definition of double-consciousness. If racial uplift was premised on changing white perceptions of the race, the didacticism of the good conduct campaigns put the onus on individual black Americans to do so by adopting bourgeois mores. In cases like this one, the politics of respectability and the newsreel's pedagogical address appear to have reinforced rather than to have countered what Jane Gaines described as the "execution of power through the trajectory of the eye."

In addition to these straightforwardly didactic examples of direct address, *All-American*'s pedagogical mode was further evident throughout the newsreel's celebrations of black achievement. These stories, which comprised the vast majority of the reel's content, drew on two fundamental aspects of the newsreel's visual rhetoric: display and evidence.

Although these elements were common in mainstream newsreels, *All-American* put these rhetorical devices to very different uses.

Nowhere was the rhetoric of display more marked than in *All-American*'s representations of celebrity. The celebration of extraordinary achievement and the glorification of outstanding individuals were commonplace in newsreels of the 1930s and 1940s. From presidential inaugurations, sporting events, and the ubiquitous ticker tape parade, the newsreel honored celebrity achievement more than the achievements themselves. These media events—and their newsreel records—visually marked the distance between the heroic individual and the crowds that cheered them on while simultaneously collapsing that distance by offering audiences a close-up look at their heroes.

In contrast to these public scenes of adoration, *All-American News* focused its cameras on more quotidian—although, in the context of the politics of respectability, no less important—successes. Unlike the spectacular displays of celebrity, these displays were lessons in hard work and perseverance. Stories like those of Flournoy English, who was awarded $100 by the quartermaster for making an efficiency suggestion, or of two firemen promoted to the rank of lieutenant, "the first negro firemen thus promoted in New York City," celebrated the achievements of regular African Americans.[68] Stories like these gave *All-American* the supportive feel of a community newsletter and suggested that members of the audience might even be able to see themselves or people they knew celebrated on screen. A letter to the New Orleans poet Marcus Bruce Christian from his wife Ruth in Chicago illustrated this sense of community at work in the newsreel's audience. Ruth described seeing an old friend, Dr. Buggs, in an issue of *All-American News.* Buggs was apparently "the only Negro at Wayne University."[69] Rather than stress the differences between the audience and the personality in the news, these stories implicitly, and sometimes explicitly, stressed their sameness. Even those African American celebrities who might command public shows of admiration—such as Joe Louis—were typically shown in private settings. Louis, for example, was shown with his daughter as she demonstrated her abilities on the piano. Stories like this one humanized black celebrities while reflecting the pride many African Americans felt in the achievements of their race brethren. Charles Wilson's voiceover commentary expressed this sense of pride: "The baby is mighty proud of her daddy, and aren't we all?"[70] While mainstream newsreels often displayed celebrity with the effect of marking the distance between the outstanding individual and the audience, stories like this one portrayed African American celebrities as regular people.[71] As such, they were models of racial uplift as well as race pride. The achievements of Joe Louis were, like those of Flournoy English, exemplary and implicitly pedagogical—for *All-American,* achievement was something to emulate, not simply contemplate.

All-American's stories of achievement reflected the philosophy of racial uplift—that through hard work and dedication, individual African Americans could overcome many of the obstacles that American society put in their path. Unlike the civil rights discourse promoted by the NAACP and others, racial uplift placed the onus for change on African Americans. This philosophy of self-help was dramatically reinforced by stories in *All-American News* dedicated to African Americans who had overcome physical challenges. One such story profiled a blind man who had "beaten his handicap" to become an accomplished student.[72] Another told the story of Clifford Blount, a man born without arms who became a successful stenographer with his own letter writing business. *All-American* showed Blount brushing his teeth, shaving, and tying his tie with his feet, while the commentator remarked that he "did everything except ask for help" and called him a "shining example of courage."[73] When viewed in the context of *All-American News*' display of black achievement, it is difficult to read these stories of individual triumph in the face of huge impediments as anything but lessons in the politics of racial uplift. Overcoming racism and inequality was implicitly aligned with the challenges of physical disabilities. Instead of challenging the United States to remove the obstacles to equality, this alignment suggested that African Americans could individually overcome racism. By displaying the achievements of men like Blount, *All-American* offered its viewers a lesson in perseverance and courage, but, by failing to question a deeply unjust United States, the newsreels also gave a lesson in accommodation.

Closely tied to the newsreel's display of the spectacle of achievement was the medium's evidentiary power. In mainstream news film, the evidentiary power of the camera confirmed the news, but, more importantly, it also made it visible. While most Americans learned of major world events through radio or newspapers, the twice-weekly newsreel capitalized on its visual power to display the events of the day for its audience. The ability to "see-for-yourself" the pomp of the president's inaugural parade or the face of Lindbergh's kidnapper formed the basis of the newsreel's appeal—and the pleasures of looking that it offered. Indeed, as we have seen, this evidentiary function worked to signify the presence of the cameraman—and by extension the audience—in the field of news events. In doing so, it both established and reiterated the authority of the newsreel to represent the world and the prerogative of the audience to view it.

All-American put the evidentiary power of the newsreel to a slightly different purpose—to testify not only to the presence of the newsreel camera but also to the presence of African Americans in the field of news events. Given the almost complete absence of African American news and personalities in the mainstream newsreel, *All-American* provided evidence of the presence of black men and women in the war effort and beyond. This evidentiary function was crucial to the mission of the newsreel as it related to the politics of uplift—African American "contributions to America and freedom" needed to be recorded and exhibited in order for them to be used as evidence in the struggle for dignity and respect.

Nowhere was the importance of the evidentiary function of the newsreel more vivid than in *All-American*'s use of Signal Corps footage. These films attested to the presence of African Americans in the military. Such evidence proved critical to the fight for Double Victory. Not only did these films offer a morale-boosting lesson in patriotism for African American audiences, but the sacrifices they showed also may have helped bolster the argument for greater respect from white America. The films of the 92nd Infantry Division were particularly important in this task, as the "Fighting 92nd" was the only African American unit to see combat in Europe during World War II. *All-American* featured several items on the 92nd Division in 1944 and 1945. These stories stressed the presence of black troops in the field of battle (Figure 20). In one item covering the 92nd in Italy, *All-American*'s voiceover declared that the division was "making history" and that "whenever the Signal Corps [made] a movie of a battle, the 92nd [would] be in the middle of it."[74] Later stories further underscored the sacrifices of these troops. The newsreels showed the di-

Figure 20. U.S. Signal Corps footage of the 92nd Infantry Division in Italy provided visual evidence of the presence of African Americans in the military. Still from *All-American News*, 123 (1945).

vision advancing under fire in Italy, featuring images of shelling and of wounded African American soldiers.[75] And after victory in Europe had been won, an item showed the 92nd honoring its dead. A somber musical score accompanied these scenes, and *All-American*'s commentator noted that "tribute [was] paid to those who gave their lives for liberty."[76] These records of sacrifice made visible the contributions African Americans were making to the war effort—providing the dramatic evidence that ought to have been decisive in the struggle for Double Victory.

As we have seen, the use of Signal Corps films became a topic of heated debate in the black press in 1944 as critics began to view *All-American*'s apparently exclusive prerogative to show footage of black soldiers with suspicion. Indeed, given the way in which these images dramatically demonstrated the African American community's wartime sacrifice, it is easy to see why many lamented the fact that they were not reaching white audiences. Nevertheless, *All-American* proudly used the footage and made a habit of noting the source of those scenes in its intertitles. At times, the newsreel went further, explicitly noting the presence of Signal Corps photographers in its voiceover commentary. On one occasion, when the Signal Corps recorded scenes of General Clark hosting several newly promoted black officers, *All-American* noted that these were "scenes the Signal Corps was proud to record."[77] These references to the Signal Corps suggested that the army itself acknowledged the participation and sacrifices of African American soldiers, even if mainstream newsreels did not. *All-American*'s references to the Signal Corps' willingness to film African American soldiers argued that black audiences could be proud that their community's efforts were being witnessed by the United States government. Such pride points to the complicated relationship between pedagogy, visibility, and racial uplift at work in *All-American News.* The Signal Corps films may have been lessons in race pride and models for uplift, but these lessons placed heavy emphasis on the white gaze of the Signal Corps cameras. Once again, in its use of this footage, *All-American* seemed to reinforce as much as it countered that "sense of always looking at one's self through the eyes of others."

The politics of visibility—underscored by the newsreel's own visual rhetoric of display and evidence—was key to *All-American*'s pedagogical mode and its message of racial uplift. Black middle-class notions of respectability as represented in the newsreel were very much concerned with the crucial trajectories of power inherent in looking at race. Not only did the pedagogical address offer models of behavior and bolster race pride, it also addressed the "race problem" in visual terms. Yet there were clear limits to this strategy. The employment of display and evidentiary power could not contain the realities of Jim Crow. As African American audiences watched *All-American News* in segregated theaters, they must have been acutely aware of this reality. The company portrayed the segregated world of which it was a product. In the films of *All-American,* black troops, black celebrities, and black middle-class bond buyers appeared in a virtually monochromatic world. But while the newsreel showed the fact of segregation, it failed to probe that reality. Racism, poverty, and social and political marginalization were simply not discussed. Indeed, racism worked like a "structuring absence" in the films of *All-American News.* It—like the eye of the newsreel's opening credits—framed the achievements of African Americans.

Given the segregated nature of the United States military, stories about black soldiers inevitably confronted—if only obliquely—the question of racism in the United States. Despite their sacrifices, African American military personnel remained second-class citizens, and *All-American News* could not help but represent this fact. Thus, even stories that celebrated African American wartime sacrifice were often freighted with the unspoken irony of segregation and inequality. A vivid example of this appeared in a story about a celebrated athlete turned naval enlistee.[78] In this story, Buddy Young, star halfback for the University of Illinois football team, was shown in training at the Great Lakes Naval Base in Michigan. The commentary declared Young to be "on Uncle Sam's team now." The piece went on to show Young in lessons and at work on the base. But while the story ostensibly applauded Young for doing his patriotic duty and implicitly called on its audience to do the same, the story was tinged with irony. Despite Young's physical abilities, his talents were applied to apparently mundane tasks, such as laundry and delivering the mail (Figure 21). As the voiceover stated, "Those muscles Buddy developed throwing forward passes come in pretty useful now—sailor whites get plenty dirty" and "The general needs to send a message. Who gets the job? Buddy Young, the fastest guy on the base." Instead of showing African Americans in a heroic light, this story cast black naval enlistees—even those with exceptional talents—as the errand boys and laundry workers of a segregated military. It was scenes like these that pointed to the limits of *All-American News.* In the context of a Jim Crow military and a Jim Crow motion picture industry, *All-American* was left to try and put a positive spin on some uncomfortable facts.

Stories such as this one raise the question of how audiences responded to *All-American News.* It is hard to believe that audiences would have easily accepted the demotion of a star athlete to errand boy as a model of achievement and object of race pride. Historian of black film Thomas Cripps notes that, by the 1940s, race movie audiences were growing increasingly aware of the genre's failures and limits:

> Watching them accompanied a mood of perverse pleasure in calculatedly laughing in all the wrong places—a sort of black nationalist politics of inappropriate behavior. In this sense their laughter was indeed politically purposeful, a way of telling each other that they

Figure 21. "Those muscles Buddy developed throwing forward passes come in pretty useful now—sailor whites get plenty dirty." *All-American News,* 125 (1945).

> *knew* not only the absurdity of racism but the absurdity of making movies to accommodate it.[79]

Indeed, laughter became a critical way for *All-American*'s audiences to express their opinion on the newsreel. Although black audiences may have appreciated seeing their prominent citizens on screen and hearing about the achievements of regular African Americans, they resisted the series when they saw it as condescending. Audience members voiced their disapproval by laughing inappropriately or by refusing to laugh when the newsreels made their own attempts at comedy.

Letters to the editor in the black press indicate that some audience members were particularly uncomfortable with the comedy duo "Butterbeans and Susie," a broad vaudeville-type skit reminiscent of the minstrel tradition, which ran for some time at the end of the newsreel. Sergeant Melvin Williamson wrote to the *Chicago Defender* to call these comedic interludes "tiresome and worn out." He pointed out that such comedy detracted from the newsreel and created the "impression that any serious news concerning the Negro would be utterly ridiculous."[80] Another letter sent to the *New York Amsterdam News* and signed only A. Private registered a similar complaint. In an otherwise positive review of the newsreel, the author said that, to him, these scenes were not "funny or comical at all."[81]

But at times, *All-American*'s audience was ready to laugh at the absurdity of racial inequality. Indeed, *All-American*'s pedagogical address could underline such ironies and, in so doing, raise the ire of audiences. In one scene designed to instruct veterans on their benefits, George Hollan of the Veteran's Administration staged an interview with a newly returned black soldier.[82] The wooden dialogue began with the GI saying, "I'm a regular vet, what can you do for me?" The answers Hollan gave did not please all audiences. According to Alfred E. Smith, author of the "Adventures in Race Relations" column for the *Chicago Defender*, "when these 'benefits' boiled down to the fact [the veteran was] entitled to free burial in a national cemetery, the all-Negro audience practically laughed the news reel out of the theater, and it was sarcastic laughter."[83] In cases like this one, *All-American*'s attempts to promote race pride and the philosophy of uplift ran up against the realities of racism and inequality. Audience laughter in the face of *All-American*'s pedagogical address suggests that African Americans understood the implicated nature of the newsreel's relationship to segregation and accommodation.

Unlike mainstream newsreels that all but ignored black America, *All-American News* acknowledged—if only implicitly—the fact of segregation. The struggle for racial uplift necessarily took place in the context of a racist society. It is in this context that we must view *All-American*'s pedagogical address. Instead of ignoring Jim Crow America, the newsreel offered instruction on how to better oneself within it. By displaying African American achievement and evidence of the community's contribution to the war effort, the newsreel aimed to show the path to racial uplift—a path that put the onus on individuals to rise above the obstacles of racism rather than confront an unjust society. As we have seen, visibility was crucial to the newsreel's pedagogy. From *All-American*'s opening credits, the film's lessons in respectability, patriotism, and courage were framed by the newsreel's watchful eye—an eye that could stand in for the proud eyes of the black community as well as the critical eyes of white America. Ironically, in a series premised so much on the politics of the visible, it was what went unrepresented that may have overshadowed the newsreel's own message. The reality of racism cast doubt on the value of *All-American*'s pedagogical address.

Conclusion

As the war came to an end, *All-American News* struggled to remain relevant. Glucksman and Barnett worked to keep the newsreel alive and to make sure African Americans and others had the opportunity to see the accomplishments of their community on screen. Forays into television and sponsored film kept *All-American* going into the 1950s, but never again did *All-American* regain its wartime prominence. The growing consciousness of the civil rights movement made the politics of racial uplift increasingly out of place in the post-war United States, while changes in Hollywood made an all-black newsreel seem like a relic of an accommodationist era now past. But it is too simple to dismiss *All-American News* as simply an agent of accommodation and of the Jim Crow society that it reflected. As Edward Wheeler points out in his work on racial uplift in the South, accommodation and uplift were far from an endorsement of the racial status quo. Wheeler argues that accommodation "had a subversive quality." While uplift reflected bourgeois notions of respectability and white standards of achievement, it was also "a denial of what white society meant by accommodation, for it spoke of a possibility to move beyond the limits prescribed by the dominant society."[84] In the context of the United States' increasingly visual public sphere, *All-American* made the black community visible. By displaying evidence of the achievements of African Americans who overcame racism and inequality, as well as by urging and instructing others to do the same, *All-American* offered the possibility of progress, however incremental. Indeed, *All-American*'s pedagogical address was premised on the idea that African Americans could and should achieve a better life in the United States. Moreover, by representing a segregated United States, *All-American News* did what no other film was able to do during World War II. It showed the reality of race relations in the United States. Unlike its mainstream cousins who simply whitewashed over the question of race or fictional race movies that posited surreal all-black worlds, *All-American* represented a Jim Crow

America. Although it failed to confront the question of racism inherent in its own images, *All-American* made an uncomfortable reality visible.

All-American never reached the white audiences Glucksman, Barnett, and the newsreel's early supporters had hoped. As such, it is tempting to dismiss it as having little effect on the campaign for Double Victory, the mainstream newsreel, or on debates within the visual public sphere more broadly. Nevertheless, *All-American* did afford African American audiences their own opportunities to look at and to engage with the news on screen. However circumscribed, this black collective spectatorship was a chance for African Americans to look at their own community through something other than what Jane Gaines called the "distorted lens" of Hollywood.[85] Even if *All-American*'s pedagogical address could never escape the Du Boisian "sense of always looking at one's self through the eyes of others," the critical responses to it demonstrate the extent to which African American audiences understood the power of the politics of visibility in the United States. Between the images of racial uplift and the dismissive laughter of audiences, we can identify a counterpublic that recognized both the power of the new mediated public sphere epitomized by the news parade and its own subordinate status within it.

Conclusion

News Parades Gone By?

This book began with two contemporaneous views of the historical potential of the newsreel: Robert McElravy's optimism that the newsreel would offer the "small boy of the future . . . 'canned' history of the most graphic and thrilling sort" and Robert Littell's dismay that those "bottled samples of what is happening now" were merely "trivial, lazy, and misleading." While McElravy's commonsense view of the newsreel's value to posterity is appealing, it has proven difficult to sustain in the face of the relative paucity and accessibility of newsreel footage. Instead of the exhaustive library McElravy envisioned, the newsreel archive is incomplete, only partially accessible, and often arbitrary in what remains. Archivists at the University of South Carolina, the University of California, Los Angeles, the National Archives, and elsewhere work hard to preserve their newsreel collections and make them available to the public, but these collections represent only a fraction of the footage shot before World War II and include very few of the complete newsreels released in the United States in the same period.[1] Nevertheless, while the newsreel archive does not represent the kind of complete and incontrovertible record that McElravy imagined and Littell hoped for, it does hold valuable lessons for media scholars and historians. The history of the newsreel system illuminates a crucial moment in the transformation of American society and can, in turn, make the glimpses of the past preserved in the archive useful. To make the most of the newsreel archive, we must go beyond the static metaphors McElravy and Littell evoked to describe it. The "canned history" and the "bottled samples" they discuss are but partial traces of the news parade. These newsreel texts simply cannot be fully legible when taken on their own. Understanding the newsreel and its remaining footage demands the restoration of the context in which Americans viewed these images and the role the newsreel played in an increasingly mediated public sphere. As we saw in chapter 2, the newsreel's realism was not confined to the image on the screen. Instead, the power and meaning of newsreels lay largely in how they circulated among the publics they addressed and helped to create. Only by looking at the newsreel system as a whole—its modes of production, distribution, exhibition, and collective spectatorship—can we begin to understand this circulation and, in turn, the filmic texts that remain in the archive. Such a holistic analysis also offers a model for how we must approach our current media moment and important lessons for making sense of new transformations of our public sphere. Finally, understanding the newsreel as a system allows us to reconsider the place of newsreel footage in the archive. Newsreel images do not simply speak for themselves to reveal the truth about individual moments in the past. Instead, they reflect the logic of the news parade itself.

Newsreel as Media System

Examining the news parade in all its facets reveals exactly how the newsreel changed the way Americans saw the world, their place in it, and their relationships to one another. Doing so brings news film to the center of the histories of visual culture and collective identity in the pre–World War II era, properly recognizing the power and influence of one of the most prolific media forms of the twentieth century. The newsreel transformed notions of American identity and civic participation by linking these things to the shared experience of collective spectatorship. As we have seen, however, not all Americans had equal access to these experiences. This book's multiperspectival analysis of the newsreel also reveals how it served as a site for the creation as well as the contestation of new publics and counterpublics.

Such an approach ought not be limited to the newsreel or to the 1930s. Examining the public dimensions of different media at different historical moments can offer important insight into the role communication and technology play in society. Indeed, this book broadly suggests the power and potential of decentering the text in the study of media. The text is a crucial, but nevertheless partial, aspect of media that rely on circulation to make meaning. By shifting the focus to examine texts within these broader systems of circulation, film and media studies are better able to account for contested meanings and counternarratives.

The news parade's complex relationship with the politics of visibility in the United States was one such site of contestation. It shows both the extent to which the screen mediated the public sphere and exactly what was at stake for newsreel audiences in the 1930s and 1940s. Whether it was covering Lindbergh's transatlantic flight or the Sino–Japanese War, the newsreel's modes of production, distribution, and address combined with the sites of its exhibition to engender a new relationship among audience members and between them and the world. While newsreels showed Lindbergh's ticker tape parade passing through New York's Canyon of Heroes, the rhetoric of the news parade joined audiences in the theater with the virtual crowd on screen to imagine a mediated American identity defined by the shared experience of watching the news and the privileges of looking.

Embodied by the figure of the newsreel cameraman, this collective spectatorship was framed as active and participatory but also implicitly male, white, and Western. As detailed in chapter 3, the newsreel's imperial gaze helped distance the American viewer from the feminized and infantilized Asian victims of the Sino–Japanese conflict. At the same time the newsreel spectator was offered the privilege of watching the war through the active, masculine gaze of the cameraman hero. This privilege was mirrored in the space of the newsreel theaters themselves—as architects like S. Charles Lee flattered audiences with references to technology, transportation, and modernity, offering them a virtual journey to exotic and dangerous places. These allusions stressed the shared identity of the audience as American but did not ensure consensus. Indeed, there were limits to the privileges of newsreel spectatorship. As *All-American News'* critical audience apparently recognized, the mediated public sphere of the news parade made little room for African Americans—either as visible members of U.S. society or as participants in the newsreel's masculine and imperial gaze. Nevertheless, the contestation of *All-American*'s politics of visibility demonstrates the extent to which political and visual representation had become powerfully linked by the 1940s. The development of an African American counterpublic that debated the means and ends of the black community's representation on screen and off reflected the news parade's central place in the public sphere by mid-century. As the newsreel's collective spectatorship came to define American identity and participation in the public sphere, the news parade became a site for struggle over recognition and rights.

The Legacy and Lessons of the Newsreel System

No simple line can be drawn between the splintered public sphere of American society today and the mediated publics of the newsreel era, but echoes remain. The public sphere has undergone a number of changes since the advent of the newsreel; the rise of television, cable news, and the internet—to name just a few significant developments—have all shaped and reflected the changing terrain in which American publics have encountered one another. Nevertheless, aspects of the newsreel mode of address persist in our contemporary media environment. The continuous, non-narrative sequence that characterized the news parade was taken up by broadcast news and further developed with the advent of twenty-four-hour news channels in the 1980s. Although news channels have more recently moved away from this model and toward an emphasis on opinion and punditry, the non-narrative sequence persists in the form of the "news crawl" or ticker—featuring a constantly updated series of headlines—at the bottom of the screen on most cable news networks. On social media too, the so-called "streams" of constantly updating content on platforms like Facebook and Twitter mimic the newsreel's passing pageant of world events—both momentous and trivial. Indeed, as our news cycle and attention spans apparently shorten, the news parade may still be an apt and useful metaphor for how Americans see the world.

The newsreel's emphasis on the power and privilege of mediated looking also continues to play a central role in how news media offer Americans a spectacular view of themselves and the world. The rise of television after World War II transformed the mediated public sphere as the shared experience of the newsreel's collective spectatorship shifted increasingly to the private realm of the home.[2] Despite this shift, the role of the visual and of visibility in struggles over identity and politics in the public sphere grew even more potent. Spectacular media events drew Americans together in new forms of mediated collectivity.[3] The civil rights movement of the 1950s and 1960s famously understood this, using television as the means to spread powerful images of racist police violence in order to indict the Jim Crow South and insist on legal equality for African Americans.[4] As the familial viewing of television has transformed again in recent years into the individualized looking of cell phone screens, the nature of collective spectatorship has once again shifted, but the importance and power of images to serve as sites for public engagement has persisted. The key role that digital video footage has played in the rise of the Black Lives Matter movement and other contemporary struggles over the politics of racism, mass incarceration, and police violence demonstrate the extent to which this remains true today. The technology has changed, but for many—including marginalized groups—the circulation of mediated images continues to be central to debate and resistance in the public sphere.

While there are important continuities with the newsreel, it is important to acknowledge that the public sphere is undergoing a new process of profound change brought on by globalization, technology, and political upheaval. While it may be too soon to fully understand these changes, we can look to the period under consideration in this book to reflect on the moment of transformation itself. Even as things appear to change, there are significant parallels between the newsreel era and today. Just as the introduction of the newsreel was met with early optimism only to be followed by disillusionment and worry, social media has followed a similar trajectory, with early boosters having extolled the promise of a convergence culture empowering individuals and communities online and more recent commentators lamenting the apparently irrevocably fractured and partisan news landscape it has helped to produce.[5] Indeed, the 2016 election campaign in the United States demonstrated the extent to which the public sphere has been divided into multiple publics—with siloed communities on platforms like Twitter and Facebook as well as partisan media ecologies offering space for not only competing ideologies and identities, but sometimes wholly separate sets of "facts" on which to base those positions. The rise of so-called "fake news" and "alternative facts," as well as competing media spheres, show that it may no longer be possible to speak of a single public sphere. But while these divisions have generated a good deal of anxiety around the possibilities for shared public discourse, some of the counterpublics fostered by social media have propelled important movements for social change. Just as Lippmann and Dewey debated the role of the news in relation to how its content shaped public opinion but missed how new media were transforming the public sphere itself, this study of the newsreel should be a reminder that as we think through the role of fake news and social media, we must not simply look at the content available on these platforms nor at the technologies of access in isolation. As with the newsreel, the content of social media, the means by which information and ideas circulate in these new contexts, as well as how these platforms create and foster communities and new publics must be understood together.

Indeed, the interdisciplinary and interconnected study of media is more important than ever. While many of today's commentators focus on the power of new media technologies to reshape our understanding of notions such as truth and facts, it is crucial to contextualize technological changes alongside cultural, social, and political ones. As this study shows, the "real" is a historically contingent concept. In the 1930s, notions of the real were radically transformed by the newsreel and an increasingly visual public sphere. By emphasizing visuality as a means of participation in the public sphere, the newsreel helped transform the nature of democratic citizenship. The shared experience of spectatorship now formed the basis for new publics. In this new configuration, the act of looking rather than the image itself was the source of realism. The collective looking engendered by the newsreel image in turn became a site for shared identity.

As the public sphere is apparently shifting once again—this time to reflect the increasingly subjective postures of social media—we would do well to recognize the power that new media formations have to shape how we see the world in ways we may not yet be able to anticipate. As noted earlier, the debate between Walter Lippmann and John Dewey centered on the role of the mass media in shaping public opinion in an industrialized society. Both Lippmann and Dewey focused on the potential of print media to meet these new challenges. In doing so, they both failed to appreciate the advent of an increasingly visual public sphere. Their shared concern over the public's ability to "know" enough to make informed public opinions in an increasingly complex world overlooked the growing importance of seeing and looking. The public sphere of the

1930s was increasingly dominated by images and the shared experience of spectatorship.

Likewise, the current anxiety about "alternative facts" and the fracturing of the public sphere might be better understood as a process of change rather than collapse. This transformation may feel like a crisis—as the inadequacy of journalism to meet the needs of mass society did for Lippmann—but this may be because we can only see the failure of those concepts and institutions with which we are familiar. It is much harder to discern the new formations that will take hold. This is not to suggest a Pollyannaish faith in new technology and the changes it augurs. The rise of the newsreel system, and the visual public sphere that came with it, profoundly transformed ideas about realism, representation, and identity—and it did so in ways that challenged existing relations of power while creating and reentrenching others. As chapter 5 shows, the new visual public sphere of the newsreel changed the terrain over which African Americans would need to assert their rights—offering new tools, but providing new obstacles as well. As established norms and institutions of journalism seem ill-equipped to respond to the splintering of the public sphere, new media platforms are taking hold. While techno-futurists (and venture capitalists) speak of these technologies "disrupting" old models, the history of the newsreel demonstrates the need to understand technological change in a wider context and resist technologically determinist explanations. Just as the newsreel was a response to broader cultural changes even as it helped transform the public sphere, new media like Twitter and Facebook should also be examined as responses to social, political, and cultural disruptions, not just as catalysts.

Finally, while it may be impossible to fully anticipate how new publics will emerge in response to our current cultural and political convulsions, the history of the newsreel reassures us that audiences are rarely simply at the mercy of new media cultures. While the newsreel's visual representation of the news, and its display in an arena of commodified leisure such as the movie theater, transformed reality into a series of consumable images, this did not make audiences into passive consumers. One of the key insights of this book is that the newsreel's collective spectatorship was a form of active participation in the public sphere—not a passive position at all. Instead, the newsreel image became a site where publics and counterpublics came together to engage with the news and one another. At a time when technological pessimists worry about the threats social media pose to democracy, the history of the newsreel points to the active role audiences will play in integrating technology into the public sphere.

Newsreel System and the Archive

The last several years have seen a significant increase in the accessibility of U.S. newsreel archives. Much of the National Archives (NARA) holdings of *Universal Newsreel* are now available online at Archive.org and other streaming sites, the Moving Image Research Collection (MIRC) at the University of South Carolina is making an ever increasing amount of its collection of *Fox News* films available through its own Digital Video Repository, and UCLA is in the process of digitizing the *Hearst Metrotone News* collection with a view to making the films more accessible to researchers in the near future.[6] The growing availability of these news film collections means the public has unprecedented access to vivid moving images of the past. While this new access is a boon for scholars, students, and documentarians, it also raises significant questions for how best to understand these films and their historical potential. As newsreels become more accessible, the danger of seeing these films simply as "canned history" becomes more acute, and it is more important than ever to view this material in the wider context of the newsreel system.

There are significant challenges when working with the newsreel archive. Far from being an orderly catalog of neatly "bottled samples" of the past, the newsreel record is an uneven mix of outtakes, edited footage, and complete release prints. The fragmentary nature of the newsreel record is largely a result of the studios' own archival priorities and practices. Rather than preserve whole newsreels, most companies routinely cut the original negatives for each story and archived them separately—often removing intertitles and other elements. Because studio sound—music, effects, and narration—was recorded on a separate optical track, in many cases these were not preserved at all. The remaining film, along with outtake footage that was never released, makes up the bulk of the extant newsreel archive. These film elements were saved for potential reuse—first as B-roll and library footage for the studios themselves and later for licensing and for sale to commercial footage libraries. Rather than preserving newsreels, the studios preserved footage. The legacy of this principle of organization and preservation remains in newsreel archives today. By stripping the footage of its narration, titles, and sound effects and by separating the stories, the archiving process atomized the events captured on film—removing key context and evidence of how these events were framed for historical audiences. While archivists have done a remarkable job of piecing together the fragments and in some cases have used dope sheets, scripts, and other materials to shed light on the context surrounding archival footage, the initial logic of the footage library still persists. This logic caters to filmmakers and others looking for footage by keyword, enabling them to locate images to serve as illustrations for historical documentaries and other projects. For researchers looking to these films as historical texts in themselves—as documents to be analyzed, contextualized, and understood—the archival process that dismantled these newsreels has severely hampered such efforts.

With the increased accessibility of historical news film, it is important that scholars and others contend with the particular challenges presented by the newsreel archive and contextualize individual films within a broader understanding of the newsreel system. The recent collection *Rediscovering U.S. Newsfilm: Cinema, Television, and the Archive* is a timely contribution to the study of the newsreel and to a recognition of the challenges of working with historical news film. The collection includes archivist introductions to key newsreel collections and advice for researchers, a critical typology of the news film archival elements and terminology, and even a discussion of the perils and research possibilities of the outtake.[7] All of this is a welcome addition to the field and to a more thoughtful evaluation of the newsreel archive itself.

I hope this book helps further these reflections and aids in contextualizing the extant newsreel footage and the archive itself in the newsreel system as a whole. Indeed, the archive must be seen as an extension of that system. The prevalence of outtakes and of dislocated footage in newsreel collections is evidence of the newsreel's own logic—a logic that was voracious in its desire to capture the world on film, but one that did so in the present tense. Despite early proclamations, the newsreel was not aimed at collecting images for posterity but at presenting audiences with a passing pageant of their world. Thus, what remains in the archive for historians and scholars is not perfectly preserved "canned history," nor is it a simple record of the past's most important events, people, and so on. What remains is a trace of the news parade itself—its modes of production, representation, and *preservation.* Just as audiences in the 1930s experienced newsreel stories as part of the news parade, historians today must view the footage in the archive as part of the newsreel system. While the newsreel archive is not the comprehensive storehouse of information that McElravy imagined, it has much more to offer than just moving images to illustrate historical narratives. But in order to better understand these images, we need to think differently about the history of the newsreel and differently about the newsreel archive as well.

Acknowledgments

This book is the product of many years of work and the help of many, many friends and colleagues. There were times when it seemed this book would not make it to this stage, and I am deeply indebted to my editor at the University of Minnesota Press, Doug Armato, for his patience and wisdom in guiding this book to publication.

This book began its life as a dissertation in American studies at Brown University. I would like to thank professors Philip Rosen and Susan Smulyan for their friendship, guidance, mentorship, and insightful commentary on my work at every stage. Lynne Joyrich provided crucial and useful commentary as a reader of the dissertation. I would also like to thank Mary Jo Buhle who—along with my dissertation committee—provided formative guidance in my preliminary field exams. Thanks to my graduate school colleagues—in both American studies and modern culture and media studies—for the many challenging discussions and sometimes heated debates that helped to shape my scholarship into what it has become. Special thanks go to Wesley Hiers, Jessica Johnson, Marcia Chatelain, Angela Mazaris, Ani Mukherji, and Elizabeth de Montfort Walker.

I have had the joy and frustration of being an itinerant academic for the last ten years. Over that time I have had the support of wonderful colleagues and friends while teaching at Brown University, Colby College, Franklin & Marshall College, the University of British Columbia, Emily Carr University for Art and Design, and Simon Fraser University. The limited institutional support afforded visiting assistant professors, limited term lecturers, or sessional instructors has made me all the more grateful for the help I received from individual academic units and colleagues. I would especially like to thank Steven Wurtzler, Carla Willard, Eric Usner, Chris Pavsek, Zoë Druick, and Alla Gadassik for their friendship and support. I would like to acknowledge the help of Amy Mulnix, director of the Faculty Center at Franklin & Marshall, and Heather Fitzgerald, coordinator of the Writing Centre at Emily Carr, for organizing writing groups that offered me the opportunity to focus on this manuscript at various points in its development. Thank you as well to the colleagues in those workshops for their encouragement with this project. A very special thank you goes to Mikaela Luttrell Rowland for being the writing partner I needed—her enthusiasm and insight were crucial in completing this work, and her passion and commitment to her principles are an inspiration to me.

This book has been shaped by a growing community of scholars interested in nontheatrical, useful, and orphan cinema. I would particularly like to acknowledge the work of Dan Streible and the Orphan Film Symposium for showing me that my work might have a home in film studies. I would also like to thank Charles Acland, Haidee Wasson, Gerda Cammaer, Zoë Druick, Joanne Stober, Mark Cooper, Sara Beth Levavy, Ross Melnick, and Mark Williams as well as all my colleagues in the Nontheatrical Film and Media Scholarly Interest Group at the Society for Cinema and Media Studies. It is exciting to be part of this growing field of film scholarship.

In 2014, I was honored to participate in a postgraduate research seminar at the Visual Studies Research Institute of the University of Southern California. I would like to thank Jason Hill and Vanessa Schwartz for inviting me to contribute my work to the seminar, along with all of the seminar participants and especially Michael Renov for his insightful comments as respondent to my work. I would like to particularly acknowledge Vanessa Schwartz and her crucial insights into my research—it was our conversation about the newsreel and the public sphere during my time in Los Angeles that allowed me to see how this work could evolve from dissertation to book.

I would like to thank the staffs of the many libraries and archives I visited in the course of this project. I would particularly like to thank Greg Wilsbacher and the rest of the staff at the Moving Image Research Collections at the University of South Carolina, Mark Quigley and all the staff at the UCLA Film and Television Archive, and everyone at the National Archives at College Park. The Brown Graduate School, the Social Sciences and Humanities Council of Canada, and the American Heritage Center at the University of Wyoming provided financial support that allowed me to perform my research. Funding for the indexing of this book was provided by the SFU University Publications Fund. Special thanks to Lisa Oberhofer of BBC Motion Gallery for assisting me in securing research copies of the *All-American Newsreels,* Michelle Delaney of the Photographic History Collection at the National Museum of American History for providing me with photographs of the Trans-Lux Cinemas, and Gibson R. Yungblut for giving me access to his private collection of materials related to the Cincinnati Union Station.

Finally, I would like to thank my family for their many years of encouragement and especially Andrea Gin for giving me her unwavering emotional, intellectual, financial, and motivational support in this project. It is not an exaggeration to say that this book would not exist but for her love and understanding.

Notes

Introduction

1 "The Camera Pressman," *Moving Picture World,* September 23, 1911, 868.

2 Robert C. McElravy, "Humanizing History," *Moving Picture World,* February 9, 1918, 791.

3 Robert Littell, "A Glance at the Newsreel," *American Mercury,* November 1933, 263–71.

4 Raymond Fielding, *The American Newsreel, 1911–1967* (Norman: University of Oklahoma Press, 1972), 132.

5 Mark Cooper et al., eds., *Rediscovering U.S. Newsfilm: Cinema, Television, and the Archive* (New York: Routledge, 2018). See also Sara Beth Levavy, "Immediate Mediation: A Narrative of the Newsreel and The Film" (PhD diss., Stanford University, 2013); Jane Collings, "Streamlining the National Body: Newsreel Spectatorship in the New Era" (PhD diss., UCLA, 1995); Fielding, *The American Newsreel, 1911–1967*; Raymond Fielding, *The March of Time, 1935–1951* (New York: Oxford University Press, 1978); Sumiko Higashi, "Melodrama, Realism, and Race: World War II Newsreels and Propaganda Film," *Cinema Journal* 37, no. 3 (1998); Luke McKernan, *Topical Budget: The Great British News Film* (London: British Film Institute, 1992); Luke McKernan, *Yesterday's News: The British Cinema Newsreel Reader* (London: Wallflower Press, 2006).

6 Thomas Cripps, *Slow Fade to Black: The Negro in American Film, 1900–1942* (New York: Oxford University Press, 1977); Thomas Cripps, *Black Film as Genre* (Bloomington: Indiana University Press, 1978); Thomas Cripps, *Making Movies Black: The Hollywood Message Movie from World War II to the Civil Rights Era* (New York: Oxford University Press, 1993); Thomas Doherty, *Pre-Code Hollywood: Sex, Immorality, and Insurrection in American Cinema,*

1930–1934 (New York: Columbia University Press, 1999); Thomas Doherty, *Projections of War: Hollywood, American Culture, and World War II,* rev. ed. (New York: Columbia University Press, 1999); Douglas Gomery, *The Hollywood Studio System* (New York: St. Martin's Press, 1986); Robert Sklar, *Movie-Made America: A Cultural History of American Movies,* rev. ed. (New York: Vintage Books, 1994); Jacqueline Najuma Stewart, *Migrating to the Movies: Cinema and Black Urban Modernity* (Berkeley: University of California Press, 2005).

7 Important work on the preservation and study of these ephemeral film forms has been presented at the Orphan Film Symposium from 1999 to 2018. See also, Joseph Clark, "Double Vision: World War II, Racial Uplift, and the All-American Newsreel's Pedagogical Address," in *Useful Cinema,* ed. Charles R. Acland and Haidee Wasson (Durham, N.C.: Duke University Press, 2011), 263–88; Vinzenz Hediger and Patrick Vonderau, eds., *Films That Work: Industrial Film and the Productivity of Media* (Amsterdam: Amsterdam University Press, 2009); Karen L. Ishizuka and Patricia R. Zimmermann, eds., *Mining the Home Movie: Excavations in Histories and Memories,* (Berkeley: University of California Press, 2007); Kirsten Ostherr, *Medical Visions: Producing the Patient Through Film, Television, and Imaging Technologies* (New York: Oxford University Press, 2013); Jennifer Lynn Peterson, *Education in the School of Dreams: Travelogues and Early Nonfiction Film* (Durham, N.C.: Duke University Press, 2013); Charles Tepperman, *Amateur Cinema: The Rise of North American Movie Making, 1923–1960* (Oakland: University of California Press, 2014); Patricia R. Zimmermann, *Reel Families: A Social History of Amateur Film* (Bloomington: Indiana University Press, 1995); Devin Orgeron, Marsha Orgeron, and Dan Streible, eds., *Learning with the Lights Off: Educational Film in the United States* (New York: Oxford University Press, 2012).

8 Stella Bruzzi, *New Documentary: A Critical Introduction* (New York: Routledge, 2000); Jane M. Gaines and Michael Renov, eds., *Collecting Visible Evidence* (Minneapolis: University of Minnesota Press, 1999); William Guynn, *A Cinema of Nonfiction* (London: Associated University Presses, 1990); Bill Nichols, *Representing Reality: Issues and Concepts in Documentary* (Bloomington: Indiana University Press, 1991); Bill Nichols, *Introduction to Documentary* (Bloomington: Indiana University Press, 2001); Michael Renov, ed., *Theorizing Documentary* (New York: Routledge, 1993); Philip Rosen, *Change Mummified: Cinema, Historicity, Theory* (Minneapolis: University of Minnesota Press, 2001); Alan Rosenthal, ed., *New Challenges for Documentary* (Berkeley: University of California Press, 1988); Barry Keith Grant and Jeannette Sloniowski, *Documenting the Documentary: Close Readings of*

Documentary Film and Video (Detroit, Mich.: Wayne State University Press, 1998); Brian Winston, *Claiming the Real: The Griersonian Documentary and Its Legitimations* (London: British Film Institute, 1995).

9 John Grierson, *Grierson on Documentary,* ed. Forsyth Hardy (New York: Praeger Publishers, 1971); Jeremy Hicks, *Dziga Vertov: Defining Documentary Film* (New York: I.B. Tauris, 2007); Siegfried Kracauer, *Theory of Film: The Redemption of Physical Reality* (New York: Oxford University Press, 1960); Paul Rotha, *Documentary Film,* 3rd ed. (1937; repr., London: Faber and Faber, 1952).

10 Jean-Louis Comolli and Jean Narboni, "Cinema/Ideology/Criticism 1" in *Screen Reader 1: Cinema/Ideology/Politics* (London: Society for Education in Film and Television, 1977); Jean-Louis Comolli and Jean Narboni, "Cinema/Ideology/Criticism 2," in *Screen Reader 1: Cinema/Ideology/Politics* (London: Society for Education in Film and Television, 1977); Stephen Heath, *Questions of Cinema* (Bloomington: Indiana University Press, 1981); Colin MacCabe, "Theory and Film: Principles of Realism and Pleasure," in *Narrative, Apparatus, Ideology: A Film Theory Reader,* ed. Philip Rosen (Cambridge, Mass.: MIT Press, 1986); Philip Rosen, ed., *Narrative, Apparatus, Ideology: A Film Theory Reader* (Cambridge, Mass.: MIT Press, 1986); Paul Willemen, "On Realism in the Cinema," in *Screen Reader 1: Cinema/Ideology/Politics* (London: Society for Education in Film and Television, 1977).

11 Jane Feuer, "The Concept of Live Television: Ontology as Ideology," in *Regarding Television,* ed. E. Ann Kaplan (Frederick, Md.: University Publications of America, 1983), 14. See also, John Ellis, *Visible Fictions: Cinema, Television, Video* (London: Routledge, 1982); Margaret Morse, *Virtualities: Television, Media Art, and Cyberculture* (Bloomington: Indiana University Press, 1998); Margaret Morse, "News as Performance: The Image as Event," in *The Television Studies Reader,* ed. Robert C. Allen and Annette Hill (New York: Routledge, 2004); Susan Murray and Laurie Ouellette, *Reality TV: Remaking Television Culture* (New York: New York University Press, 2004); Lauren Rabinovitz and Susan Jeffords, eds., *Seeing through the Media: The Persian Gulf War* (New Brunswick, N.J.: Rutgers University Press, 1994); Elayne Rapping, *The Looking Glass World of Nonfiction TV* (Boston, Mass.: South End Press, 1987); Robert Stam, "Television News and Its Spectator," in *Regarding Television,* ed. E. Ann Kaplan (Frederick, Md.: University Publications of America, 1983); Raymond Williams, *Television: Technology and Cultural Form* (Middletown, Conn.: Wesleyan University Press, 1992).

12 Daniel Dayan and Elihu Katz, *Media Events: The Live Broadcasting of History* (Cambridge, Mass.: Harvard University Press, 1992), 120.

13 John Dewey, *The Public and Its Problems,* (Athens, Ohio: Swallow Press, 1954); Walter Lippmann, *The Phantom Public,* reprint ed. (New Brunswick, N.J.: Transaction Publishers, 1993).

14 For a phenomenological rather than historical account of collective spectatorship, see Julian Hanich, "Watching a Film with Others: Towards a Theory of Collective Spectatorship," *Screen* 55, no. 3 (September 1, 2014): 338–59.

15 Walter Lippmann, *Public Opinion,* reissue ed. (New York: Free Press, 1997), 19.

16 Sue Curry Jansen, "Phantom Conflict: Lippmann, Dewey, and the Fate of the Public in Modern Society," *Communication and Critical/Cultural Studies* 6, no. 3 (September 1, 2009): 221–45; Dell P. Champlin and Janet T. Knoedler, "The Media, the News, and Democracy: Revisiting the Dewey-Lippmann Debate," *Journal of Economic Issues* 40, no. 1 (March 1, 2006): 135–52; Dave Tell, "Reinventing Walter Lippmann: Communication and Cultural Studies," *Review of Communication* 13, no. 2 (April 1, 2013): 108–26.

17 Lippmann, *Public Opinion,* 158.

18 Edward Bernays, *Propaganda,* (Brooklyn, N.Y.: Ig Publishing, 2004), 12.

19 Susan Douglas, *Listening In: Radio and the American Imagination, From Amos 'n' Andy and Edward R. Murrow to Wolfman Jack and Howard Stern* (New York: Times Books, 1999); Michele Hilmes and Jason Loviglio, eds., *Radio Reader: Essays in the Cultural History of Radio* (New York: Routledge, 2002); Michele Hilmes, *Radio Voices: American Broadcasting, 1922–1952* (Minneapolis: University of Minnesota Press, 1997); Jason Loviglio, *Radio's Intimate Public: Network Broadcasting and Mass-Mediated Democracy* (Minneapolis: University of Minnesota Press, 2005); Susan Smulyan, *Selling Radio: The Commercialization of American Broadcasting, 1920–1934* (Washington, D.C.: Smithsonian Institution Press, 1994).

20 Douglas, *Listening In,* 218.

21 Loviglio, *Radio's Intimate Public,* xvi.

22 Craig Calhoun, ed., *Habermas and the Public Sphere,* reprint ed. (Cambridge, Mass.: MIT Press, 1993); Nancy Fraser, *Transnationalizing the Public Sphere,* ed. Kate Nash, (Cambridge: Polity, 2014); Lewis Edwin Hahn, *Perspectives on Habermas* (Chicago, Ill.: Open Court Publishing, 2000); Jürgen Habermas, *The Structural Transformation of the Public Sphere: An Inquiry into a Category of Bourgeois Society,* reprint ed. (Cambridge, Mass.: MIT Press, 1991).

23 Michael Warner, *Publics and Counterpublics* (New York: Zone Books, 2005), 118–19.

24 Warner, 8.

25 Jean Baudrillard, *Simulations* (New York: Semiotext(e), 1983); Guy Debord, *Society of the Spectacle* (Detroit, Mich.: Black and Red, 1983); Marshall

McLuhan, *Understanding Media: The Extensions of Man* (New York: Signet, 1966); Margaret Morse, "News as Performance: The Image as Event," in *The Television Studies Reader,* ed. Robert C. Allen and Annette Hill (New York: Routledge, 2004).

26 Debord, *Society of the Spectacle,* sec. 1.

27 Miriam Hansen, "Early Cinema, Late Cinema: Permutations of the Public Sphere," *Screen* 34, no. 3 (September 21, 1993): 205.

28 Hansen, 207–8.

29 Miriam Hansen, *Babel and Babylon: Spectatorship in American Silent Film* (Cambridge, Mass.: Harvard University Press, 1991), 50.

30 Julian Hanich, "Watching a Film with Others: Towards a Theory of Collective Spectatorship," *Screen* 55, no. 3 (September 1, 2014): 359.

31 Warner, *Publics and Counterpublics,* 72.

32 Hansen, "Early Cinema, Late Cinema," 208.

33 Warner, *Publics and Counterpublics,* 90.

34 Josh Braun, "Social Media and Distribution Studies," *Social Media + Society* 1, no. 1 (April 1, 2015): 1.

1. News Parade

1 Howard Thompson Lewis, ed., *Cases on the Motion Picture Industry,* Harvard Business Reports, vol. 8 (New York: McGraw-Hill, 1930), 113.

2 "Films on Lindbergh Set Speed Record," *New York Times,* June 14, 1927; "Short Feature Service Guide: Newsreel Number," *Motion Picture News,* June 24, 1927; "'Talking' News Reels Sent Grosses up; Roxy, $104,000 and Capitol, $65,100," *Variety,* June 22, 1927.

3 Silas Bent, "Lindbergh and the Press," *Outlook,* April 1932; Andrew Scott Berg, *Lindbergh* (New York: Berkeley Books, 1999); Daniel J. Boorstin, *The Image: A Guide to Pseudo-Events in America,* 25th anniversary ed. (New York: Vintage, 1987); Kenneth S. Davis, *Hero: Charles A. Lindbergh and the American Dream* (Garden City, N.Y.: Doubleday, 1959).

4 "N.Y. Dailies Give Remarkable Space to Lindbergh's Arrival," *Variety,* June 15, 1927, 1.

5 "Films on Lindbergh."

6 Raymond Fielding, *The American Newsreel, 1911–1967* (Norman: University of Oklahoma Press, 1972), 48.

7 "Short Feature Service Guide."

8 "Picture Men Await Lindbergh Verdict on Many Contracts," *Moving Picture World,* May 28, 1927, 248.

9 L. C. Moen, "Newsreels in Scramble for Lindbergh 'Beat,'" *Motion Picture News,* June 10, 1927.

10 "News Reels' Records and Costs of Handling Lindy's Views," *Variety,* June 22, 1927, 10.

11 Charles Peden, *Newsreel Man* (New York: Doubleday, Doran, 1932), 20.

12 "Films on Lindbergh."

13 "Films on Lindbergh."

14 Truman Talley, "How Lindbergh Put Newsreels Over," *Motion Picture News,* June 24, 1927.

15 Ironically, it seems that the Fox crew filmed Lindbergh's takeoff by serendipity, as they had likely been at Roosevelt Field that day to film for a planned release dedicated to Admiral Byrd's upcoming attempt to win the Orteig Prize. With Byrd's attempt delayed due to damage to his aircraft, the unlikely Lindbergh beat him to the prize. Cf. Greg Wilsbacher, "Beaten by Your Own Scoop: Early Synch-Sound Newsreels, Admiral Byrd, and the Orteig Prize" (paper, Society for Cinema and Media Studies Conference, Atlanta, Ga., March 30–April 3, 2016).

16 The *Fox Movietone News* special, "Lindbergh's Flight from N.Y. to Paris," is available for study in the moving image collection of the Museum of Modern Art.

17 "Lindbergh on Movietone," *Variety,* May 25, 1927, 9.

18 "Crowds Cheer News in Times Square," *New York Times,* May 22, 1927.

19 Mordaunt Hall, "The Screen," *New York Times,* June 15, 1927.

20 "'Talking' News Reels Sent Grosses up."

21 "Films on Lindbergh."

22 "Short Feature Service Guide."

23 David Bordwell, Janet Staiger, and Kristin Thompson, *The Classical Hollywood Cinema: Film Style and Mode of Production to 1960* (New York: Columbia University Press, 1985); Douglas Gomery, *The Hollywood Studio System* (New York: St. Martin's Press, 1986); Richard Maltby, *Hollywood Cinema,* 2nd ed. (New York: Blackwell Publishing, 2003).

24 Gomery, *Hollywood Studio System,* 6.

25 Gomery, 2.

26 Lewis, *Cases on the Motion Picture Industry,* 102.

27 Lewis, 126.

28 As detailed in chapter 4, the newsreel cameraman was a heavily gendered occupation. I use the historical term "cameraman" to reflect both the lack of women in the profession during this period and the way the job was specifically associated with masculinity.

29 Lewis, *Cases on the Motion Picture Industry,* 127.

30 Shipping Memorandum from Universal, internal memo in Universal Newsreel Production File, vol. 6, no. 222 in Production Files of the Universal Newsreel Library, 1929–1967; 200-UN, MCA/Universal Pictures Collection, 1929–1967; National Archives at College Park, Maryland.

31 Sugrue, "The Newsreels," *Scribner's Magazine,* April 1937, 17.

32 Selden C. Menefee, "The Movies Join Hearst," *The New Republic,* October 9, 1935, 241.

33 Numerous examples of these dope sheets can be found in Production Files in the Fox Movietone News Collection, Newsfilm Library, University of South Carolina and in Production Files of the Universal Newsreel Library, 1929–1967; 200-UN, MCA/Universal Pictures Collection, 1929–1967; National Archives at College Park, Maryland.

34 Janet Marble, "Reeling up the Newsreels," *Christian Science Monitor,* June 19, 1935; Sugrue, "The Newsreels," 17.

35 Gomery, *Hollywood Studio System,* 11–12.

36 For more on these newsreel theaters, see chapter 4.

37 Lewis, *Cases on the Motion Picture Industry,* 128; Sugrue, "The Newsreels," 17.

38 Sugrue, "The Newsreels," 17.

39 *Hearst Metrotone News,* synopsis sheet, vol. 1, no. 300, September 13, 1931 in Hearst Metrotone News Collection, UCLA Film and Television Archive, Los Angeles.

40 Internal correspondence, Universal Newsreel Production File, vol. 5, no. 126 in Production Files of the Universal Newsreel Library, 1929–1967; 200-UN, MCA/Universal Pictures Collection, 1929–1967; National Archives at College Park, Maryland.

41 The Montreal-based Associated Screen News was one of the principle producers of news films in Canada before World War II. ASN did not release its own regular newsreel but instead shot footage for American studios like Universal Newsreel and printed release prints for distribution in Canada. For more on the relationship between the ASN and U.S.-based studio newsreels, see Joseph Clark, "From Canada and Back Again: Montreal's Associated Screen News and the Transnational Flow of Non-Fiction Film before WWII," in *Rediscovering U.S. Newsfilm: Cinema, Television, and the Archive,* ed. Mark Cooper et al. (New York: Routledge, 2018), 173–85.

42 David Bordwell and Kristin Thompson, *Film Art: An Introduction,* 4th ed. (New York: McGraw-Hill, 1993), 10. See also Bordwell, Staiger, and Thompson, *The Classical Hollywood Cinema*; Maltby, *Hollywood Cinema*; Thomas Schatz, *The Genius of the System: Hollywood Filmmaking in the Studio Era* (New

York: Pantheon Books, 1988); Michael Storper, "Flexible Specialization and Post-Fordist Industrialization," in *Post-Fordism: A Reader,* ed. Ash Amin (Malden, Mass.: Blackwell, 1994).

43 Fielding, *American Newsreel,* 191.

44 *Fox Movietone News,* unidentified issue, 1936, in Hearst Metrotone News Collection, UCLA Film and Television Archive, Los Angeles.

45 *News of the Day,* synopsis sheet, vol. 9, no. 301, 1938, in Hearst Metrotone News Collection, UCLA Film and Television Archive, Los Angeles.

46 *Universal Newsreel,* synopsis sheet, vol. 5, no. 125, February 1933, in Production Files of the Universal Newsreel Library, 1929–1967; 200-UN, MCA/Universal Pictures Collection, 1929–1967; National Archives at College Park, Maryland.

47 *Hearst Metrotone News,* synopsis sheet, vol. 6, no. 205, October 9, 1934, in Hearst Metrotone News Collection, UCLA Film and Television Archive, Los Angeles.

48 David Holbrook Culbert, *News for Everyman: Radio and Foreign Affairs in Thirties America* (Westport, Conn.: Greenwood Press, 1976); Susan Douglas, *Listening In: Radio and the American Imagination, from Amos 'n' Andy and Edward R. Murrow to Wolfman Jack and Howard Stern* (New York: Times Books, 1999); Michele Hilmes, *Radio Voices: American Broadcasting, 1922–1952* (Minneapolis: University of Minnesota Press, 1997); Michele Hilmes and Jason Loviglio, eds., *Radio Reader: Essays in the Cultural History of Radio* (New York: Routledge, 2002); Jason Loviglio, *Radio's Intimate Public: Network Broadcasting and Mass-Mediated Democracy* (Minneapolis: University of Minnesota Press, 2005).

49 Gilbert Seldes, "Newsreels and Pictures," *New Republic,* March 11, 1931, 95.

50 John Erskine, "Newsreels Should Be Seen and Not Heard," *American Mercury,* June 1935, 219.

51 For examples of newsreel fraud, see Fielding, *American Newsreel.*

52 "Movietone," *Variety,* May 4, 1927, 27.

53 Mary Ann Doane, "The Voice in the Cinema: The Articulation of Body and Space," *Yale French Studies* 60 (1980): 42.

54 Stella Bruzzi, *New Documentary: A Critical Introduction* (New York: Routledge, 2000); Bill Nichols, *Representing Reality: Issues and Concepts in Documentary* (Bloomington: Indiana University Press, 1991). One can compare these discussions with debates over the role of the presenter in television news, cf. Margaret Morse, "News as Performance: The Image as Event," in *The Television Studies Reader,* ed. Robert C. Allen and Annette Hill (New York: Routledge, 2004); Robert Stam, "Television News and Its Spectator," in

Regarding Television: Critical Approaches—an Anthology, ed. E. Ann Kaplan (Frederick, Md.: University Publications of America, 1983).

55 See Jane Collings, "Streamlining the National Body: Newsreel Spectatorship in the New Era" (PhD diss., UCLA, 1995); Thomas Doherty, *Projections of War: Hollywood, American Culture, and World War II,* rev. ed. (New York: Columbia University Press, 1999); Sumiko Higashi, "Melodrama, Realism, and Race: World War II Newsreels and Propaganda Film," *Cinema Journal* 37, no. 3 (1998): 38–61.

56 The live broadcast of sporting events had been a key part of radio listening since the early 1920s. Cf. Susan Douglas, *Listening In.*

57 *Universal Newsreel,* vol. 6, no. 291, October 19, 1934, in Edited Motion Picture Releases of the Universal Newsreel Library, 1929–1967; 200-UN, MCA/Universal Pictures Collection, 1929–1967; National Archives at College Park, Maryland.

58 *Hearst Metrotone News,* synopsis sheet, vol. 7, no. 228, 1935, in Hearst Metrotone News Collection, UCLA Film and Television Archive, Los Angeles.

59 Vanessa Schwartz, *Spectacular Realities: Early Mass Culture in Fin-De-Siècle Paris* (Berkeley: University of California Press, 1998), 6. See also Leo Charney and Vanessa R Schwartz, eds., *Cinema and the Invention of Modern Life* (Berkeley: University of California Press, 1995); T. J. Clark, *The Painting of Modern Life: Paris in the Art of Manet and His Followers* (Princeton, N.J.: Princeton University Press, 1984); Jonathan Crary, *Techniques of the Observer: On Vision and Modernity in the Nineteenth Century* (Cambridge, Mass.: MIT Press, 1990); Jib Fowles, "Stereography and the Standardization of Vision," *Journal of American Culture* 17, no. 2 (1994); Robert J. Silverman, "The Stereoscope and Photographic Depiction in the 19th Century," *Technology and Culture* 34, no. 4 (1993).

60 Schwartz, *Spectacular Realities,* 192.

61 Tom Gunning, "The Cinema of Attractions: Early Film, Its Spectator and the Avant-Garde," in *Early Cinema: Space, Frame, Narrative,* ed. Thomas Elsaesser (London: British Film Institute, 1990); Tom Gunning, "'Now You See It, Now You Don't': The Temporality of the Cinema of Attractions," *The Velvet Light Trap,* no. 32 (1993); Tom Gunning, "An Aesthetic of Astonishment: Early Film and the (In)Credulous Spectator," in *Viewing Positions: Ways of Seeing Film,* ed. Linda Williams (New Brunswick, N.J.: Rutgers University Press, 1995).

62 Gunning, "'Now You See It," 6.

63 Gunning, 6.

64 Gunning, "'Now You See It," 4; Gunning, "An Aesthetic of Astonishment."

65 Steve Neale, "Triumph of the Will: Notes on Documentary and Spectacle," *Screen* 20, no. 1 (1979): 66.

66 Neale, "Triumph of the Will," 85.

67 Roland Barthes, *Camera Lucida* (New York: Hill and Wang, 1981), 88–89. For more of the debate on photographic indexicality and what, if anything, it guarantees, see Geoffrey Batchen, *Burning with Desire: The Conception of Photography* (Cambridge, Mass.: MIT Press, 1997); Andre Bazin, "The Ontology of the Photographic Image," in *What Is Cinema? Volume I* (Berkeley: University of California Press, 1967); John Tagg, *The Burden of Representation: Essays of Photographies and Histories* (Boston: University of Massachusetts Press, 1988).

68 John Ellis, *Visible Fictions: Cinema, Television, Video* (London: Routledge, 1982), 58–59. For more on the debate over indexicality and the film document, see Bruzzi, *New Documentary*; Jane M. Gaines and Michael Renov, eds., *Collecting Visible Evidence* (Minneapolis: University of Minnesota Press, 1999); John Grierson, "The Course of Realism," in *Grierson on Documentary*, ed. Forsyth Hardy (London: Faber and Faber, 1979); William Guynn, *A Cinema of Nonfiction* (London: Associated University Presses, 1990); Nichols, *Representing Reality*; Michael Renov, ed., *Theorizing Documentary* (New York: Routledge, 1993); Philip Rosen, *Change Mummified: Cinema, Historicity, Theory* (Minneapolis: University of Minnesota Press, 2001); Brian Winston, *Claiming the Real: The Griersonian Documentary and Its Legitimations* (London: British Film Institute, 1995).

69 *Hearst Metrotone News*, vol. 1, no. 212, November 9, 1929, in Hearst Metrotone News Collection, UCLA Film and Television Archive, Los Angeles.

70 *Universal Newsreel*, synopsis sheet, vol. 5, no. 190, in Production Files of the Universal Newsreel Library, 1929–1967; 200-UN, MCA/Universal Pictures Collection, 1929–1967; National Archives at College Park, Maryland.

71 *Hearst Metrotone News*, vol. 9, no. 217, 1937, in Hearst Metrotone News Collection, UCLA Film and Television Archive, Los Angeles. See also *Universal Newsreel*, synopsis sheets, vol. 8, no. 432; vol. 9, no. 606; vol. 13, no. 974 in Production Files of the Universal Newsreel Library, 1929–1967; 200-UN, MCA/Universal Pictures Collection, 1929–1967; National Archives at College Park, Maryland.

72 The popular image of the newsreel cameraman is discussed further in chapter 3.

73 Robert Littell, "A Glance at the Newsreel," *The American Mercury*, November 1933, 271.

74 Press sheet for "The News Parade," Fox Films, May 1928, in clippings file,

Billy Rose Theatre Collection, New York Public Library for the Performing Arts.

75 MGM, "Advertisement," *Motion Picture Daily,* December 29, 1937, 3.

76 *Hearst Metrotone News,* synopsis sheet, vol. 6, no. 226, 1934, in Hearst Metrotone News Collection, UCLA Film and Television Archive, Los Angeles.

77 Hayden White, *Metahistory: The Historical Imagination in Nineteenth-Century Europe* (Baltimore: Johns Hopkins University Press, 1973); Hayden White, *Tropics of Discourse: Essays in Cultural Criticism* (Baltimore: Johns Hopkins University Press, 1978); Hayden White, *Content of the Form: Narrative Discourse and Historical Representation* (Baltimore: Johns Hopkins University Press, 1987).

78 Rosen, *Change Mummified,* 245.

79 Rosen, 240.

80 John Dewey, *The Public and Its Problems* (Athens: Swallow Press, 1954), 180–81; Walter Lippmann, *Public Opinion,* reissue ed. (New York: Free Press, 1997), 228–29.

81 Mary Ryan, "The American Parade: Representations of the Nineteenth-Century Social Order," in *The New Cultural History,* ed. Lynn Hunt (Berkeley: University of California Press, 1989), 138. See also, Susan G. Davis, *Parades and Power: Street Theatre in Nineteenth-Century Philadelphia* (Berkeley: University of California Press, 1988).

82 See Boorstin, *The Image*; Richard Wightman Fox and T. J. Jackson Lears, eds., *The Culture of Consumption: Critical Essays in American History, 1880–1980* (New York: Pantheon Books, 1983); Michael Kammen, *American Culture, American Tastes: Social Change and the 20th Century* (New York: Knopf, 1999); Roland Marchand, *Advertising and the American Dream: Making Way for Modernity, 1920–1940* (Berkeley: University of California Press, 1985); Michael Schudson, *Advertising, the Uneasy Persuasion: Its Dubious Impact on American Society* (New York: Basic Books, 1984); James B. Twitchell, *Adcult USA: The Triumph of Advertising in American Culture* (New York: Columbia University Press, 1996).

83 "Lindbergh Home," *Pathé News,* unused material, 1927, catalog ref. #2072.06, archived at www.britishpathe.com, downloaded on February 22, 2007.

84 Walter Benjamin, "The Work of Art in the Age of Mechanical Reproduction," in *Illuminations,* ed. Hannah Arendt (New York: Schocken Books, 1969), 251.

85 Benjamin, "The Work of Art."

86 For information on the crowd, visual culture, and the street, see Schwartz, *Spectacular Realities*; Lauren Rabinovitz, *For the Love of Pleasure: Women, Movies and Culture in Turn-of-the-Century Chicago* (New Brunswick, N.J.: Rutgers University Press, 1998).

2. Newsreel Realism

1 Thomas M. Pryor, "An Adventurous Life for the Newsreel Man," *New York Times,* January 1, 1939.

2 "Ad. Pathé Weekly," *Moving Picture World,* September 23, 1911; "Ad. Herst-Selig News Pictorial," *Moving Picture World,* March 14, 1914; "Ad. Selig Polyscope Company," *Moving Picture World,* January 2, 1915.

3 Raymond Fielding, *The American Newsreel, 1911–1967* (Norman: University of Oklahoma Press, 1972), 146–47.

4 Stephen Bush, "War Films," *Motion Picture World,* September 19, 1914.

5 Emanuel Cohen, "The Business of International News by Motion Pictures," *Annals of the American Academy of Political and Social Science* 128, no. 1 (1926): 76.

6 Fielding, *American Newsreel.*

7 "Are Newsreels News?," *The Nation,* October 2, 1935; Robert Littell, "A Glance at the Newsreel," *American Mercury,* November 1933; Selden C. Menefee, "The Movies Join Hearst," *New Republic,* October 9, 1935; Anthony North, "Let's Wait for the Newsreel," *New Outlook,* October 1934; Thomas Sugrue, "The Newsreels," *Scribner's,* April 1937.

8 "Are Newsreels News?," 370.

9 "Are Newsreels News?," 370.

10 Thomas Doherty, *Pre-Code Hollywood: Sex, Immorality, and Insurrection in American Cinema, 1930–1934* (New York: Columbia University Press, 1999), 214.

11 Littell, "Glance at the Newsreel," 264.

12 Littell, "Glance at the Newsreel," 271.

13 One notable exception to this tendency was the Russian filmmaker and theorist Dziga Vertov, who saw the newsreel as a potentially powerful tool for educating and persuading the masses. Cf. Jeremy Hicks, *Dziga Vertov: Defining Documentary Film* (New York: I.B. Tauris, 2007); Vlada Petric, "Dziga Vertov as Theorist," *Cinema Journal* 1, Fall (1978).

14 Paul Rotha, *Documentary Film,* 3rd ed. (London: Faber and Faber, 1952), 88.

15 John Grierson, "The Course of Realism," in *Grierson on Documentary,* rev. ed., ed. Forsyth Hardy (London: Faber and Faber, 1966), 201.

16 Grierson, "Course of Realism," 201.

17 For more on Grierson's famous definition of documentary, see Brian Winston, *Claiming the Real: The Griersonian Documentary and Its Legitimations* (London: British Film Institute, 1995).

18 Grierson, "Course of Realism," 201.

19 Grierson, 207.

20 Philip Rosen, *Change Mummified: Cinema, Historicity, Theory* (Minneapolis: University of Minnesota Press, 2001), 251.

21 Ian Aitken, *Film and Reform: John Grierson and the Documentary Film Movement* (New York: Routledge, 1990); Ian Aitken, *Realist Film Theory and Cinema: The Nineteenth-Century Lukácsian and Intuitionist Realist Traditions* (Manchester: Manchester University Press, 2006).

22 John Hillier and Alan Lovell, *Studies in Documentary* (London: Secker and Warburg, 1972).

23 Aitken, *Film and Reform,* 191.

24 See Karl Marx, *Capital: A Critique of Political Economy,* vol. 1 (New York: International Publishers, 1967); Karl Marx, "Preface to a Contribution to the Critique of Political Economy (the '1859 Introduction')," in *Karl Marx and Frederick Engels, Selected Works* (New York: International Publishers, 1972).

25 Georg Lukács, "Realism in the Balance," in *Aesthetics and Politics* (New York: Verso, 1977), 33.

26 Georg Lukács, "Narrate or Describe?," in *Writer and Critic and Other Essays* (New York: Grosset and Dunlap, 1970), 146.

27 Ian Aitken has argued that Lukács's writing on cinema suggests a different notion of cinematic realism than his literary criticism—namely that he accepts naturalism as a "categorical aesthetic quality of the filmic medium." Nevertheless, like Grierson, Lukács's notion of cinematic realism retains the key notion of a Hegelian totality that cannot be appreciated by simply superficial representation. Cf. Aitken, *Realist Film Theory and Cinema,* 91.

28 Miles Orvell, *The Real Thing: Imitation and Authenticity in American Culture, 1880–1940* (Chapel Hill: University of North Carolina Press, 1989), xv.

29 Guy Debord, *Society of the Spectacle* (Detroit: Black and Red, 1983).

30 See, for example, a selection of texts from 1970s film theory, which made realism a central and influential point of critique: Stephen Heath, *Questions of Cinema* (Bloomington: Indiana University Press, 1981); Colin MacCabe, "Theory and Film: Principles of Realism and Pleasure," in *Narrative, Apparatus, Ideology: A Film Theory Reader,* ed. Philip Rosen (Cambridge, Mass.: MIT Press, 1986); Philip Rosen, ed., *Narrative, Apparatus, Ideology: A Film Theory Reader* (Cambridge, Mass.: MIT Press, 1986); Paul Willemen, "On Realism in the Cinema," in *Screen Reader 1: Cinema/Ideology/Politics* (London: SEFT, 1977). For earlier debates about cinematic realism, see Andre Bazin, *What Is Cinema? Volume I* (Berkeley: University of California Press, 1967); Andre Bazin, *What Is Cinema? Volume II* (Berkeley: University of California Press, 1972); Sergei Eisenstein, *Film Form,* trans. Leyda Jay (New York:

Harcourt Brace, 1969); Siegfried Kracauer, *Theory of Film: The Redemption of Physical Reality* (New York: Oxford University Press, 1960).

31 Zoë Druick, *Projecting Canada: Government Policy and Documentary Film at the National Film Board of Canada* (Montreal: McGill-Queen's University Press, 2007); Amy Kaplan, *The Social Construction of American Realism* (Chicago: University of Chicago Press, 1988); Orvell, *The Real Thing: Imitation and Authenticity in American Culture, 1880–1940*; Christopher P. Wilson, *The Labor of Words: Literary Professionalism in the Progressive Era* (Athens: University of Georgia Press, 1985).

32 "Newsreels Set for a Cleanup in Washington," *Motion Picture Daily,* March 3, 1933.

33 Memo from Charles E. Ford to Allyn Butterfield, February 24, 1933, Universal Newsreel Production File, vol. 5, no. 125 in Production Files of the Universal Newsreel Library, 1929–1967; 200-UN, MCA/Universal Pictures Collection, 1929–1967; National Archives at College Park, Maryland.

34 "Extra Special: Roosevelt Inaugurated," *Universal Newsreel,* March 4, 1934, in Edited Motion Picture Releases of the Universal Newsreel Library, 1929–1967; 200-UN, MCA/Universal Pictures Collection, 1929–1967; National Archives at College Park, Maryland.

35 "Speed Battle of Newsreels Sets Records," *Motion Picture Daily,* March 7, 1933, 6.

36 "Speed Battle," 6.

37 Jane Feuer, "The Concept of Live Television: Ontology as Ideology," in *Regarding Television,* ed. E. Ann Kaplan (Frederick, Md.: American Film Institute, 1983), 14.

38 *Universal Newsreel,* script, vol. 5, no. 125, February 1933, in Production Files of the Universal Newsreel Library, 1929–1967; 200-UN, MCA/Universal Pictures Collection, 1929–1967; National Archives at College Park, Maryland.

39 Daniel Dayan and Elihu Katz, *Media Events: The Live Broadcasting of History* (Cambridge, Mass.: Harvard University Press, 1992).

40 These questions were raised by contemporary observers as well as historians. For contemporary accounts, see *Editor and Publisher,* March 5, 1932; "Editorials Stress Need of New Laws," *New York Times,* March 3, 1932; Silas Bent, "Lindbergh and the Press," *Outlook,* April 1932. For historical accounts that raise similar questions, see Kenneth S. Davis, *Hero: Charles A. Lindbergh and the American Dream* (Garden City, N.Y.: Doubleday, 1959); Paula Fass, *Kidnapped: Child Abduction in America* (New York: Oxford University Press, 1997); Jim Fisher, *The Lindbergh Case* (New Brunswick, N.J.: Rutgers University Press, 1987); Jim Fisher, *The Ghosts of Hopewell: Setting the Re-*

cord Straight in the Lindbergh Case (Carbondale: Southern Illinois University Press, 1999); Lloyd C. Gardner, *The Case That Never Dies: The Lindbergh Kidnapping* (New Brunswick, N.J.: Rutgers University Press, 2004).

41 Davis, *Hero*; Fisher, *Lindbergh Case.*

42 Charles Peden, *Newsreel Man* (New York: Doubleday, Doran and Company, 1932), 114–15.

43 Fass, *Kidnapped,* 119–21.

44 Davis, *Hero.*

45 Quoted in Fass, *Kidnapped,* 124.

46 Bent, "Lindbergh and the Press," 212.

47 Fass, *Kidnapped,* 98–99.

48 Fass, 123.

49 Peden, *Newsreel Man,* 116; Roy Edwards and Fred Fordham (Universal cameramen), cameraman's caption sheet for March 2, 1932, *Universal Newsreel,* vol. 4, no. 20, Production Files of the Universal Newsreel Library, 1929–1967; 200-UN, MCA/Universal Pictures Collection, 1929–1967; National Archives at College Park, Maryland.

50 Kathleen Battles, *Calling All Cars: Radio Dragnets and the Technology of Policing* (Minneapolis: University Of Minnesota Press, 2010), 99.

51 Detailed production records and extant copies of virtually of all issues of the *Universal Newsreel* at the National Archives at College Park make it possible to better trace its continuing coverage of the Lindbergh story.

52 *Universal Newsreel,* vol. 4, nos. 20–40, Production Files of the Universal Newsreel Library, 1929–1967; 200-UN, MCA/Universal Pictures Collection, 1929–1967; National Archives at College Park, Maryland.

53 Script, "Nation Aroused at Revolting Kidnapping of Lindbergh Baby," *Universal Newsreel,* vol. 4, no. 20, Production Files of the Universal Newsreel Library, 1929–1967; 200-UN, MCA/Universal Pictures Collection, 1929–1967; National Archives at College Park, Maryland.

54 Script, "Lindberghs Enlist Underworld's Aid for Baby's Return," *Universal Newsreel,* vol. 4, no. 21, Production Files of the Universal Newsreel Library, 1929–1967; 200-UN, MCA/Universal Pictures Collection, 1929–1967; National Archives at College Park, Maryland.

55 "Nation Aroused."

56 "Lindbergh Son Seized by Kidnapers," *Los Angeles Times,* March 2, 1932; "Lindbergh Baby Is Stolen: Seized While Sleeping in Home at Hopewell, N. J.," *Chicago Tribune,* March 2, 1932; "Lindbergh Baby Kidnapped from Home of Parents on Farm near Princeton; Taken from His Crib; Wide Search On," *New York Times,* March 2, 1932.

57 Tom Gunning, "The Exterior as *Intérieur*: Benjamin's Optical Detective," *Boundary* 2 30, no. 1 (2003): 127.

58 Synopsis sheet, *Universal Newsreel*, vol. 4, no. 20, Production Files of the Universal Newsreel Library, 1929–1967; 200-UN, MCA/Universal Pictures Collection, 1929–1967; National Archives at College Park, Maryland.

59 "Nation Aroused."

60 "Lindberghs Enlist."

61 Script, "U.S. Calls 1400 Cities to Assist in Search for Lindbergh Baby," *Universal Newsreel*, vol. 4, no. 23, Production Files of the Universal Newsreel Library, 1929–1967; 200-UN, MCA/Universal Pictures Collection, 1929–1967; National Archives at College Park, Maryland.

62 Peden, *Newsreel Man*, 117.

63 Roy Edwards and Fred Fordham (Universal cameramen), cameraman's caption sheet for March 2, 1932, *Universal Newsreel*, vol. 4, no. 20, Production Files of the Universal Newsreel Library, 1929–1967; 200-UN, MCA/Universal Pictures Collection, 1929–1967; National Archives at College Park, Maryland.

64 "Nation Aroused."

65 "Film of Baby Aids Hunt," *New York Times*, March 3, 1932.

66 "Lindberghs Enlist."

67 Fass, *Kidnapped*, 101.

68 "Editorials Stress Need of New Laws," 10.

69 "Nation Aroused."

70 Script, "Shocked Populace Shares Sorrow of Bereft Lindberghs," *Universal Newsreel*, vol. 4, no. 40, Production Files of the Universal Newsreel Library, 1929–1967; 200-UN, MCA/Universal Pictures Collection, 1929–1967; National Archives at College Park, Maryland.

71 See chapter 4 for more on the newsreel cinema as public forum.

72 Synopsis sheet, *Hearst Metrotone News*, vol. 6, no. 201, September 25, 1934, in Hearst Metrotone News Collection, UCLA Film and Television Archive, Los Angeles.

73 "Huge Wire Service Set up for Trial," *New York Times*, January 2, 1935; "Life in Flemington Is Transformed as It Becomes World News Centre," *New York Times*, January 2, 1935.

74 "Highlights of Trial Will Be Broadcast," *New York Times*, January 2, 1935.

75 Quoted in "Trial by Newspapers Is Charged by Editor," *New York Times*, January 5, 1935.

76 Quoted in Fass, *Kidnapped*, 127.

77 "Hauptmann Trial Produces Battle Between Attorneys," *Universal Newsreel*, vol. 6, no. 317, Production Files of the Universal Newsreel Library, 1929–1967;

200-UN, MCA/Universal Pictures Collection, 1929–1967; National Archives at College Park, Maryland.

78 Synopsis sheets, *Hearst Metrotone News,* vol. 6, no. 281; *Hearst Metrotone News,* vol. 6, no. 288, in Hearst Metrotone News Collection, UCLA Film and Television Archive, Los Angeles.

79 Script, "Evidence Grows Stronger in Lindbergh Kidnap Case," *Universal Newsreel,* vol. 6, no. 287, Production Files of the Universal Newsreel Library, 1929–1967; 200-UN, MCA/Universal Pictures Collection, 1929–1967; National Archives at College Park, Maryland.

80 "Hauptmann Smiles as State Nears Completion of Case," *Universal Newsreel,* vol. 6, no. 321, Production Files of the Universal Newsreel Library, 1929–1967; 200-UN, MCA/Universal Pictures Collection, 1929–1967; National Archives at College Park, Maryland.

81 "Chain of Testimony Links Hauptmann Closer to Crime," *Universal Newsreel,* vol. 6, no. 319, Production Files of the Universal Newsreel Library, 1929–1967; 200-UN, MCA/Universal Pictures Collection, 1929–1967; National Archives at College Park, Maryland.

82 "Expert Says Hauptmann Wrote All Ransom Notes; $14,600 in Bills Identified," *New York Times,* January 12, 1935.

83 "Lindbergh Case Reaches Climax," *Hearst Metrotone News,* vol. 6, no. 203, October 1, 1935, in Hearst Metrotone News Collection, UCLA Film and Television Archive, Los Angeles.

84 "Evidence Grows Stronger."

85 "Hauptmann Smiles."

86 Alexander Woollcott, "Hauptmann's Odd Smile Described by Woollcott," *Los Angeles Times,* January 29, 1935. See also Willard Edwards, "'Liar' Cries Bruno in Court," *Chicago Tribune,* January 29, 1935; Russell B. Porter, "Hauptmann Admits Lying and Says Wilentz Lies Too; Still Protests Innocence," *New York Times,* January 29, 1935.

87 "Hauptmann Smiles."

88 Script, *Universal Newsreel,* vol. 7, no. 324, Production Files of the Universal Newsreel Library, 1929–1967; 200-UN, MCA/Universal Pictures Collection, 1929–1967; National Archives at College Park, Maryland.

89 Synopsis sheet, "First Films of Hauptmann on the Witness Stand," *Hearst Metrotone News,* vol. 6, no. 288, in Hearst Metrotone News Collection, UCLA Film and Television Archive, Los Angeles.

90 "Hauptmann Testifies at Last," *Universal Newsreel,* vol. 7, no. 324, Universal Newsreel Library, 1929–1967; 200-UN, MCA/Universal Pictures Collection, 1929–1967; National Archives at College Park, Md.

91 Script, "Hauptmann Testifies at Last," *Universal Newsreel,* vol. 7, no. 324, Production Files of the Universal Newsreel Library, 1929–1967; 200-UN, MCA/Universal Pictures Collection, 1929–1967; National Archives at College Park, Maryland.

92 "Hauptmann's Reel Arouses Wilentz Ire," *Motion Picture Daily,* February 2, 1935.

93 "Wilentz Demands Suppression of Newsreels Taken by 'Trickery' During Trial Session," *New York Times,* February 2, 1935.

94 "Universal Refuses to Halt Trial Movie," *New York Times,* February 6, 1935.

95 "Hauptmann's Reel," 2.

96 "Newsreel Ordered out of Flemington," *Motion Picture Daily,* February 5, 1935; Fass, *Kidnapped.*

97 "Reels Release Advance Films of Hauptmann," *Motion Picture Daily,* February 15, 1935.

98 Cf. Neil Harris, *Humbug: The Art of P. T. Barnum* (Chicago: University of Chicago Press, 1981).

3. "Heroes of the Lens"

1 For more on the history of masculinity in U.S. popular culture, see Steven Cohan and Ina Rae Hark, eds., *Screening the Male: Exploring Masculinities in Hollywood Cinema* (New York: Routledge, 1993); Michael Denning, *Mechanic Accents: Dime Novels and Working-Class Culture in America* (New York: Verso, 1987); Miriam Hansen, *Babel and Babylon: Spectatorship in American Silent Film* (Cambridge, Mass.: Harvard University Press, 1991); Kristin L. Hoganson, *Fighting for American Manhood: How Gender Politics Provoked the Spanish-American and Philippine-American Wars* (New Haven, Conn.: Yale University Press, 1998); Tom Pendergast, *Creating the Modern Man: American Magazines and Consumer Culture, 1900–1950* (Columbia: University of Missouri Press, 2000); Erin A. Smith, *Hard-Boiled: Working-Class Readers and Pulp Magazines* (Philadelphia: Temple University Press, 2000).

2 Irving Crump, *The Boys' Book of Newsreel Hunters* (New York: Dodd, Mead, 1933).

3 John J. Floherty, *Men without Fear* (Philadelphia: J.B. Lippincott, 1940); Leland Jamieson, "News-Reel Rescue," *Blue Book Magazine,* February 1934; Charles Peden, *Newsreel Man* (New York: Doubleday, Doran, 1932); Frank Richardson Pierce, "The Sky Fool," *Air Trails,* December 1928; Thomas M. Pryor, "An Adventurous Life for the Newsreel Man," *New York Times,* January 1, 1939; Wallace West, *Paramount Newsreel Men with Admiral Byrd in Little America* (Racine, Wisc.: Whitman Publishing, 1934).

4 Ron Goulart, *Ron Goulart's Great History of Comic Books* (Chicago: Contemporary Books, 1986).

5 "Metro News," Metro Goldwyn Mayer, 1929, in Hearst Silent Vault Material, UCLA Film and Television Archive, Los Angeles.

6 Script, "Cameraman Risks Life To Film 'Sub' in Striking Speed Tests, " *Universal Newsreel,* vol. 5, no. 190, Production Files of the Universal Newsreel Library, 1929–1967; 200-UN, MCA/Universal Pictures Collection, 1929–1967; National Archives at College Park, Maryland.

7 Crump, *Boys' Book,* 101.

8 Bonnie S. Brennen, "From *Headline Shooter* to *Picture Snatcher*: The Construction of Photojournalists in American Film, 1928–39," *Journalism* 5, no. 4 (2004).

9 "The Cameraman," Metro Goldwyn Mayer, 1928.

10 Crump, *Boys' Book,* 27.

11 "Metro News," Metro Goldwyn Mayer, 1929, in Hearst Silent Vault Material, UCLA Film and Television Archive, Los Angeles.

12 Press sheet, "The News Parade," Fox Films, 1928, in clippings file, Performing Arts Library, New York Public Library.

13 For more on the relationship between the public and celebrity, see Richard Dyer, *Heavenly Bodies: Film Stars and Society* (New York: St. Martin's Press, 1986); Hansen, *Babel and Babylon*; Sean Redmond and Su Holmes, *Stardom and Celebrity: A Reader* (London: Sage, 2007); Jackie Stacey, *Star Gazing: Hollywood Cinema and Female Spectatorship* (London: Routledge, 1994).

14 West, *Paramount Newsreel Men.*

15 Synopsis sheet, "Famous Explorers Go to Africa for Metrotone," *Hearst Metrotone News,* vol. 1, no. 210, in Hearst Metrotone News Collection, UCLA Film and Television Archive, Los Angeles.

16 Pascal James Imperato and Eleanor M. Imperato, *They Married Adventure: The Wandering Lives of Martin and Osa Johnson* (New Brunswick, N.J.: Rutgers University Press, 1992); Fatimah Tobing Rony, *The Third Eye: Race, Cinema, and Ethnographic Spectacle* (Durham, N.C.: Duke University Press, 1996); Jennifer Lynn Peterson, *Education in the School of Dreams: Travelogues and Early Nonfiction Film* (Durham, N.C.: Duke University Press, 2013).

17 Synopsis sheet and script, "Red Cross Unit Bombed in Ethiopia," *Universal Newsreel,* vol. 8, no. 432, Production Files of the Universal Newsreel Library, 1929–1967; 200-UN, MCA/Universal Pictures Collection, 1929–1967; National Archives at College Park, Maryland.

18 Crump, *Boys' Book,* 187.

19 E. Ann Kaplan, *Looking for the Other: Feminism, Film, and the Imperial Gaze* (New York: Routledge, 1997), 9.

20 For more on the relationship between orientalism and gender in the United States, see Gail Bederman, *Manliness and Civilization: A Cultural History of Gender and Race in the United States* (Chicago: University of Chicago Press, 1995); Matthew Frye Jacobson, *Barbarian Virtues: The United States Encounters Foreign Peoples at Home and Abroad, 1876–1917* (New York: Hill and Wang, 2000); Amy Kaplan and Donald E. Pease, eds., *Cultures of United States Imperialism* (Durham, N.C.: Duke University Press, 1993); Robert Lee, *Orientals: Asian Americans in Popular Culture* (Philadelphia: Temple University Press, 1999); David Palumbo-Liu, *Asian/American: Historical Crossings of a Racial Frontier* (Stanford, Calif.: Stanford University Press, 1999); Mary Louise Pratt, *Imperial Eyes: Travel Writing and Transculturation*, 2nd ed. (New York: Routledge, 2008); Mari Yoshihara, *Embracing the East: White Women and American Orientalism* (New York: Oxford University Press, 2003).

21 The number of civilian causalities in Nanking remains a subject of controversy; most scholars put these numbers in the hundreds of thousands, while some revisionist Japanese historians argue the number is much lower. Cf. Iris Chiang, *The Rape of Nanking: The Forgotten Holocaust of World War II* (New York: Basic Books, 1997); Joshua A. Fogel, *The Nanjing Massacre in History and Historiography*, (Berkeley: University of California Press, 2000); Masahiro Yamamoto, *Nanking: Anatomy of an Atrocity* (Westport, Conn.: Praeger, 2000).

22 "Sensational Pictures of War in China," *News of the Day*, vol. 8, no. 301, September 1, 1937, in Hearst Metrotone News Collection, UCLA Film and Television Archive, Los Angeles.

23 "Bombing of Shanghai," *Universal Newsreel*, vol. 9, no. 595, in Universal Newsreel Library, 1929–1967; 200-UN, MCA/Universal Pictures Collection, 1929–1967; National Archives at College Park, Maryland.

24 Lobby card, *Universal Newsreel*, vol. 9, no. 595, in Universal Newsreel Library, 1929–1967; 200-UN, MCA/Universal Pictures Collection, 1929–1967; National Archives at College Park, Maryland.

25 "Newsreels Bring Horror of Sino–Japanese Hostilities," *Motion Picture Daily*, September 4, 1937.

26 Wayne S. Cole, *Roosevelt and the Isolationists, 1932–45* (Lincoln: University of Nebraska Press, 1983); James C. Schneider, *Should America Go to War? The Debate over Foreign Policy in Chicago, 1939–1941* (Chapel Hill: University of North Carolina Press, 1989).

27 *News of the Day,* vol. 9, no. 217, November 11, 1937, in Hearst Metrotone News Collection, UCLA Film and Television Archive, Los Angeles.

28 "Chinese in Offer to Buy 'U' War Shots," *Motion Picture Daily,* September 10, 1937.

29 Hadley Cantril and Mildred Strunk, *Public Opinion, 1935–1946* (Princeton, N.J.: Princeton University Press, 1951), 1081.

30 "Bombing of Shanghai."

31 Ali Behdad, *Belated Travelers: Orientalism in the Age of Colonial Dissolution* (Durham, N.C.: Duke University Press, 1994); Jacobson, *Barbarian Virtues;* Kaplan, *Looking for the Other;* Edward Said, *Orientalism* (London: Penguin, 2003); Ella Shohat and Robert Stam, *Unthinking Eurocentrism: Multiculturalism and the Media* (New York: Routledge, 1994).

32 Robert Lee, *Orientals,* 10.

33 Script, "Japanese Take Shanghai," *Universal Newsreel,* vol. 9, no. 622, in Production Files of the Universal Newsreel Library, 1929–1967; 200-UN, MCA/Universal Pictures Collection, 1929–1967; National Archives at College Park, Maryland.

34 "News Parade of 1937," *News of the Day,* vol. 9, no. 228, December 22, 1937, in Hearst Metrotone News Collection, UCLA Film and Television Archive, Los Angeles.

35 Malek Alloula, *The Colonial Harem,* trans. Myrna Godzich and Wlad Godzich (Minneapolis: University of Minnesota Press, 1986); Said, *Orientalism;* Lynne Thornton, *Women as Portrayed in Orientalist Painting,* (Paris: Art Creation Realisation, 1996).

36 "The Camera Overseas: 136,000,000 People See this Picture of Shanghai's South Station," *Life Magazine,* October 4, 1937.

37 *News of the Day,* vol. 9, no. 200 (excerpt), September 15, 1937, in Hearst Metrotone News Collection, UCLA Film and Television Archive, Los Angeles.

38 Cf. Jacobson, *Barbarian Virtues.*

39 *News of the Day,* vol. 8, no. 301, September 1, 1937; *News of the Day,* vol. 9, no. 217, November 11, 1937; in Hearst Metrotone News Collection, UCLA Film and Television Archive, Los Angeles.

40 Lobby card, *Universal Newsreel,* vol. 9, no. 595, in Production Files of the Universal Newsreel Library, 1929–1967; 200-UN, MCA/Universal Pictures Collection, 1929–1967; National Archives at College Park, Maryland.

41 Caption sheet, *Universal Newsreel,* vol. 9, no. 606, in Production Files of the Universal Newsreel Library, 1929–1967; 200-UN, MCA/Universal Pictures Collection, 1929–1967; National Archives at College Park, Maryland.

42 Joan M. Schwartz and James R. Ryan, *Picturing Place: Photography and the*

Geographical Imagination (New York: Palgrave Macmillan, 2003); Paul S. Landau and Deborah D. Kaspin, eds., *Images and Empires: Visuality in Colonial and Postcolonial Africa* (Berkeley: University of California Press, 2002); James R. Ryan, *Picturing Empire: Photography and the Visualization of the British Empire* (Chicago: University of Chicago Press, 1997).

43 Fatimah Tobing Rony, "Those Who Squat and Those Who Sit: Iconography of Race in the 1895 Films of Felix-Louis Regnault," *Camera Obscura*, no. 10 (1992): 283.

44 Kaplan, *Looking for the Other*, 69–70.

45 Kaplan, 79.

46 It is important to remember that although the newsreel offered audiences a neutral position from which to the view the war, as we'll see in chapter 4, real audiences were not always willing to adopt such a point of view. In the case of the Sino–Japanese War, Chinese American audiences in particular sought to use newsreel images of the conflict to sway U.S. public opinion against Japan. Cf. "Chinese in Offer."

47 Quoted in Hamilton Darby Perry, *The Panay Incident: Prelude to Pearl Harbor* (Toronto: MacMillan, 1969), 47.

48 Perry, *Panay Incident*, 58.

49 Perry, *Panay Incident*, 113. "U.S. Gunboat Sunk by Japanese Bombs," *New York Times*, December 13, 1937.

50 "U.S. Gunboat Sunk."

51 "U.S. Demands Full Satisfaction from Japan with Guarantee against Further Attacks," *New York Times*, December 14, 1937.

52 "U.S. Naval Display Reported Likely Unless Japan Guarantees Our Rights; Butchery Marked Capture of Nanking," *New York Times*, December 18, 1937.

53 "Camera Men Took Many Panay Pictures," *New York Times*, December 19, 1937.

54 "Rush Plans Set for Panay Film," *Motion Picture Daily*, December 28, 1937.

55 "First Panay Films Shown around Noon," *Motion Picture Daily*, December 31, 1937.

56 "First Panay Films," 6.

57 "Panay Films Today!, Advertisement," *New York Times*, December 30, 1937, L15.

58 Universal, "Advertisement," *Motion Picture Daily*, December 27, 1937.

59 MGM, "Advertisement," *Motion Picture Daily*, December 29, 1937; Fox Movietone, "Advertisement," *Motion Picture Daily*, December 29, 1937.

60 "The Newsreel Parade," *Motion Picture Daily*, December 31, 1937.

61 "Panay Film Ready; Bears out Charges," *New York Times*, December 30, 1937.

62 "First Panay Films"; "'U' Says 564 Panay Prints Not Enough," *Motion Picture Daily,* January 4, 1938.

63 "Advertisement," *New York Times,* December 30, 1937, L15.

64 Universal, "Advertisement," 3.

65 "Alley Broadcasts on U.S. Panay Sinking," *Motion Picture Daily,* December 18, 1937.

66 "Norman Alley at Warwick Tells of Panay Experience," *Motion Picture Daily,* December 30, 1937.

67 "Panay Film Speeds across Continent," *New York Times,* December 29, 1937.

68 *News of the Day,* vol. 9, no. 230, December 30, 1937, in Hearst Metrotone News Collection, UCLA Film and Television Archive, Los Angeles.

69 "Bombing of the Panay," *Universal Newsreel,* December 30, 1937, in Universal Newsreel Library, 1929–1967; 200-UN, MCA/Universal Pictures Collection, 1929–1967; National Archives at College Park, Maryland.

70 *News of the Day,* vol. 9, no. 230, December 30, 1937, in Hearst Metrotone News Collection, UCLA Film and Television Archive, Los Angeles.

71 "Norman Alley at Warwick."

72 "Bombing of the Panay."

73 "U.S. Demands Full Satisfaction." President Roosevelt did not, however, invoke the U.S. Neutrality Act—which would have placed an arms embargo on both sides—because to do so would have effectively aided the Japanese, who produced their own weapons, while seriously harming China's ability to defend itself. See Robert Dallek, *Franklin D. Roosevelt and American Foreign Policy, 1932–1945* (New York: Oxford University Press, 1979); Robert A. Divine, *The Illusion of Neutrality* (Chicago: University of Chicago Press, 1962); Justus D. Doenecke and Mark A. Stoler, *Debating Franklin D. Roosevelt's Foreign Policies, 1933–1945* (New York: Rowman and Littlefield, 2005).

74 "Bombing of the Panay."

75 Cantril and Strunk, *Public Opinion,* 1081; Divine, *Illusion of Neutrality,* 210.

76 Cantril and Strunk, *Public Opinion,* 1135; Doenecke and Stoler, *Debating Franklin D. Roosevelt's,* 32.

77 *Too Hot to Handle,* directed by Jack Conway (USA: Metro-Goldwyn-Mayer, 1938).

78 Goulart, *Great History of Comic Books.*

79 Dallek, *Franklin D. Roosevelt and American Foreign Policy*; Divine, *Illusion of Neutrality*; Doenecke and Stoler, *Debating Franklin D. Roosevelt's*; Schneider, *Should America Go to War?*

80 Goulart, *Great History of Comic Books.*

81 Vic Bloom, "'Speed' Martin Newsreel Cameraman," *The Funnies,* 54 (New

York: Dell Comics, 1941), 58, in Library of Congress, Serial and Government Publications Division, Washington, D.C.

82 Vic Bloom, "'Speed' Martin Newsreel Cameraman," *The Funnies,* 55 (New York: Dell Comics, 1941), 48, in Library of Congress, Serial and Government Publications Division, Washington, D.C.

83 Vic Bloom and Bob Hebbert, "'Speed' Martin Newsreel Cameraman," *The Funnies,* 61 (New York: Dell Comics, 1941), 2, in Library of Congress, Serial and Government Publications Division, Washington, D.C.

84 Vic Bloom and Bob Hebbert, "'Speed' Martin Newsreel Cameraman," *The Funnies,* 61 (New York: Dell Comics, 1941), 7, in Library of Congress, Serial and Government Publications Division, Washington, D.C.

85 Vic Bloom, "'Speed' Martin Newsreel Cameraman," *The Funnies,* 55 (New York: Dell Comics, 1941), 48–54, in Library of Congress, Serial and Government Publications Division, Washington, D.C.

86 Vic Bloom, "'Speed' Martin Newsreel Cameraman," *The Funnies,* 54 (New York: Dell Comics, 1941), 56, in Library of Congress, Serial and Government Publications Division, Washington, D.C.

4. "Come Along. We're Going to the Trans-Lux to Hiss Roosevelt"

1 Peter Arno, "Come Along, We're Going to the Trans-Lux to Hiss Roosevelt," *New Yorker,* September 19, 1936, 16.

2 Quoted in Sarah Wernick, "Masters of the Quick Guffaw," *Smithsonian,* June 1995.

3 Douglas Gomery, *Shared Pleasures: A History of Movie Presentation in the United States* (Madison: University of Wisconsin Press, 1992), 145.

4 "War News Brings Boom to Newsreel Theatres," *Motion Picture Herald,* January 24, 1942, 21.

5 "Cornerstone of New Depot Is Placed," *Cincinnati Times-Star,* November 21, 1931; "Railroad Station Features Theatre," *Motion Picture Herald,* May 15, 1937; "New Newsreel House Opens Sept. 5 in Airlines Terminal Building," *New York Sun,* n.d., 1941, in clipping file Theatres: U.S.: N.Y.: Trans-Lux, Billy Rose Theater Collection, New York Public Library; "War News Brings Boom to Newsreel Theatres," *Motion Picture Herald,* January 24, 1942; Alfred Fellheimer and Steward Wagner, "Cincinnati Union Terminal," *Architectural Forum,* June 1933; Christine Grenz, *Trans-Lux: Biography of a Corporation* (Norwalk, Conn.: Trans-Lux Corporation, 1982).

6 Grenz, *Trans-Lux,* 10.

7 Jean-Louis Baudry, "Ideological Effects of the Basic Cinematic Apparatus,"

in *Narrative, Apparatus, Ideology: A Film Theory Reader*, ed. Philip Rosen (New York: Columbia University Press, 1986), 295.

8 For an excellent overview of 1970s film theory and many of its most important works, see Philip Rosen, ed., *Narrative, Apparatus, Ideology: A Film Theory Reader* (Cambridge, Mass.: MIT Press, 1986).

9 Robert C. Allen and Douglas Gomery, *Film History: Theory and Practice* (New York: Alfred A. Knopf, 1985); Gomery, *Shared Pleasures.*

10 Robert C. Allen, "Manhattan Myopia; or, Oh! Iowa!," *Cinema Journal* 35, no. 3 (1996); Mary Carbine, "'The Finest Outside the Loop': Motion Picture Exhibition in Chicago's Black Metropolis, 1905–1928," *Camera Obscura* 23 (1990); Ben Singer, "Manhattan Nickelodeons: New Data on Audiences and Exhibitors," *Cinema Journal* 34, no. 3 (1995); Gregory A. Waller, "Another Audience: Black Moviegoing, 1907–16," *Cinema Journal* 31, no. 2 (1992); Gregory A. Waller, *Main Street Amusements: Movies and Commercial Entertainment in a Southern City, 1896–1930* (Washington, D.C.: Smithsonian Institution Press, 1995).

11 Jean-Louis Baudry, "The Apparatus: Metaphysical Approaches to the Impression of Reality in the Cinema," in *Narrative, Apparatus, Ideology: A Film Theory Reader*, ed. Philip Rosen (New York: Columbia University Press, 1986), 313.

12 Kathryn H. Fuller, *At the Picture Show: Small-Town Audiences and the Creation of Movie Fan Culture* (Charlottesville: University Press of Virginia, 1996); Jeffrey Klepotic, "'Like Nickels in a Slot': Children of the American Working Classes at the Neighborhood Movie House," *Velvet Light Trap* 48, Fall (2001).

13 Richard Maltby, "Sticks, Hicks and Flaps: Classical Hollywood's Generic Conception of Its Audiences," in *Identifying Hollywood's Audiences: Cultural Identity and the Movies* (London: British Film Institute, 1999).

14 See David Bordwell, "Contemporary Film Studies and the Vicissitudes of Grand Theory," Vance Kepley Jr., "Whose Apparatus? Problems of Film Exhibition and History," and Stephen Prince, "Psychoanalytic Film Theory and the Problem of the Missing Spectator," in David Bordwell and Noël Carroll, eds., *Post Theory: Reconstructing Film Studies* (Madison: University of Wisconsin Press, 1996).

15 Judith Mayne, *Cinema and Spectatorship* (New York: Routledge, 1993), 16–17.

16 Miriam Hansen, *Babel and Babylon: Spectatorship in American Silent Film* (Cambridge, Mass.: Harvard University Press, 1991), 6.

17 Hansen, *Babel and Babylon*, 7. For more on the collective and contextual nature of spectatorship, see Jacqueline Stewart, "Negroes Laughing at Themselves?

Black Spectatorship and the Performance of Urban Modernity," *Critical Inquiry* 29, no. 4 (June 1, 2003): 650–77, https://doi.org/10.1086/377724.

18 "Trans-Lux," *Time Magazine,* March 23, 1931.

19 "Inside Stuff—Pictures," March 25, 1931. In clipping file Theatres: U.S.: N.Y.: Trans-Lux, Billy Rose Theater Collection, New York Public Library.

20 Grenz, *Trans-Lux.*

21 For the complete history of the Trans-Lux Corporation, see Grenz, *Trans-Lux.*

22 Grenz, *Trans-Lux,* 5.

23 Trans-Lux Corporation, "Annual Report," (1928), 6, in Mudd Stacks, Yale University Library, New Haven, Connecticut.

24 Jack Burton, *The Story of Trans-Lux* (New York: Trans-Lux, 1929), 14–15.

25 Burton, *Story of Trans-Lux,* 20.

26 Given its use of the telegraph, the Trans-Lux ticker can also be seen as an early precursor to television.

27 Trans-Lux, "Annual Report," (1928), in Mudd Stacks, Yale University Library, New Haven, Connecticut.

28 Promotional brochure, Trans-Lux Movies Corporation, "Modern Theatre," 7, Billy Rose Theater Collection, New York Public Library.

29 Burton, *Story of Trans-Lux,* 30–1.

30 Trans-Lux, "Modern Theatre," 9.

31 Trans-Lux, "Modern Theatre," 8.

32 Burton, *Story of Trans-Lux,* 32.

33 Peter B. B. Andrews, "A New 'Miniature' Makes Its Bow," *Nation's Business,* March 1931, 111.

34 Trans-Lux, "Modern Theatre," 9.

35 Trans-Lux, "Annual Report," (1936), 5, in Mudd Stacks, Yale University Library, New Haven, Connecticut.

36 "The Theatres of Tomorrow Are Here Today!," *New York Herald Tribune,* May 14, 1931.

37 Terry Ramsaye, "The Short Picture—Cocktail of the Program," *Motion Picture Herald,* March 14, 1931, 59.

38 Giovanna Franci, Rosella Mangaroni, and Esther Zago, *A Journey through American Art Deco: Architecture, Design, and Cinema in the Twenties and Thirties* (Seattle: University of Washington Press, 1997); Ghislaine Wood, "Art Deco and Hollywood Film," in *Art Deco 1910–1939,* ed. Charlotte Benton, Tim Benton, and Ghislaine Wood (Boston: Bullfinch Press, 2003).

39 Wood, "Art Deco and Hollywood Film," 325.

40 Charlotte Benton, Tim Benton, and Ghislaine Wood, *Art Deco 1910–1939* (Boston: Bullfinch Press, 2003); Franci, Mangaroni, and Zago, *A Journey through*

American Art Deco: Architecture, Design, and Cinema in the Twenties and Thirties; David Gebhard, *The National Trust Guide to Art Deco in America* (New York: Preservation Press, 1996); Bevis Hillier and Stephen Escritt, *Art Deco Style* (New York: Phaidon, 1997).

41 Gebhard, *National Trust Guide,* 11.

42 James L. Holton, "Trans-Lux to Move Its Theatre Block North on Madison Ave.," *New York World-Telegram,* September 7, 1933.

43 Trans-Lux Program for week starting Friday, September 11, 1941. In clipping file Theatres: U.S.: N.Y.: Trans-Lux (Broadway at 49th St.), Billy Rose Theater Collection, New York Public Library.

44 Gebhard, *National Trust Guide,* 9.

45 "Grand Central Theatre in New York, N.Y.—Cinema Treasures," accessed May 9, 2019, http://cinematreasures.org/theaters/3766/.

46 "Railroad Station Features Theatre," 36.

47 "Miscellany," *New York Herald Tribune,* September 14, 1938.

48 South Station Theatre, "Handbill," https://www.flickr.com/photos/italiangerry/1692840759/lightbox/.

49 In part because of its architectural importance, the building was not razed after it fell into disuse in the 1970s. After a number of failed plans to demolish the building in favor of a mall and other developments, the main concourse was preserved and restored as part of the Cincinnati Museum Center. The Newsreel Theatre was also restored and is used, largely in its original condition, for meetings and film screenings. I was able to visit the center in the Spring of 2006. Thanks to Gibson Yungblut, local historian and expert on the history of Union Terminal, for his informative tour of the terminal and for providing materials from his private collection of memorabilia and records of the station's architecture and history.

50 "Cornerstone of New Depot."

51 Fellheimer and Wagner, "Cincinnati Union Terminal."

52 Cherry Greve, "Artistic Viewpoint of New Railroad Terminal," *Cincinnati Times-Star,* March 25, 1933.

53 Wolfgang Schivelbusch, *The Railway Journey: Trains and Travel in the Nineteenth Century,* trans. Anselm Hollo (Oxford: Basil Blackwell, 1979), 48. See also Lynne Kirby, *Parallel Tracks: The Railroad and Silent Cinema* (Durham, N.C.: Duke University Press, 1997).

54 For more on this history, see Jennifer Lynn Peterson, *Education in the School of Dreams: Travelogues and Early Nonfiction Film* (Durham, N.C.: Duke University Press, 2013).

55 Noël Burch, *Life to Those Shadows,* trans. Brewster Ben (Berkeley: University of California Press, 1990).

56 Lauren Rabinovitz, *For the Love of Pleasure: Women, Movies, and Culture in Turn-of-the-Century Chicago* (New Brunswick, N.J.: Rutgers University Press, 1998), 145.

57 See Charles Musser, *The Emergence of Cinema: The American Screen to 1907* (New York: Maxwell Macmillan International, 1990), 260–65; Rabinovitz, *For the Love of Pleasure,* 145–57.

58 Promotional pamphlet, in clipping file Theatres: U.S.: N.Y.: Newsreel Theatres, Billy Rose Theater Collection, New York Public Library.

59 Lee quoted in Maggie Valentine, *The Show Starts on the Sidewalk: An Architectural History of the Movie Theatre, Starring S. Charles Lee* (New Haven, Conn.: Yale University Press, 1994), 95.

60 Valentine, *Show Starts,* 188.

61 Valentine, 192.

62 Valentine.

63 S. Charles Lee, New Theatre Sketches: Town Perspective Sketch, box 5, folder 5, S. Charles Lee Papers, 1919–1962, Department of Special Collections, University of California, Los Angeles.

64 Contemporary media scholars have adopted the notion of scale from geography as a way to think through the binding capacities of modern communications. See Nick Couldry and Anna McCarthy, eds., *Mediaspace: Place, Scale and Culture in a Media Age* (New York: Routledge, 2004); Anna McCarthy, *Ambient Television: Visual Culture and Public Space* (Durham, N.C.: Duke University Press, 2001).

65 Much of feminist film theory, for example, posits the implicitly masculine gaze of the spectator, which consumes the feminized screen object. See Patricia Erens, ed., *Issues in Feminist Film Criticism* (Bloomington: Indiana University Press, 1990); Laura Mulvey, *Visual and Other Pleasures* (Bloomington: Indiana University Press, 1989); Sue Thornham, ed., *Feminist Film Theory: A Reader* (Edinborough: Edinborough University Press, 1999).

66 Hansen, *Babel and Babylon,* 7.

67 "Fox Warns Mgrs to Keep an Eagle Eye on Newsreels," *Motion Picture Herald,* March 7, 1931; "Movie Audiences Cool to Walker," *New York Times,* September 12, 1932; "War News Films Stir No Demonstrations, but Applause and Hisses Greet Some Pictures," *New York Times,* September 4, 1939; Jimmy Fiddler, "In Hollywood: 10 Best in Newsreels," *Washington Post,* February 3, 1937; Alice Highes, "A Woman's New York," *Washington Post,* July 10, 1937; Arthur Krock, "The Paramount Issue: Roosevelt," *New York Times,* Octo-

ber 4, 1936; H. I. Phillips, "The Once Over: Private Purkey," *Washington Post,* November 20, 1941.

68 Highes, "A Woman's New York," 110.

69 "Movie Audiences Cool to Walker," 2.

70 W. E. Hill, "Neighborhood Movie," *Los Angeles Times,* January 19, 1936.

71 H. I. Phillips, "The Once Over: Interview with a Hisser," *Washington Post,* August 29, 1936, X7.

72 Dante Vezzoli, "Discourtesy to Candidates," *New York Times,* October 7, 1936.

73 "Manager Asks End to Newsreel Boos," *Hartford Courant,* November 3, 1940.

74 Jimmie Fidler, "Jimmie Fidler in Hollywood," *Los Angeles Times,* October 24, 1940.

75 "Fox Warns."

76 "Fox Warns."

77 Martin Quigley, "The Exhibitor's Screen—How Shall It Be Used?," *Motion Picture Herald,* February 5, 1938, 7.

78 Quigley, "Exhibitor's Screen," 8.

79 Lucius Beebe, "The Man Who Edits the News Reels," *New York Herald Tribune,* June 24, 1934; Creighton Peet, "Trans-Lux," *Outlook and Independent,* March 25, 1931.

80 "Githens Takes Charge of Newsreel Theatres," *Motion Picture Herald,* August 31, 1935.

81 Archer Winsten, "German U.F.A. Newsreels Cause Small Tempest," *New York Post,* n.d., 1940, from clipping file in Billy Rose Theater Collection, New York Public Library.

82 Audience Reaction to "Peace by Hitler," *March of Time* vol. 7, no. 13, recorded at Radio City Music Hall, August 13, 1941, in Jack Glenn Papers, Collection 9059, American Heritage Center, University of Wyoming.

83 See Raymond Fielding, "Mirror of Discontent: The March of Time and Its Politically Controversial Film Issues," *Western Political Quarterly* 12, no. 1 (1959); Raymond Fielding, *The March of Time, 1935–1951* (New York: Oxford University Press, 1978).

84 "Showing of Film on Nazis Guarded," *New York Times,* January 21, 1938.

85 Janet Staiger, *Perverse Spectators: The Practices of Film Reception* (New York: New York University Press, 2000), 55.

86 Staiger, *Perverse Spectators,* 54.

87 "War News Brings Boom," 21.

88 Lee Shippey, "Lee Side O' L.A.," *Los Angeles Times,* January 7, 1942, A4.

89 Anti-Japanese sentiment was already running high less than a month after Pearl Harbor. Barely a month later on February 19, 1944, President Roosevelt

passed Executive Order 9066 authorizing the internment of tens of thousands of American citizens of Japanese ancestry.

90 Scholars like bell hooks have outlined how groups might engage in an "oppositional gaze" under these kinds of circumstances. bell hooks, "The Oppositional Gaze: Black Female Spectators," in *Black Looks: Race and Representation* (Boston, Mass.: South End Press, 1992), 115–31.

5. Double Vision

1 "Fletcher Henderson at Apollo; All-Negro Newsreel on Screen," *People's Voice,* November 7, 1942, microfilm, reel 81, 268, in Tuskegee Institute News Clipping File, Division of Behavioral Science Research, Carver Research Foundation, Tuskegee Institute.

2 These thirty-nine issues were among forty-five reportedly discovered in a New York City garage by Ephraim Horowitz in the early 1990s. The CBS News Archive purchased the 35-mm originals and an uncataloged viewing copy is available at the Schomburg Center for Research in Black Culture in New York City (Cf. Robyn E. Wheeler, "News for All Americans—History of All-American News, a Series of 45 Newsreels About Blacks Made in the 1940s," *American Visions,* February–March [1993], http://findarticles.com/p/articles/mi_m1546/is_n1_v8/ai_13560600). Fred MacDonald of MacDonald and Associates, a private Chicago-based historical film archive that was sold to the Library of Congress in 2010, claimed he owned the rights to these same films. In correspondence to the author, MacDonald stated he purchased a collection of *All-American News* from a retired ABC News technician. MacDonald received a Beta Master of these films—an almost identical collection as that held by the CBS News Archive—but was told that before they could be delivered to him, the film originals were lost.

3 W. E. B. Du Bois, *The Souls of Black Folk* (Boston: Bedford Books, 1997), 9.

4 Michael Warner, *Publics and Counterpublics* (New York: Zone Books, 2005), 119.

5 In addition to producing films and theatrical revues, Glucksman wrote a guide for theater managers. Cf. E. M. Glucksman, *General Instructions Manual for Theatre Managers* (Chicago: Chicago Show Printing, 1930).

6 Pearl Bowser, "Pioneers of Black Documentary Film," in *Struggles for Representation: African American Film and Video,* ed. Phyllis R. Klotman and Janet K. Cutler (Bloomington: Indiana University Press, 1999).

7 See Thomas Cripps, *Slow Fade to Black: The Negro in American Film 1900–1942* (New York: Oxford University Press, 1977); Thomas Cripps, *Making Movies Black: The Hollywood Message Movie from World War II to the*

Civil Rights Era (New York: Oxford University Press, 1993); Jesse Algernon Rhines, *Black Film/White Money* (New Brunswick, N.J.: Rutgers University Press, 1996).

8 Cripps, *Slow Fade.*

9 "Negro Newsreel Seen by 4,000,000," *American Cinematographer,* November 1943, 408.

10 Letter from Claude Barnett to *All-American News,* August 14, 1948, microform, part 2, series D, roll 4, in Claude A. Barnett papers, Chicago History Museum Research Center.

11 Letter from Emmanuel Glucksman to Claude Barnett, April 5, 1949, microform, part 2, series D, roll 4, in Claude A. Barnett papers, Chicago History Museum Research Center.

12 Scripts for the "The Negro in Education" and "The Negro in Industry" can be found in microform, part 2, series D, roll 5, Claude A. Barnett papers, Chicago History Museum Research Center.

13 Press release, "Six Dramatic Movies to Portray Negro America in Nation's Motion Picture Theatres," microform, part 2, series D, roll 3, in Claude A. Barnett papers, Chicago History Museum Research Center.

14 "Negro Newsreel to Be Produced Weekly in U.S.," *Atlanta Daily World,* October 19, 1942; "1st Newsreel for Negroes Now Ready," *New York Amsterdam Star-News,* October 31, 1942.

15 Ted Watson, "Says Negro Newsreel Will Explain Race to Whites," *Atlanta Daily World,* November 16, 1942.

16 "The Courier's Double 'V' for Double Victory Campaign Gets Country-Wide Support," *Pittsburgh Courier,* February 14, 1942. See also Lawrence P. Scott and William M. Womack, *Double V: The Civil Rights Struggle of Tuskegee Airmen* (East Lansing: Michigan State University Press, 1998); Ronald Takaki, *Double Victory: A Multicultural History of America in World War II* (Boston: Back Bay, 2001).

17 Frank White, "'All-American News'—a Negro Newsreel," *Pittsburgh Courier,* April 10, 1943.

18 Kevin K. Gaines, *Uplifting the Race: Black Leadership, Politics, and Culture in the Twentieth Century* (Chapel Hill: University of North Carolina Press, 1996); Evelyn Brooks Higginbotham, *Righteous Discontent: The Women's Movement in the Black Baptist Church, 1880–1920* (Cambridge, Mass.: Harvard University Press, 1993); Edward L. Wheeler, *Uplifting the Race: The Black Minister in the New South, 1865–1902* (Lanham, Md.: University Press of America, 1986). For more on the connection between the notion of racial uplift and early cinema, see Allyson Nadia Field, *Uplift Cinema: The Emergence of African*

American Film and the Possibility of Black Modernity (Durham, N.C.: Duke University Press, 2015).

19 Gaines, *Uplifting the Race,* 4.

20 Higginbotham, *Righteous Discontent.*

21 Field, *Uplift Cinema,* 256.

22 See Claude A. Barnett, "The Role of the Press, Radio, and Motion Picture and Negro Morale," *Journal of Negro Education* 12, no. 3 (1943); Rayford W. Logan, "Negro Youth and the Influence of the Press, Radio, and Cinema," *Journal of Negro Education* 9, July (1940); Mary A. Morton, "The Federal Government and Negro Morale," *Journal of Negro Education* 12, no. 3 (1943); L. D. Reddick, "Educational Programs for the Improvement of Race Relations: Motion Pictures, Radio, the Press and Libraries," *Journal of Negro Education* 13, no. 3 (1944).

23 See Jacqueline Najuma Stewart, *Migrating to the Movies: Cinema and Black Urban Modernity* (Berkeley: University of California Press, 2005).

24 Cited in Barbara Stones, *America Goes to the Movies: 100 Years of Motion Picture Exhibition* (Hollywood: National Association of Theatre Owners, 1993), 212.

25 Cited in Peter Noble, *The Negro in Films* (London: Skelton Robinson, 1948), 99.

26 Noble, *Negro in Films,* 99.

27 Stones, *America Goes to the Movies,* 211.

28 Cripps, *Slow Fade.*

29 Cripps, *Slow Fade,* 329.

30 "Typed Offerings Disgust Him," *Atlanta Daily World,* October 5, 1942, microfilm, in Tuskegee Institute News Clipping File, Division of Behavioral Science Research, Carver Research Foundation, Tuskegee Institute.

31 Cripps, *Slow Fade*; Thomas Cripps, *Black Film as Genre* (Bloomington: Indiana University Press, 1978); Cripps, *Making Movies Black*; Thomas Doherty, *Projections of War: Hollywood, American Culture, and World War II,* rev. ed. (New York: Columbia University Press, 1999).

32 Reddick, "Educational Programs for the Improvement," 367.

33 Reddick, "Educational Programs for the Improvement."

34 "Poll Shows What Folk Think of Hollywood Treatment of Negro," *Kansas City Call,* March 26, 1943, microfilm, in Tuskegee Institute News Clipping File, Division of Behavioral Science Research, Carver Research Foundation, Tuskegee Institute.

35 Herman Hill, "Walter White Is Winning His Fight for Better Roles," *Pittsburgh Courier,* August 8, 1942, microfilm, in Tuskegee Institute News Clip-

ping File, Division of Behavioral Science Research, Carver Research Foundation, Tuskegee Institute.

36 "Distorted Roles of Negro on Screen Must Go, Says White," *Atlanta Daily World*, October 13, 1943, microfilm, in Tuskegee Institute News Clipping File, Division of Behavioral Science Research, Carver Research Foundation, Tuskegee Institute.

37 Morton, "Federal Government and Negro Morale," 357.

38 Cripps, *Making Movies Black*, 129.

39 Doherty, *Projections of War*, 210.

40 Noble, *Negro in Films*; Henry T. Sampson, *Blacks in Black and White: A Source Book on Black Films* (Metuchen, N.J.: Scarecrow Press, 1977).

41 "Negroes' War Efforts Get H'wood Brushoff; Writers Complaining," *Variety*, March 15, 1944, 32.

42 "More Negro Scenes Cut out in Dixie Set New Problems for Pix Producers," *Variety*, July 12, 1944, 32.

43 Lawrence F. Lamar, "Newsreel of the Negro in Army Camps Out Soon," *Chicago Defender*, October 17, 1942, microfilm, in Tuskegee Institute News Clipping File, Division of Behavioral Science Research, Carver Research Foundation, Tuskegee Institute.

44 Sampson, *Blacks in Black and White*, 66.

45 "'We've Come A Long, Long Way' Depicts Advances of Race and Fight for Freedom," *Philadelphia Tribune*, January 20, 1945, microfilm, in Tuskegee Institute News Clipping File, Division of Behavioral Science Research, Carver Research Foundation, Tuskegee Institute.

46 "Film on Negro Life Is Called Insulting," *Chicago Defender*, February 19, 1944, microfilm, in Tuskegee Institute News Clipping File, Division of Behavioral Science Research, Carver Research Foundation, Tuskegee Institute.

47 "Here's a Film Everyone Should See, Writes Defender Columnist," *Chicago Defender*, February 26, 1944, microfilm, in Tuskegee Institute News Clipping File, Division of Behavioral Science Research, Carver Research Foundation, Tuskegee Institute.

48 Letter from Truman K. Gibson Jr. to Claude Barnett, December 14, 1942, microform, part 2, series D, roll 4, Claude A. Barnett papers.

49 Lauren Rebecca Sklaroff, "Constructing G. I. Joe Louis: Cultural Solutions to the 'Negro Problem' during World War II," *Journal of American History* 89, no. 3 (2002).

50 Harry McAlpin, "OWI Deal Bars Negro in Major Newsreels," *Chicago Defender*, January 2, 1943.

51 Harry McAlpin, "Silver Lining," *Chicago Defender*, February 13, 1943.

52 Barnett, "Role of the Press," 478.

53 "Newsreels 'Cut' Negro Fighters," *New York Amsterdam News,* January 8, 1944, A1; "Newsreels Blackout Race Troops," *Atlanta Daily World,* January 9, 1944; "Newsreels and the Negro in the War," *Journal and Guide,* January 15, 1944, microfilm, in Tuskegee Institute News Clipping File, Division of Behavioral Science Research, Carver Research Foundation, Tuskegee Institute.

54 "Newsreels 'Cut' Negro Fighters."

55 "Newsreels Blackout."

56 "Omissions from Newsreels," *Crisis,* February 1944, 39.

57 "Newsreels 'Cut' Negro Fighters."

58 "No Agreement with Newsreels, NAACP Is Assured by War Dep't," *Atlanta Daily World,* February 2, 1944.

59 "No Agreement with Newsreels."

60 Roy Wilkins, "The Watchtower," *New York Amsterdam News,* January 15, 1944, 7A.

61 "99th Fliers in Newsreels on Broadway," *People's Voice,* February 12, 1944, microfilm, in Tuskegee Institute News Clipping File, Division of Behavioral Science Research, Carver Research Foundation, Tuskegee Institute.

62 W. E. B. Du Bois, "The Souls of Black Folk," in *Three Negro Classics* (New York: Avon Books, 1965), 215.

63 Jane Gaines, *Fire and Desire: Mixed-Race Movies in the Silent Era* (Chicago: University of Chicago Press, 2001), 12.

64 Luther Hill, "Newsreel to Back 'Good Conduct' Campaign," *Pittsburgh Courier,* May 13, 1944.

65 "Churchman Makes Good Conduct Plea," *All-American News,* 113 (1944) in CBS News Archive.

66 Higginbotham, *Righteous Discontent,* 196.

67 "Teenagers Show 'Good' Conduct," *All-American News,* 123 (1945) in CBS News Archive.

68 "Flournoy English Wins Award for Efficiency," *All-American News,* 116 (1944) and "Firemen Promoted in New York City," *All-American News,* 120 (1945) in CBS News Archive.

69 Letter to Marcus Bruce Christian from Ruth, June 1, 1945, in "Letters from the Archives of Marcus Bruce Christian," *Chickenbones: A Journal of Literary and Artistic African American Themes,* http://www.nathanielturner.com/ruthenjoysnegrolifechicago.htm (accessed August 5, 2008).

70 "Champs Baby Punches Ivories," *All-American News,* 117 (1945) in CBS News Archive.

71 As Richard Dyer has pointed out, representations of stardom often rely on

tensions between celebrities being both like us and exceptional, close to us and far away. In *All-American,* these tensions took on special relevance with respect to the politics of racial uplift. See Richard Dyer, *Heavenly Bodies: Film Stars and Society* (New York: St. Martin's Press, 1986).

72 "Blind Man Fine student," *All-American News,* 221 (1945) in CBS News Archive.

73 "Armless, He Is a Success," *All-American News,* 140 (1945) in CBS News Archive.

74 "92nd in Italy Rout Nazis," *All-American News,* 108 (1944) in CBS News Archive.

75 "92nd Infantry in Italy," *All-American News,* 131 (1945) in CBS News Archive.

76 "92nd Honors Its Dead," *All-American News,* 138 (1945) in CBS News Archive.

77 "Gen. Clark Host to New Officers," *All-American News,* 115 (1944) in CBS News Archive.

78 "Buddy Young now a 'GOB,'" *All-American News,* 125 (1945) in CBS News Archive.

79 Cripps, *Making Movies Black,* 150.

80 Melvin R. Williamson, "Soldiers Criticize All-American News," *Chicago Defender,* August 26, 1944, 12.

81 A. Private, "Likes 'All American News,'" *New York Amsterdam News,* May 27, 1944, 6A.

82 "Hollan Explains Vet Policy," *All-American News,* 142 (1945) in CBS News Archive.

83 Alfred E. Smith, "Adventures in Race Relations," *Chicago Defender,* August 11, 1945.

84 Wheeler, *Uplifting the Race,* xvii.

85 Jane Gaines, *Fire and Desire,* 12.

Conclusion

1 For more on the efforts to preserve newsreels, see Mark Garrett Cooper et al., eds., *Rediscovering U.S. Newsfilm: Cinema, Television, and the Archive* (New York: Routledge, 2018). See below for further discussion on this question.

2 Anna McCarthy, *The Citizen Machine: Governing by Television in 1950s America* (New York: New Press, 2010); Karal Ann Marling, *As Seen on TV: The Visual Culture of Everyday Life in the 1950s* (Cambridge, Mass.: Harvard University Press, 1996); Michael Curtin, *Redeeming the Wasteland: Television Documentary and Cold War Politics* (New Brunswick, N.J.: Rutgers University Press, 1995); Janet Thumin, *Small Screens, Big Ideas: Television in the 1950s* (London: I.B. Tauris, 2002).

3 Daniel Dayan and Elihu Katz, *Media Events: The Live Broadcasting of History* (Cambridge, Mass.: Harvard University Press, 1992); Daniel J. Boorstin, *The Image: A Guide to Pseudo-Events in America,* 25th anniversary ed. (New York: Vintage, 1987); Ien Ang, *Living Room Wars: Rethinking Media Audiences for a Postmodern World* (New York: Routledge, 1996).

4 Aniko Bodroghkozy, *Equal Time: Television and the Civil Rights Movement* (Urbana: University of Illinois Press, 2013); Sasha Torres, *Black, White, and in Color: Television and Black Civil Rights* (Princeton, N.J.: Princeton University Press, 2003).

5 Josh Braun, "Social Media and Distribution Studies," *Social Media + Society* 1, no. 1 (April 1, 2015); Dell P. Champlin and Janet T. Knoedler, "The Media, the News, and Democracy: Revisiting the Dewey-Lippmann Debate," *Journal of Economic Issues* 40, no. 1 (March 1, 2006): 135–52; Irfan Chaudhry, "#Hashtags for Change: Can Twitter Promote Social Progress in Saudi Arabia?," *International Journal of Communication* 8 (January 2014): 943–61; Adrian Chen, "The Fake-News Fallacy," *New Yorker* 93, no. 26 (September 4, 2017): 78–83; Lynn Schofield Clark, "Constructing Public Spaces | Participants on the Margins: Examining the Role That Shared Artifacts of Engagement in the Ferguson Protests Played Among Minoritized Political Newcomers on Snapchat, Facebook, and Twitter," *International Journal of Communication* 10, no. 0 (January 6, 2016): 26; Peter Dahlgren, "The Internet, Public Spheres, and Political Communication: Dispersion and Deliberation," *Political Communication* 22, no. 2 (April 1, 2005): 147–62; Malcolm Gladwell, "Small Change," *New Yorker,* October 4, 2010; Nicholas Negroponte, *Being Digital* (New York: Vintage Books, 1996); "From Fake News to Disappearing Ad Revenue, Journalism Fights for Survival in a Post-Truth Era," *WIRED,* accessed August 14, 2017, https://www.wired.com/2017/02/journalism-fights-survival-post-truth-era/; "How Facebook Is Changing the Way Its Users Consume Journalism," *New York Times,* accessed August 14, 2017, https://www.nytimes.com/2014/10/27/business/media/how-facebook-is-changing-the-way-its-users-consume-journalism.html; "How Social Media Is Changing Journalism," Bedrosian Center | USC, accessed August 14, 2017, https://bedrosian.usc.edu/blog/how-social-media-is-changing-journalism/; "Your Filter Bubble Is Destroying Democracy," *WIRED,* accessed August 14, 2017, https://www.wired.com/2016/11/filter-bubble-destroying-democracy/.

6 Cooper, *Rediscovering U.S. Newsfilm.*

7 Cooper.

Index

Index by Denise E. Carlson

Page numbers in italics refer to illustrations.

African Americans: excluded from mainstream newsreels, 179–80, 182–85, 188, 194, 199; film portrayals of, 17, 176–78, 205–6; middle-class, 172–73, 190, 196; showcasing accomplishments of, 17, 167–68, 170–71, 179–81, 186–88, 191–94, 200; during World War II, 17, 171–74, 179, 181–85, 194–200, *195*, *198*. See also *All-American News* (newsreel); audiences: African American; civil rights movement; race; race movies; race relations; racial uplift; racism

Aitken, Ian, 55–56, 229n27

Alexander, William, 169

All-American News (newsreel), 167–201; accommodation in, 17, 193, 197–200, *198*; audience response, 11, 197–200, 205; counterpublics of, 168–69, 201; direct address, 186–92, *191*; extant collection, 246n2; Jim Crow cinema and, 173–86, 199, 200–201; opening sequence, 186–89, *187*; pedagogical address, 17, 168, 172–73, 186–201, *191*; racial uplift through, 167–68, 169–73, 186, 187–91, 193–96, 199, 250–51n71; Signal Corps footage in, 181–82, 194–96, *195*. *See also* African Americans

Allen, Robert C., 132

Alley, Norman, cameraman, 91; *Panay* Incident filmed by, 109, 110, 112, 113–15, *115*, 116, 124–25

Alley, Paul: voiceovers by, 101

Althusser, Louis, 131

Ament, Walton, 184

Arno, Peter: cartoon by, 127, 128, 130, 155

art deco style, 141–45, 149. *See also* newsreel theaters: architecture

assassination: attempt on Crown Prince Humbert of Italy, 41; of King Alexander of Yugoslavia, 36

Asians. *See* China; Far East locales; Japan/Japanese people; orientalist discourses; Sino–Japanese War

Associated Negro Press, 169

Associated Screen News (Canada), 223n41

audiences, 9, 15–16, 154–55; African American, 16–17, 173, 175, 176, 201; for *All-American News*, 11, 197–200, 205; direct address to, 13, 32–42,

49, 55, 186–92, *191*, 205; engaging, 50–51, 66, 130, 131; experiencing the news, 18, 59, 91, 100, 102, 107; for Hauptmann trial newsreels, 78–89; for Lindbergh son's kidnapping newsreels, 66–67, 68–77; mediated distance from real events, 93–94, 96–99, 108–10, 115–18, 125–26, 165, 238n46; reactions, 24, 128, 155–64, 168; relationship to reality, 11, 46–47, 59, 120; for Roosevelt 1933 inauguration newsreels, 61–66. *See also* collective spectatorship; gaze: audience's; news: watching; public sphere; reception; spectatorship

Barnett, Claude, 169, 170, 171, 182–83, 188, 200, 201
Barthes, Roland, 40
Battles, Kathleen, 69
Baudry, Jean-Louis, 131, 132, 133
Benjamin, Walter, 46, 47, 72
Bent, Silas, 68, 74–75, 76
Bernays, Edward, 8
blacks. *See* African Americans
Blount, Clifford, 193
Bordwell, David, 31
Bourdelle, Pierre: murals in Cincinnati's Union Terminal, 148–49
Bradley, F. H., 56
Buell, Jed, 176
Burch, Noël, 38, 151
Bush, Stephen, 52
Butterbeans and Susie (comedy duo), 198
Byrd, Richard, 97

Calvalcanti, Alberto, 54
Cameraman, The (motion picture), 95
cameramen, 91–126; capturing spectacular footage, 28–29, 31, 35, 41, 93–95, 98, 100, 119; celebrity interviews, 96–97; in comic books, 118, 121–25, *122, 124, 125*, 126; as explorers, 92–93, 119–20; heroism of, 13–17, 95, 97, 105–10, 116–18, 121–22, 126, 205; masculinity of, 15, 93–100, 107, 108–9, 125–26, 222n28; in motion pictures, 43–44, 95, 96, 99, 117–21, 126; mythic status, 94, 96, 100, 106–7; in war zones, 14–15, 41, 92, 98–117, 205
Capra, Frank, 181
celebrity: culture of, 19–20, 66, 76; interviews with, 96–97; representations of, 192, 193, 250–51n71
Chiang Kai-Shek, 101
China. *See* Nanking, Japanese attack on; Shanghai, Japanese attack on; Sino–Japanese War
Cincinnati Union Terminal: newsreel theater in, 146–49, *146, 147, 150*, 151, 243n49
cinema: of attractions, 38–39, 45; classical Hollywood, 12, 132–33, 141; of exotic places, 150–51; indexicality of, 37, 40–41, 52; realism in, 59, 229n27. *See also* documentaries; ethnographic motion pictures; motion picture industry; newsreels; newsreel theaters
civil rights movement, 172, 184, 193, 200, 206–7, 209. *See also* Double Victory (Double V) campaign; Du Bois, W. E. B.; racial uplift
Cochrane, R. H., 87
Cohen, Emanuel, 52
collective spectatorship, 7–11, 46–48,

65–66, 113, 134, 201; of news parade, 12–14, 17, 134; participation in the public sphere through, 91, 117, 126, 206–7, 209–10; shared experience of, 204, 205, 206, 208–9. *See also* audiences; news: watching; spectatorship
colonialism, 107–8. *See also* orientalist discourses
comic books, 118. *See also* Speed Martin comic book series
Condon, John "Jafsie," 82; testimony at Hauptmann trial, 83, 84, 87
counterpublics, 10–11, 17–18, 168–69, 201, 204, 207, 210. *See also* public sphere
Cripps, Thomas, 176, 178, 197–98
Crump, Irving: *Boys' Book of Newsreel Hunters,* 93, 94, 95–96, 99–100
culture: of authenticity, 58; of celebrity, 19–20, 66, 76; media, 10, 17; of speed, 15

Darrow, Clarence, 79
Davis, Kenneth, 68
Dayan, Daniel, 7
Debord, Guy, 11, 59
Dewey, John: Lippmann's debate with, 7, 8, 45, 208–9
display: rhetoric of, 186–87, 191–92, 196; tension between evidence and, 5, 14, 36–42, 44–45, 49, 59, 66–78, 80–81, 200
distribution: of Lindbergh transatlantic flight newsreels, 23–24; modes of, 13, 25–32, 43, 47, 204, 205; networks of, 38, 42, 69–70, 92, 129; power of, 21, 59; realism in, 59–60, 66, 89; of Roosevelt inauguration newsreels, 63–65
Doane, Mary Ann, 35
documentaries, 6, 44–45, 53–56. *See also* ethnographic motion pictures; motion picture industry
Doherty, Thomas, 179
Double Victory (Double V) campaign, 16, 169–73, 177, 184, 188, 194–95, 201. *See also* African Americans: during World War II; racial uplift
Douglas, Susan, 9
Du Bois, W. E. B.: double consciousness concept, 168, 188–89, 191, 201
Durdin, F. Tillman, 111
Dyer, Richard, 250–51n71

Eberson, John: cinema theaters designed by, 141
editors, 28–29, 31, 37, 60
education. *See All-American News* (newsreel): pedagogical address; newsreels: educational role
Edwards, Roy, cameraman, 74
Eisenstein, Sergei, 54
Ellis, John, 40–41
Embassy Newsreel Theatre (New York City), 128, 134, 139
English, Flournoy, 192, 193
Erskine, John, 34
ethnographic motion pictures, 42, 97–98, 107–8. *See also* documentaries; motion picture industry
evidence: newsreels as, 40–42; as realism, 14, 66–77; rhetoric of, 186–87, 191–92, 193–94, 196. *See also* display: tension between evidence and
exhibition, 18, 38, 135, 188; history of, 129–31; of motion pictures, 26, 138–42; rear projection, 134–40;

system of, 13, 31, 38, 92, 204–5. *See also* newsreel theaters

Far East locales, 92, 100–102, 104, 108–9, 113–21, 123, 125–27
Fass, Paula, 68, 74
Fellheimer, Alfred: newsreel cinemas designed by, 146, 148
Feuer, Jane, 6–7, 64
Fidler, Jimmie, 159
Field, Allyson Nadia, 173
Fielding, Raymond, 5, 21
Fighting 92nd Infantry Division, 194–95, *195*. *See also* African Americans: during World War II
films. *See* cinema; documentaries; ethnographic motion pictures; motion picture industry; newsreels
Flaherty, Robert, 54
Fonck, René: transatlantic flight attempt, 22
footage, newsreel: archives, 203, 210–12; flow of, 27–29, 30, 32, 42; home movies of Lindbergh son, 69–70, 73–76. *See also* cameramen: capturing spectacular footage
Ford, Charles E., 60–61, 63, 103
Fordist manufacturing models, 31, 32, 42
Fox Films, 43–44, 96, 128
Fox Movietone News (newsreel), 24–25, 27, 32–34, 43–44, 60, 87, 112–13, 128
Fox News (newsreel), 23–24, 26–27, 29, 210, 222n15
Freeman, Mervyn, cameraman, 41, 94–95
Furber, Percy, 135

Gaines, Jane, 6, 189, 191, 201
Gaines, Kevin, 172
gaze: audience's, 4, 81, 85, 93, 121, 126; camera's, 71, 75, 190–91; imperial, 14, 100–109, 114–15, 126, 165, 205; masculine, 108, 132, 205, 244n65; newsreel's, 73, 76, 96; oppositional, 246n90; white, 190–91, 196. *See also* looking
Gebhard, David, 145
gender, 15, 48, 93, 244n65; orientalist discourses around, 103–5, 107–9
Germans/Germany, 121, 122–23, 160–63. *See also* Riefenstahl, Leni
Gibson, Truman K., Jr., 181–82
Githens, French, 160–61, 163
Glucksman, Emmanuel, 169, 170–71, 188, 200, 201, 246n5
Goldberg, Bert and Jack, 176, 180
Gomery, Douglas, 26, 132
Grand Central Station (New York City): newsreel theater in, 145
Gregg, John A. (Bishop), 190
Grierson, John, 53, 54–57, 58, 59, 89
Gunning, Tom, 38, 72

Habermas, Jürgen, 10
Hale's Tour (travelogue), 151
Hall, Mordaunt, 24
Hanich, Julian, 12
Hansen, Miriam, 11–12, 133, 156
Hauptmann, Bruno Richard: trial coverage, 51, 77–89, *85*, *86*
Hawley, Adelaide: voiceovers by, 33
Hearst Metrotone News (newsreel), 27, 30, 33, 41, 60, 67, 97, 210; critics of, 52–53; Hauptmann trial coverage, 78, 80, 81–82, 83–84, 87, 89; year-end reviews, 37, 43–44. See also *News of the Day* (Hearst newsreel)
Hegel, Georg Wilhelm Friedrich, 56, 57, 229n27

Higginbotham, Evelyn Brooks, 172, 173, 190
Hill, Edwin C.: voiceovers by, 33
Hill, W. E., 158
Hillis, Newell, 135
Hitler, Adolf, 161–63, 177, 180. *See also* Riefenstahl, Leni
Hollan, George, 199
Hollywood. *See* cinema: classical Hollywood; motion picture industry
hooks, bell, 246n90
Horowitz, Ephraim, 246n2
Hughes, Alice, 157
Hughes, Langston, 181

I Cover the War (motion picture), 99
identity, 3, 189; American collective, 7–8, 9, 11–12, 18, 48, 165, 204–8
inequality, racial, 197, 199–200; contesting, 17, 168, 176, 193, 207. *See also* Jim Crow society; racism
Ingres, Jean Auguste Dominque, 104
International Newsreel (Hearst), 27, 29; Lindbergh's transatlantic flight coverage, 22, 23; promotional motion picture, 94, 96; Sino–Japanese War coverage, 91, 109
isolationism, U.S., 102, 117–18, 121, 162. *See also* neutrality, U.S. policy of, during Sino–Japanese War

Japan/Japanese people, 121, 123, 164, 165, 245–46n89. *See also* Nanking, Japanese attack on; orientalist discourses; *Panay* Incident; Shanghai, Japanese attack on; Sino–Japanese War
Jim Crow society, 187, 196, 207; *All-American News* showing, 173–86, 199, 200–201; motion picture industry, 17, 168, 173–86, 197. *See also* inequality, racial; segregation
Johnson, Martin and Osa, 97

Kaminsky, Alexander H., 79
Kant, Immanuel, 56
Kaplan, E. Ann, 100, 108
Katz, Elihu, 7
Kennedy, John B.: voiceovers by, 33
King, John Paul: voiceovers by, 114, 116
Kinograms (newsreel), 27, 29
Krainukov, George, cameraman, 91, 106

Lacan, Jacques, 131
Lamb, Thomas W.: newsreel theaters designed by, 141, 142–43, 155
Lee, Robert, 103
Lee, S. Charles: newsreel theaters designed by, 141, 151–54, 155, 205
Lehr, Lew: voiceovers by, 33
Leibowitiz, Samuel, 79
Lewis, John: newsreel audience reactions to, 157
Lindbergh, Anne Morrow, 66, 74, 75, 79, 84, 87
Lindbergh, Charles, newsreel coverage of: at Hauptmann trial, 79, 80, 82–83, 84, 87; isolationist stance, 162; kidnapping of son, 50–51, 66–77; transatlantic flight, 19–25, 28, 40, 46, 47, 66, 205, 222n15
Lindsey, A. D., 56
Lippmann, Walter: Dewey's debate with, 7, 8, 45, 208–9; John Grierson on, 55; on Lindbergh son's kidnapping, 68, 74–75, 76
Littell, Robert, 1, 2, 7, 18, 53, 203
looking, 128, 167, 194; act of, 39–40, 51, 72, 78, 88–89, 91–126, 208; audience's, 107, 128, 201; culture of,

66, 76; newsreel's emphasis on, 7, 14–15, 17, 45, 69–70; police's, 71–73; power and privilege of, 5, 11–12, 16, 48, 89, 91–93, 205, 206–7; relations of, 18, 46; trajectories of, 186–87. *See also* gaze
Louis, Joe, 192–93
Loviglio, Jason, 9
Lukács, Georg, 57–58, 59, 89, 229n27

MacDonald, Fred, 246n2
Maltby, Richard, 132
March of Time, The (documentary series), 161–63
Marx, Karl: commodity form concept, 57
Mayell, Eric, cameraman: *Panay* Incident footage, 109, 110, 114, 124–25
Mayne, Judith, 133
McAlpin, Harry, 182
McCallister, Richard, 127
McDaniels, Hattie, 176
McElravy, Robert C., 1, 2, 7, 17, 18, 203, 212
McNamee, Graham: voiceovers by, 33, 36, 64–65, 115, 116–17
media/media events, 76, 244n64; culture of, 10, 17; Hauptmann trial coverage, 77–89; history of, 3–7, 11; newsreels as system of, 204–6; reality of, 15, 93; role in democracy, 7–8, 12. *See also* motion picture industry; newspapers; press, the; radio; social media; television
Menken, Arthur, cameraman: *Panay* incident filmed by, 110
Micheaux, Oscar, 175–76
Micheaux, Solomon Lightfoot (Elder), 180
military, segregation in, 172, 179, 181–82, 197–200. *See also* African Americans: during World War II
mobility, newsreel's association with, 15, 16, 130, 145, 148–49. *See also* speed; travel, newsreel's association with
modernism, 58–59, 154
modernity, 72, 128; cameraman symbolizing, 97, 107; newsreel's association with, 15–16, 45, 130, 141–44, 148, 164–65, 205; of newsreel theater architecture, 139–42, 144–45, 151–52, 155
Morton, Mary, 178
motion picture industry: Big Five studios, 4, 26–27, 30, 31–32, 129, 174, 181; culture of, 5–6, 20; newsreel cameramen motion pictures, 43–44, 95, 96, 99, 117–21, 126; segregation in, 17, 168, 169–73, 173–86, 188, 197, 201; studio system, 11–12, 26–27, 29, 31. *See also* cinema; documentaries; ethnographic motion pictures; Far East locales; newsreels; race movies
Movie Ticker. *See* Trans-Lux Corporation: Movie Ticker
Movietone News (Fox newsreel). See *Fox Movietone News* (newsreel)
Muse, Clarence, 176
Muth, Russell, cameraman, 96

Nanking, Japanese attack on, 14, 92, 100, 101, 105, 108–9, 236n21. See also *Panay* Incident
National Association for the Advancement of Colored People (NAACP), 177–79, 180, 183–85. *See also* racial uplift

Neale, Steve, 39
Negro Soldier, The (OWI film), 181
neutrality, U.S. policy of, during Sino–Japanese War, 15, 109–11, 115, 122, 125–26, 238n46, 239n73. *See also* isolationism, U.S.
news: fake, 207–8; motion picture, 49–89; public engagement in, 8, 91, 159, 160–61, 164, 208; as spectacle, 6–7, 25, 37–38, 45, 49, 98; visual representation of, 11, 209; watching, 3, 9–10, 12, 14, 16, 128–31, 155, 165, 167
News of the Day (Hearst newsreel), 27, 33; *Panay* Incident coverage, 112–13, 114–17; Sino–Japanese War coverage, 41, 101, 103–5, 109
newspapers, 21, 194; Hauptmann trial coverage, 78, 79, 81, 87, 88; Lindbergh son's kidnapping coverage, 65, 66, 67, 68, 71, 76–83; newsreels organized like, 4, 27, 32–33. *See also* press, the
news parade, 19–48; collective spectatorship of, 12–14, 17, 134; emphasis on watching, 128, 167; as industry, 25–32; logic of, 42–48, 49, 204; metaphor of, 3, 13–14, 20, 32, 91, 206; mode of address, 32–42
News Parade, The (motion picture), 43–44, 96
newsreels: African Americans excluded from mainstream, 179–80, 182–85, 188, 194, 199; apparatus of, 131–33; archives, 2–3, 210–12; authenticity, 40, 42, 51, 58, 93, 94, 95, 100, 114, 125–26; authority, 7, 76, 93, 113, 173; censoring, 159–60; compartmentalization in, 4, 27, 32–33, 45, 49; consolidation of, 11–12, 26–27, 53, 167; critics of, 31–35, 43, 45, 49, 51–59, 65, 89, 120; educational role, 1–2, 6, 7, 17, 168, 172–73, 228n13; features, 4, 186, 192; history, 1–18; as industry, 25–32; narrative in, 44–45; popularity, 127–28; power, 51, 89, 204; present absence in, 40–48, 49, 97–98; promotion, 91–95, 98, 100–102, 113, 125–26, 129, 151; rhetoric, 144–45; silent, 4, 20, 27, 32, 34; as spectacle, 37–42; talking, 24–25, 32–36; value, 17, 203–4, 206–10, 212; war coverage, 14–15, 41, 92, 98–117, 205. *See also individual newsreel titles*
newsreel system, 3, 13–14, 18, 19–48, 204–6. *See also* distribution; exhibition; news parade; production; reception; representation
newsreel theaters, 26, 29, 127–65, 205; architecture, 15–16, 140–55, 164, 243n49; audiences, 131–34, 155–65; Trans-Lux Corporation, 134–40. *See also* theaters; *and individual newsreel theaters*
Newsreel Theatres, Inc., 15, 128
New York Stock Exchange, Movie Ticker system, 135–37
Nichol, Bill, 6
Nungesser, Charles: transatlantic flight attempt, 22

Office of War Information (OWI): films by, 179, 181–82
orientalist discourses, 15, 100, 103–5, 107–9, 205. *See also* racism
Orvell, Miles, 58

Osborn, Albert S.: testimony at Hauptmann trial, 81

Panay Incident, 109–17, *115*, 124–25, 126. *See also* Sino–Japanese War
parades. *See* news parade; ticker tape parades
Paramount News (newsreel), 27, 60, 64, 87, 89, 97, 185
Pathé News (newsreel), 2–4, 23, 27, 60, 64, 74, 87, 185
Payne, Arthur, 135
Peden, Charles, cameraman, 67
Pennsylvania Station (New York City): newsreel theater in, 145–46
Phillips, H. I., 158
photography, 40, 96, 107
politics: racial, 16–17, 167, 187, 197–98, 207; of racial uplift, 193, 194, 200, 250–51n71; of respectability, 173, 190–91, 192; struggles over, 206–7; of visibility, 16–17, 168, 173, 187–88, 196, 199–200, 201, 205
Popkin, Leo and Harry, 176
press, the, 8, 22, 37, 67–68, 75, 79, 88; criticism of newsreels by, 51, 52, 53. *See also* newspapers
production, 38, 92; factory model of, 31, 32, 42, 53; of Lindbergh transatlantic flight story, 23–24; modes of, 13, 25–32, 43, 204, 205, 212; processional nature of, 43, 47; realism in, 49–50, 55, 59–66, 88–89; Universal's network, 69–70
public sphere: divisions within, 207–8, 209; emergent, 5, 128; mediated, 7–18, 168, 201, 204, 205, 206; newsreel cinemas as, 130, 131, 155–65; participation in, 91, 117, 126, 206–7, 209–10; reshaping of, 4, 18, 207–9; visual, 200, 209. *See also* audiences; counterpublics
Purdy, Paul S., 158–59

Quigley, Martin, 160

race, 15, 48, 93; politics of, 16–17, 167, 187, 197–98, 207. *See also* African Americans; *All-American News* (newsreel)
race movies, 169–70, 174, 176–78, 180–81, 185–86, 197–98, 200
race relations, 17, 168, 174, 179, 181–82, 199, 200–201
racial uplift, 16, 201; politics of, 193, 194, 200, 250–51n71. See also *All-American News* (newsreel): racial uplift through; civil rights movement; Double Victory (Double V) campaign; National Association for the Advancement of Colored People (NAACP)
racism, 196, 197, 198; stereotypes perpetrated by, 190–91; during World War II, 164, 165, 245–46n89. *See also* inequality, racial; Jim Crow society; newsreels: African Americans excluded from mainstream; orientalist discourses; segregation
radio, 194, 225n56; advent of, 9–10; Hauptmann trial coverage, 78, 79, 81, 87, 88; Lindbergh's son kidnapping coverage, 67, 69; Roosevelt's 1933 inauguration coverage, 64, 65
realism, 49–89; course of, 51–59; in Hauptman trial coverage, 77–89; ideological function of, 6; in Lindbergh son's kidnapping coverage,

66–77; manipulation of, 120; in Roosevelt's 1933 inauguration coverage, 59–66; sources of, 34, 113, 204, 208
reality: audience's relationship to, 11, 46–47, 59, 120; changing notions of, 2–3; experience of, 9, 18; of media events, 15, 93; newsreel's effect of, 32, 36, 43, 50–51, 65; representation of, 6, 11, 59; as spectacle, 37–42; visibility of, 5, 18, 40, 41–42, 51, 89, 167
rear projection system. *See* Trans-Lux Corporation: rear projection system
reception, 11, 12–13, 15–16, 129–34. *See also* audiences: reactions
Reddick, L. D., 177
Reilly, Edward J.: Hauptmann defense attorney, 81, 87–88
Reiss, Winold: mosaics designed by, 146
Renov, Michael, 6
representation, 6, 11, 40, 69, 229n27; logic of, 20, 32, 42–48, 49, 50; mode of, 14, 88, 212; racial uplift through, 167–68; realism in, 59–60; technological means of, 38–39
respectability, 172, 173, 190–91, 192, 196, 200
Riefenstahl, Leni: *Triumph of the Will,* 39, 40, 42
Robeson, Paul, 175, 176
Rogers, Dorothy, 190–91, *191*
Rony, Fatimah Tobing, 107
Roosevelt, Eleanor, 79, 157
Roosevelt, Franklin D.: audience reactions to, 127, 157, 159, 162, 165; 1933 inauguration coverage, 50, 59–66, *62*, *63*, 86
Rosen, Philip, 44, 45, 55
Rotha, Paul, 53–54
Ryan, Mary, 45

Sack, Alfred J., 176
Said, Edward, 103
scale, use of term, 244n64
Schivelbusch, Wolfgang, 149–50
Schwartz, Vanessa, 37
Seabury, Samuel: newsreel audience reactions to, 157
segregation: in the military, 172, 179, 181–82, 197; in motion picture industry, 17, 168, 169–73, 173–86. *See also* Jim Crow society; racism
Shanghai, Japanese attack on, 14, 92, 99, 100, 101–2, 103–6, *105*, 108–9
Sino–Japanese War, 91–126; newsreel cameramen's involvement in, 14–15, 41, 92, 100–117, 205. *See also* neutrality, U.S. policy of, during Sino–Japanese War
Smith, Alfred E., 199
Smith, Courtland, 134–35, 137, 160
social media, 17, 18, 206, 207–8, 209–10
sound: introduction of, 4–5, 26–27, 52, 175; in newsreels, 13, 21, 24. *See also* newsreels: talking; voiceover commentaries
South Station (Boston): newsreel theater in, 145, 146
spectacle: news as, 6–7, 25, 37–38, 45, 49, 98; reality as, 37–42; society of, 11, 59; of war, 100–103
spectatorship, 3, 100, 119, 130, 135, 137, 156, 189; contested arena of, 163–65; linked to travel and mobility, 5, 15, 145, 149–50, 151, 154–55; scholarship

on, 131–34. *See also* collective spectatorship; gaze; looking
speed, 15, 145; newsreel's association with, 64–65, 70, 155. *See also* mobility, newsreel's association with
Speed Martin comic book series, 118, 121–25, *122, 124, 125,* 126
Staiger, Janet, 31, 163–64
Starr, Milton, 182
Stern, Bill: voiceovers by, 33
Strand Newsreel, 29
streamline moderne style, 142, 144–45, 151–52, 155. *See also* modernity
studio system. *See* motion picture industry
Sugrue, Thomas, 19
Surles, A. D., 184

Talley, Truman, 23–24, 96
technology: media, 9, 17, 208, 209–10; newsreel, 38–39, 70, 205; rear projection system, 134–40. *See also* sound
Telenews theater chain, 129
television: history, 6–7, 206–7, 242n26; liveness and timeliness, 64; presenting African American achievements, 170–71, 200
theaters: African American, 169–70, 174–75; segregated, 174, 196. *See also* newsreel theaters
Thomas, Lowell: voiceovers by, 33
Thorgersen, Ed: voiceovers by, 33
ticker tape parades, 19–20, 25, 45–46, 135–36, 192, 205
Toddy, Ted, 180
Too Hot to Handle (motion picture), 118–20, 126
Town Theatre (newsreel theater, Los Angeles), 152–54, *153*
Trans-Lux Corporation, 15; Movie Ticker, 135–37, 140, 242n26; newsreel theaters, 142–45, *143, 144,* 154; rear projection system, 134–40
travel, newsreel's association with, 16, 130, 140–55, 164–65, 205. *See also* mobility, newsreel's association with

Universal Newsreel, 27, 30, 33, 36, 99; archives of, 2, 210; cameramen's daring, 41, 94–95; Hauptmann trial coverage, 80–86, *85, 86,* 87–88; Lindbergh son kidnapping coverage, 69–77, 80; *Panay* Incident coverage, 112–17, *115*; Roosevelt's 1933 inauguration coverage, 60–66, *62, 63,* 70, 85; Sino–Japanese War coverage, 91, 101–2, 103–4, 105–6, 109

Valentine, Maggie, 152
Vance, Louise: voiceovers by, 33
Vertov, Dziga, 228n13
visibility, 16, 39; of absence, 66–77; African American struggle for, 165, 171, 173, 184, 185. *See also* politics: of visibility; reality: visibility of
visuality, 5, 9–11, 187, 208; emphasis on, 16, 17, 38, 39, 41–42; power of, 14, 37, 66–67, 68, 88, 168
voiceover commentaries, 4, 32–42, 189; cameramen extolled in, 93–94, 105–6, 114. *See also* audiences: direct address to; newsreels: talking; sound

Wagner, Steward: newsreel theaters designed by, 146
Wagner, Walter, 178

Walker, James: newsreel audience reactions to, 157
Warner, Michael, 10, 12–13, 18, 168
Warner Bros. (motion picture studio), 27
wars. *See* African Americans: during World War II; Sino-Japanese War
watching. *See* gaze; looking; news: watching; spectatorship
Watson, Ted, 171
We've Come a Long, Long Way (documentary), 180–81
Wheeler, Burton K.: audience reaction to, 162
Wheeler, Edward, 172, 200
White, Hayden, 44
White, Walter, 178
White, William Allen, 79
white angels, 169, 176
Wilentz, David T., Hauptmann trial prosecuting attorney, 82, 84, *85*, 87
Wilkins, Roy, 184–85
Williamson, Melvin: letter to the editor, 198–99
Wilson, Charles: voiceovers by, 169, 192–93
Winner, Howard, cameraman, 98–99, 106
Winston, Brian, 6
Wong, H. S. "Newsreel," cameraman, 91, 104–5; crying baby image, *105*
Wood, Ghislaine, 141
Woollcott, Alexander, 82
World War II. *See* African Americans: during World War II; Double Victory (Double V) campaign

Young, Buddy, 197, *198*
Yungblut, Gibson, 243n49

Zanuck, Darryl F., 178
Zola, Emile, 57

JOSEPH CLARK is a lecturer in film studies in the School for the Contemporary Arts at Simon Fraser University and teaches film history at Emily Carr University for Art and Design.